STUDYING
YOUTH GANGS

Violence Prevention and Policy Series

This AltaMira series publishes new books in the multidisciplinary study of violence. Books are designed to support scientifically based violence prevention programs and widely applicable violence prevention policy. Key topics are juvenile and/or adult community reentry programs, community-based addiction and violence programs, prison violence reduction programs with application in community settings, and school culture and climate studies with recommendations for organizational approaches to school violence reduction. Studies may combine quantitative and qualitative methods, may be multidisciplinary, or may feature European research if it has a multinational application. The series publishes highly accessible books that offer violence prevention policy as the outcome of scientifically based research, designed for college undergraduates and graduates, community agency leaders, school and community decision makers, and senior government policymakers.

Series Editor

Editorial Board Members

Books in the Series

Gang Cop: The Words and Ways of Officer Paco Domingo by Malcolm Klein (2004)

Measuring Prison Performance: Government Privatization and Accountability by Gerald G. Gaes, Scott D. Camp, Julianne B. Nelson, William G. Saylor (2004)

European Street Gangs and Troublesome Youth Groups edited by Scott H. Decker and Frank M. Weerman (2005)

Violence and Mental Health in Everyday Life: Prevention and Intervention Strategies for Children and Adolescents by Daniel J. Flannery (2005)

Studying Youth Gangs edited by James F. Short, Jr., and Lorine A. Hughes (2006)

Family Abuse and Violence: What Do We Know? What Can We Do? by JoAnn Miller and Dean D. Knudsen

STUDYING
YOUTH GANGS

Edited by
James F. Short, Jr.
and
Lorine A. Hughes

ALTAMIRA
PRESS

A Division of
ROWMAN & LITTLEFIELD PUBLISHERS, INC.
Lanham • New York • Toronto • Oxford

ALTAMIRA PRESS
A Division of Rowman & Littlefield Publishers, Inc.
A wholly owned subsidiary of The Rowman & Littlefield Publishing Group, Inc.
4501 Forbes Boulevard, Suite 200
Lanham, MD 20706
www.altamirapress.com

PO Box 317, Oxford, OX2 9RU, UK

British Library Cataloguing in Publication Information Available

Library of Congress Cataloguing-in-Publication Data

Studying youth gangs / edited by James F. Short and Lorine A. Hughes.
     p.   cm. — (Violence prevention and policy series)
    Includes bibliographical references and index.
    ISBN-13: 978-0-7591-0938-4 (cloth : alk. paper)
    ISBN-10: 0-7591-0938-9 (cloth : alk. paper)
    ISBN-13: 978-0-7591-0939-1 (pbk. : alk. paper)
    ISBN-10: 0-7591-0939-7 (pbk. : alk. paper)
    1. Gangs.   2. Youth and violence.   I. Short, James F.
II. Hughes, Lorine A., 1974–   III. Series.
HV6437.S78 2006
364.106′6—dc22

                                        2005037372

Printed in the United States of America

∞™ The paper used in this publication meets the minimum requirements of American
National Standard for Information Sciences—Permanence of Paper for Printed Library
Materials, ANSI/NISO Z39.48-1992.

Contents

Preface

James F. Short, Jr., and Lorine A. Hughes

GANG RESEARCHERS HAVE BECOME ISOLATED from mainstream discoveries and insights. Moreover, despite heroic empirical and descriptive efforts, the seemingly myriad forms of today's gangs defy the most elaborate typologies. Concerns such as these led Jim Short to accept an invitation from Chris Eskridge, editor of the *Journal of Contemporary Criminal Justice* (*JCCJ*), to guest edit the May 2005 issue on a topic of his choosing. Jim chose "Why Study Gangs?"

As if to demonstrate progress toward correction of such problems, the five papers accepted for that issue (out of the more than twenty received) focused primarily on methodological and theoretical, rather than substantive, issues. Revisions of four of the five, by Mark Fleisher, John Hagedorn, Malcolm Klein, and Mercer Sullivan, form the core of this book, together with Lorine Hughes's "sequel" to her *JCCJ* article.

The first three chapters are both introductory and diagnostic of the state of gang research. Short's historical and autobiographical chapter 1 discusses the challenges of studying youth gangs and briefly addresses the role played by others, as well as gang members, in processes of gang formation and identification. Sullivan's chapter 2 focuses on the problems associated with the loose manner in which the term *gang* is used by mass media, in popular discourse, and often by law enforcement personnel and scholars. His discussion of the consequences of reification of various types of groups of young people as gangs is a challenge to all who are concerned with gangs and their behavior. In chapter 3, Hughes continues her *JCCJ* paper's focus on what has been learned from quantitative and qualitative approaches to the study of gangs. Pointing to the theoretical and methodological limits of the currently dominant "variables paradigm" (see Abbott 1997, 1999), she urges a return to the contextualist tradition of the Chicago school.

Two examples of sophisticated quantitative, variables-oriented research follow. Although both examine neighborhood effects on gang behavior, they do so quite differently. Chapter 4, by Gina Hall, Terence Thornberry, and Alan Lizotte, analyzes self-reported gang membership and delinquent-behavior data from the Rochester Youth Survey as they relate to census tract characteristics. The delinquency "facilitative" effect of gang membership is confirmed, but few neighborhood effects are found. In contrast, strong (but varied) neighborhood effects on gang-motivated homicides in Chicago are reported in chapter 5. Andrew Papachristos and David Kirk examine the relationship between gang-motivated homicides and Chicago neighborhood characteristics by combining official records with data from the Project on Human Development Neighborhoods (PHDCN) (see Sampson, Morenoff, and Earls 1999). Their study confirms the importance of collective efficacy as a factor in the control of gang homicide. The findings may in part be a function of the study's measures, but the paper has implications for the manner in which social disorganization is measured among various populations, for example, black versus Hispanic, gang versus nongang. These two chapters add to already impressive findings from their parent projects.

The next three chapters discuss the use of social network analysis in gang research. Fleisher's *JCCJ* paper (chapter 6), here expanded, draws attention to the dangers of rigid conceptualization of gang boundaries, with examples from his own extensive field research. Papachristos, in chapter 7, treat network analysis more broadly, including application of both theory and method to the Erls gang, from Gerald Suttles's classic *The Social Order of the Slum* (1968). Chapter 8, by Bill Sanders and Steve Lankenau, places network analysis within a public health approach to the study of gangs.

Chapters 9 through 12 are concerned with comparative research, beginning with Klein's *JCCJ* admonitory paper. Themes of diversity and change follow, first in Pete Simi's study of racist skinhead gangs (chapter 10), then in Rob White's survey of youth gang research in Australia (chapter 11). Hagedorn's critique of traditional gang research and his advocacy for recognition of the impact of global changes on gangs concludes this section.

The next two chapters address issues of crime and gang control in quite different ways. David Olson and Brendan Dooley (chapter 13) report that recidivism rates of probationers and parolees identified as gang members are higher than those of their nongang counterparts. The extent to which gang members may have been targeted by police is unknown, but the study is one of the few that has examined the salience of gang membership within correctional populations. Chapter 14, by Irving Spergel, Kwai Ming Wa, and Rolando Sosa, describes in summary form six quasi-experimental efforts that were designed to be comprehensive community-wide programs for gang prevention, intervention, and suppression. In addition to the boldness of these efforts and their limited success, Spergel and his colleagues inform the political and organizational barriers to such programs.

The final chapter, "Moving Gang Research Forward," is based in part on earlier chapters and the lessons they convey. Beyond this, we attempt to convey our vision of how the study of gangs might be advanced substantively, methodologically, and theoretically. A priori, however, it seems clear that the amazing diversity of gangs demands study, as does their relevance to issues of crime control. We believe strongly that there is much to learn about human behavior from the study of gangs.

Acknowledgments

O UR PRIMARY DEBT, of course, is to those who join us as contributing authors. More than this, they have participated in reviewing other papers that were submitted for inclusion in the book, as well as the *JCCJ* issue. Others who were consulted in a variety of ways include Eli Anderson, Dave Curry, Scott Decker, Finn Esbensen, John Hagan, Buddy Howell, David Huizinga, Jim Marquart, Lisa McIntyre, Jody Miller, Joan Petersilia, and Charles Tittle. Bob Bursik was especially helpful and deserves special thanks. Special thanks also are due to Mark Fleisher, editor of the AltaMira Press series on Violence Prevention and Policy, and Rosalie Robertson, senior editor for AltaMira.

1

Why Study Gangs?
An Intellectual Journey

James F. Short, Jr.

R ECENT REVIEWS NOTWITHSTANDING (Coughlin and Venkatesh 2003; Vigil 2003), over the many years that the idea for this book has percolated in my mind, the study of gangs has become increasingly specialized and isolated from the mainstream.[1] Close friends have wondered why I continue to grapple with the genre. Why devote so much time and effort to studying phenomena so loosely grouped under a theoretical construct that defies definitional consensus? Is the gang really a "specific type or variety of society," as remarked by Robert E. Park so long ago (1927, vi)? What happened to the "types of gangs" described by Frederic Thrasher (1927, chapter 4)? What are gangs, after all, and why study them? Why, indeed?

While conducting self-reported delinquency research half a century ago, this question never entered my mind. Discussion of "gangs" (the noun) was customarily preceded by the adjective "delinquent." It was, therefore, important to study gang members. Thrasher's 1,313 gangs were legendary (1927),[2] and case studies of boys and their friends collected by my mentors Clifford Shaw and Henry McKay led them to subtitle their report to the nation's first crime commission, *A Study of the Community, the Family, and the Gang in Relation to Delinquent Behavior* (1931; see also Shaw 1927, 1930; Shaw and Moore 1931).[3]

Thrasher explicitly regarded his study as "exploratory" rather than definitive. "Such formulations as are presented," he writes, "must be regarded as tentative hypotheses rather than as scientific generalizations." He hoped that the book would "encourage additional study in this field and indicate some interesting lines for further research" (Thrasher 1927, xi). Yet, for two decades following these early studies, little research was devoted to gangs.[4]

Shaw and his colleagues wrote little about gangs. Except for a single case and a brief quote from Thrasher's book, they relied chiefly on their own research[5] and wrote instead about companions who had been brought to court, patterns of friendship, association of younger with older offenders, and the existence in communities—notably in "delinquency areas"—of organized crime and other forms of adult criminality. The ecological studies (*Delinquency Areas, Juvenile Delinquency and Urban Areas*) located official delinquency and delinquents in space and in the course of urban development. Together with the case studies, they documented the family, economic, and other institutional structural parameters within which urban lives were lived—parameters that shaped the ability of communities to socialize children and exercise control over their lives. The life histories (*The Jack-roller, The Natural History of a Delinquent Career, Brothers in Crime*, and others) argue convincingly that these conditions and processes help to account not only for the distribution of delinquency, but for why kids become delinquents and why some communities lack the ability to prevent delinquency.

Because gangs were *there*, we needed to know about gang members' self-reported delinquent behavior. Albert Cohen thought so, too. Publication of his seminal *Delinquent Boys: The Culture of the Gang* (1955) stimulated a great deal of theoretical interest in subcultures but raised empirical questions, as well.[6] At an annual meeting of the American Sociological Association in the mid-1950s, Cohen and I sought out Solomon Kobrin, whose article "The Conflict of Values in Delinquency Areas" (1951), anticipated theoretical issues later addressed by Richard Cloward and Lloyd Ohlin in *Delinquency and Opportunity: A Theory of Delinquent Gangs* (1960).[7] We asked Kobrin whether he had fleshed out his ideas on the consequences for delinquent subcultures of the community value conflicts he had identified. He had not, but the discussion was helpful to us as we explored "Research in Delinquent Subcultures" (Cohen and Short 1958).[8]

Later, in the fall of 1958, Ohlin, Walter Miller, Cohen, and I met in Chicago to discuss theories about gangs and subcultures. Philip Hauser and Fred Strodtbeck represented the University of Chicago at the meeting, which was also attended by professional and lay YMCA leaders and personnel associated with the Program for Detached Workers, a recently initiated effort to reach gangs on the street rather than waiting for them to become involved in traditional YMCA building-centered programs. Discussions were lively and stimulating. At the end of two days it was agreed that Strodtbeck and I, guided by theoretical ideas and issues such as those we had discussed, would prepare a proposal for National Institute of Mental Health (NIMH) for funding of research that would inform the nature of youth gangs and subcultures. Access to the gangs with which the detached workers were associated was assured, and we would be given the opportunity to identify and recruit to the program additional gangs of theoretical interest.

The Youth Studies Program at the University of Chicago

I recount this history in order to make the point that in these discussions and the scholarly treatises that animated them little attention was devoted to *why or how youth gangs should be studied.* The meager professional literature also was largely silent on these issues. It was simply assumed that studying gangs and gang members was a good way to study juvenile delinquency and a proper focus for research on delinquents and related subcultures.

The research team that was assembled at the University of Chicago also made these assumptions, and we reasoned that the best way to study gangs was by compiling data on gang members' behavior though police records, self-reports, detached worker ratings of individuals, and administration of various "tests" to members of gangs and comparison groups—their values, personality characteristics, and relationships.[9] Observational data obtained by periodic (usually weekly) interviews with detached workers and by graduate student field observation reports were primarily for the purpose of "keeping a window open" on gangs *in order to carry out more systematic inquiries by objective and projective means amenable to quantitative analysis.* We did those things, with varying degrees of success (see Short and Strodtbeck 1965/1974).

I make no apology either for the assumptions or the methodological choices that guided our inquiries. Even as we were filling out research designs and drafting protocols for interviews and testing of gang boys, however, the realization dawned that the detached worker interviews and field observer reports were generating exceptionally rich data concerning group dynamics of gangs and their members.[10] Our first published paper drew heavily on worker interviews and on data collected by paper-and-pencil instruments (Short, Strodtbeck, and Cartwright 1962).[11] Later we used field observations as ethnography for generating theoretical ideas and supplementing quantitative data obtained from interviews and various forms of "testing" (Short and Strodtbeck 1965/1974).[12]

The appearance in 1955 of Cohen's theoretical treatise *Delinquent Boys* reflected a shift in sociology's mainstream from Chicago-style inquiry to the structural/functional tradition then centered at Harvard and Columbia (Abbott 1999; Abbott and Sparrow forthcoming).[13] Richard Cloward and Lloyd Ohlin's *Delinquency and Opportunity* (1960), while acknowledging Thrasher, Shaw, and McKay, built primarily on Robert K. Merton's structural/functional paradigm and, despite Ohlin's Chicago upbringing, was solidly in that tradition.

These traditions differed both theoretically and methodologically. Chicago's focus on the ecological structure of the city, and on the diverse and sometimes conflicting forces at play within local communities, contrasted with the overarching individual-collectivist theories and survey research methodology emphasized at Harvard and Columbia. Although he acknowledged his debt to Chicago-style inquiry, Cohen's theory of the "culture of the gang" was rooted in understandings of the larger social structure and in the functionalist psychoanalytic mechanism of reaction formation. Like Cohen's and Cloward and Ohlin's theories, Walter Miller's "Lower Class Culture as a Generating Milieu of Gang Delinquency" (1958) also focused on influences *outside* the gang as driving forces of street-gang culture.

As we launched the Youth Studies Program, our research designs and strategies were guided by the theoretical ferment generated by these theories, rather than by Chicago's focus on interaction and process. Our basic research strategies were supplemented, but not abandoned, after we discovered the richness of data to be found in the unstructured worker interviews and observer reports. We lacked ethnographic expertise, and computer technology for systematic analysis of such data did not exist.[14] Insights gained from these data had the effect, however, of directing us to the importance of the temporal and spatial contexts of interpersonal interaction and group processes.

The book that came out of that research, *Group Process and Gang Delinquency* (Short and Strodtbeck 1965/1974), reflected this realization but did not fully either appreciate or implement it. Our attempts to weave together quantitative and qualitative analyses were reported in the narrative sections of the book, which illustrated but could not fully document such matters as contrasting adolescent-adult relationships in black and white communities, indigenous community institutions, and forces of local change and their relevance to youth gangs (chapter 5). We were able to document white community support of gang efforts to resist threatened black invasion, and variation among gang members in participation in such resistance (112–14, chapter 9). Reactions of leaders and other gang members to a variety of individual and group status threats and varying subcultural styles were described (chapters 8 and 9). Social abilities of gang members were evaluated in a variety of contexts, such as family relationships and gang boys' relationships with girls (chapters 2 and 10), group conflict in public settings, and employment (chapters 9 and 10). A case of group and individual decision making under extreme duress was studied (chapter 11). The final chapter brought together elements of a "group process perspective," in which we argued that the "process of interaction transforms culture" (273).

Forty years later, however, the group process perspective remains undeveloped. The research that we did has been cited frequently and appreciatively, but later gang research by sociologists and anthropologists has focused less on group processes than on correlates of individual self-reports of gang membership in school settings (e.g., Thornberry et al. 2003), depictions of gang life based on interviews with gang members (e.g., Decker and Van Winkle 1996), and broadly ethnographic accounts of one or more gangs (e.g., Hagedorn 1998a; Vigil 2002). Even the more qualitative of these tend to portray gangs in broad social and cultural strokes, with little attention to group processes and the relevance of situational contexts.

Our primary research activities took place between 1959 and 1962. With NIMH funding, a limited follow-up study became possible in 1971. Because both time and funding limitations precluded extensive fieldwork, we focused primarily on two gangs, the Nobles and the Vice Lords. Although the first publication from this study concerned "politics and youth gangs" (Short and Moland 1976), our hope was to construct a *natural history* of these two gangs, somewhat in the manner of Thrasher.

Thrasher postulated "embryonic stages" of the gang within families and among intimate companions, spontaneous playgroups, formal groups, and crowds. His "end products of gang development and the more inclusive groups into which the gang may ultimately enter" included a variety of collective behaviors as well as conventional and illicit organizational forms (Thrasher 1927, 70).

> If conditions are favorable to its continued existence, the gang tends to undergo a sort of natural evolution from a diffuse and loosely organized group into the solidified unit which represents the matured gang and which may take one of several forms. It sometimes becomes a specialized delinquent type such as the criminal gang, but usually it becomes conventionalized and seeks incorporation into the structure of the community, imitating some established social pattern such as a club, but in reality retaining many, if not all, of its original attributes. (Thrasher 1927, 58)

Lacking resources for field observations, we relied on interviews and contacts provided by prominent members of the Nobles and the Vice Lords. The choice of these two gangs, although somewhat fortuitous, proved to be fortunate. We knew that they represented opposite poles of organization, but we had neither knowledge nor appreciation of the extent to which life course development of individual members and the gangs as organizations had diverged.

When our research began, the Vice Lords had only recently quite literally established themselves as a gang. Their biographer, Boys Court caseworker Lincoln Keiser, noted that the gang "began in Harding Cottage, which housed the toughest boys in (the Illinois State Training School for Boys at St. Charles, Illinois). The club was started in the Lawndale area . . . in the fall of 1958, following the release of several members" (Keiser 1969, 1).[15] The Vice Lords later became a "gang nation" and even today are a force to be reckoned with. Their turf, when we studied them, was in Lawndale, Community Area 29, one of the west side communities that had changed rapidly from white to black residency.

By the end of our field research, in the summer of 1962, although the Nobles had expanded from twenty-five members when we first contacted them to forty-five members, the gang had become less cohesive and virtually ceased to exist. Their turf was in Douglas, Chicago Community Area 35, an area of longtime black settlement on Chicago's south side, dating from World War I.

For the Nobles, identity as a gang had always been fluid, having developed out of traditional hanging and recreational patterns of local children. In the words of a former member:

> They had a real close-knit type of thing even before they came into what you might call a gang-like element. . . . We would hang out and have a little fun, you know. After awhile the group began to grow and gather in an area called Ellis Park. A lot of girls used to be around and we (a few from the project) would go to parties over in their neighborhood. . . . [The Nobles] used to hang around in little bunches and hit on people for money and if you got into it with one of them you would have to deal with a group of them. As an outsider you would have to deal with a group of them. . . . A lot of people were not actually members of the Nobles, insofar as being in the club is concerned. . . . If they would go into the project for a party or something and they would get into a humbug, well then they would send somebody around to 36th and Ellis, the hanging place for the whole area. . . . And there was a big open courtway where a lot of people hung out over there for there was a lot of drugs over there and a lot of . . . "slick" things happened over there. . . . But when you got down to some action as an outsider you wouldn't be able to distinguish as to who [was a member and who was not]. . . . People who lived in that area saw a lot of harsh things happen while growing up. This made them a little more violent or have a little more heart than most young people growing up. They were exposed to seeing their mommas get cut or seeing all kinds of brutality and drugs. . . . They saw everything there—prostitution, people getting killed, shot down, they saw all of this. (adapted from Short and Moland 1976, 166–67)

Although the Nobles' turf remained a relatively high delinquency area, the community's population and institutions were stabilizing. Henry McKay's last published work documented vast changes in rates of delinquents for Community Areas 29 and 35 (Lawndale and Douglas). Both communities had relatively high rates of delinquents. Douglas rates for the period 1958–1961 (the latter, the midpoint of our study), were less than half the rates for 1934–1940, however, and were the most pronounced *downward* trending of such rates among Chicago community areas. In contrast, 1958–1961 rates for Lawndale were nearly four times those for 1934–1940, the most pronounced *upward* trend among community areas (McKay 1969, 377–78).

For our follow-up study, we sought information primarily from and about members of the Nobles and Vice Lords who had belonged to the gangs when we began to study them.[16] After a decade, the contrast between the two gangs was dramatic. Informants could provide information on only sixteen of the original twenty-five Nobles who were still living (three were deceased), of whom thirteen (81 percent) were employed. Little information was available on the expanded group of Nobles, clearly an indication that the group no longer had a gang identity. Most Nobles appeared to have "grown out of" the gang, as most gang members once did.

The Vice Lords were quite another matter. Their instability was overwhelming. Most had remained in Chicago when they were not incarcerated outside the city. We were able to find information on all but four of the sixty-six on our initial roster. Of the remaining sixty-two, twelve (19 percent) were dead, the circumstances of death varying from "the heroic (one young man was killed attempting to rescue a child from a fire) to the criminally violent, with a heavy weighting toward the latter" (Short and Moland 1976, 168). Fewer than half (43.5 percent) were employed; twenty-three (38 percent) were unemployed, of whom perhaps ten were involved in drug distribution; and ten were in prison when the roster was last checked, in the fall of 1973. Nearly all the young men on our original roster had served time in correctional institutions.

Other measures of socioeconomic status, such as education and type of employment, also favored the Nobles. Members of both groups indicated greater political awareness and concern than had been evident in our earlier study (the Vice Lords only slightly more so), and the Vice Lords were more approving than the former Nobles of violent means toward the achievement of civil rights (Short and Moland 1976).

This was as far as we got with our "natural history"—a modest achievement. We know little of such transformations or of the forces and processes that might account for them. Again, we may profit by going back to our forebears—and to the following chapters in this book.

The Problem of Reification

Chapter 2, by Mercer Sullivan, highlights problems associated with reification of gangs. Sullivan charges that the notion of gangs is too vague and that the focus on gangs distracts us from the broader and more intrinsically problematic topic of youth violence. Thrasher and Shaw and McKay clearly were aware of—and concerned about—reification of gangs and crime, as well. Here is Thrasher:

> Residents in the vicinity south of the stockyards were startled one morning by a number of placards bearing the inscription "The Murderers, 10,000 Strong, 48th and Ada." In this way attention was attracted to a gang of thirty Polish boys, who hang out in a district known as the Bush. (1927, 62–63)

The Murderers did more than hang out. Thrasher's description of their activities is quite vivid: They "broke into box cars" and stole merchandise, "cut out wire cables to sell as junk . . . broke open telephone boxes," "took autos for joy-riding," "purloined several quarts of whiskey from a brewery," attacked "niggers," and fought other gangs. Their primary pastimes, however, "were loafing, smoking, chewing, crap-shooting, card-playing, pool, and bowling." They also "had great fun camping, flipping freights, and pestering the railroad detectives." Local storekeepers "were indignant at their rudeness and thievery, and the neighbors regard them as an awful nuisance."[17]

Shaw, too, was concerned with reification. He was especially impressed with Tannenbaum's notion of "the dramatization of evil," a precursor of the labeling perspective, which he regularly assigned to his classes (Tannenbaum 1938). For Shaw, Stanley, his *Jack-roller*, illustrates the point, as he describes how he feels upon finding himself in a "bare, hard, and drab" reformatory cell:

> Before, I had been just a mischievous lad, a poor city waif, a petty thief, a habitual runaway; but now, as I sat in my cell of stone and iron, dressed in a gray uniform, with my head shaved, small skull cap, like all the other hardened criminals around me, some strange feeling came over me. Never before had I realized that I was a criminal. (Shaw 1930, 103)

Sullivan's point is both theoretically and methodologically significant. The empirical problem of identifying different types of youth groups that parade under the gang banner has consequences. Sullivan's methodological solution is to distinguish groups based on *types of association, identity, and law-violating behavior*. A *clique*, he suggests, is a group that shares some form of diffuse but relatively enduring bond among its members. Although they meet regularly and take part in common activities, including perhaps breaking the law, law-breaking is neither their primary purpose nor the basis for their group identity. *Action-sets* are groups of individuals that take part in particular events. They may or may not ever act together again.

Jerzy Sarnecki's study of Swedish "action-sets" is informative in this regard. Sarnecki found that nearly half of the 575 juveniles "suspected of offenses" in Borlange, Sweden, between 1975 and 1977 (later followed up through 1984) "could be linked together in a single large network" (Sarnecki 2001, 25). Within this network, clusters of youths varied in the extent to which they continued to offend together. Some appeared in "similar constellations" over the period of study, while others offended "in continually new constellations." Interviews with a small sample of these youths (n = 29) found that their friendships "showed a high degree of correspondence" with the police suspect data. The interviews also revealed, however, that they "had no conception of themselves as belonging to a 'gang'" (26).

Sarnecki later conducted a larger study of young offender suspects in Stockholm, with similar findings. Stockholm action-sets (in the sense of police "suspects") were found to be short-lived and unstable. Study of a Stockholm suburban group, the "Angen gang," found that these youth described themselves as "a bunch of mates who've known each other since [they] were little and who look out for each other" (Sarnecki 2001, 145). They spent much of the day together, simply "hanging out" or keeping in touch by mobile phones. Delinquent behavior and use of drugs and alcohol "did play an important part in the interactions between the youths in Angen," however, and, over a five-year period, "most of the larger networks, comprised of more actively delinquent youths, become instead a single large, central network with members from all over the county" (145, 151).

Sarnecki notes police estimates of as many as one hundred gangs in Stockholm but concludes that neither the networks he examined nor the "Central Network" that "drew together the vast majority of the most delinquent youths in the city" comprised gangs in Sullivan's *named gang* terms—groups that have the properties of cliques, together with names and explicit criteria of membership, that are recognized by members and others; that is, *public identity* is important both to the groups and to others.

So how does public identity occur, and why? Most gang researchers take gangs as given, as identified by the police or by social agencies, as we did in our Chicago gang research. The fact that a field search to find and contact "retreatist" and "criminal" gangs (in order to complete our research design) was unsuccessful alerted us to the fragility of theories on which that design was based. In retrospect perhaps it should have alerted us to the importance of public identity, as well. Chicago police attention at the time was focused primarily on troublemaking street gangs that posed threats to local communities and to themselves in the form of gang conflict.[18] Although we did not make systematic inquiries about the matter, it was clear that some gangs recognized that public notoriety was a factor in their reputations. Very early in our research the detached worker program director received a telephone call from a boy who identified himself as a member of a south side gang. The boy requested that a "worker" be assigned to his gang. Asked why, after a pause the boy responded, "Man, you ain't nothin' unless you got a worker." Regrettably the program did not follow through on this request from the gang that became the Blackstone Rangers, later reputed to be the toughest, best-organized gang in Chicago.

Newspaper publicity to that effect, in turn, led to the establishment of the Vice Lords, according to their biographer (Keiser 1969). The rest, as is often said, is history, as both the Blackstone Rangers and the Vice Lords developed into supergangs.[19] More systematic observations of the *process* of gang identity is found in ethnographer Richard Brymmer's study of Mexican American youth conflict gangs in a large southwestern U.S. city (Brymmer 1998).

Based on intensive fieldwork over an extended period, Brymmer describes images of gangs held by various officials and citizens. The police "saw gangs only in crowd control situations" and as a result "viewed every group of young males in the ghetto as a gang or as part of a gang" (1998, 147). Probation and parole officers, who met with their clients primarily in "one-on-one interview" situations rather than on the street, identified few gang members among them. Unlike Brymmer, they apparently also did not "use the bathroom in the 'bull pen' waiting area" which was "covered with spray-painted gang graffiti." Social work agencies and "elders of the neighborhood" viewed gangs "as large fighting units" identified with neighborhoods marked by gang graffiti. The received wisdom was that gangs were "relatively large groups of 75 to 150 members who were identified with a given 'territory' (or bounded neighborhood)." After two years of observation, however, Brymmer had never seen such a gang.

Sifting through these images, Brymmer realized that he and others who had direct contact with what they agreed was gang activity did not observe such large gangs of local "cultural mythology" but rather engaged them in the course of interaction with "'gang guys' in small groups of approximately 8 to 10 members," known locally as *palomillas*. One evening's observation, however, witnessed the transformation of palomillas into just this sort of large gang:

> I was driving around the city with a palomilla in my wagon, cruising the neighborhood and its boundaries. As we went north on a street, we passed a drive-in restaurant and hangout that had a large parking lot in which there were groups of cars surrounded by small groups of young people. The group in my car identified the various groups assembled by their palomilla names (e.g., Jose and his guys). Thirty minutes later, we were again passing south on the street, and on approaching the drive-in, the guys said, "Pull over, there is the X gang" of which they were members. The ecological scene had shifted. Rather than a series of discrete groups, there was now a wall of young males facing the street. The cars had their trunks open, and the girls were behind the wall of young males and the cars. I was ecstatic because after two years in the field, I finally saw a gang! The palomilla members in my car assumed their position in the wall, and I began to run around making field notes. The open car trunks contained massive amounts of weaponry, including semiautomatic shotguns and rifles. This gang was in fact deadly, and its members' willingness to fight had, in my view, fulfilled various definitions of a gang. What produced the symbolic and actual move from palomilla member to gang member?

When I asked what happened, the guys (now gang members and not palomilla members) said that members of the Y gang had driven by and made observations about the X gang's masculinity. This affront was accompanied by the threat that they were going to come back and kill them. (Brymmer 1998, 148)

In the event, Brymmer notes, the rival gang members did not return, and no fight occurred. Although officially unnoticed, the confrontation had transformed otherwise loosely connected groups into named gangs. Does reification then *cause* gang formation or gang behavior? We need to know a great deal more about the processes that give rise to gang formation, identity, and behavior, and about processes of individual and group adaptations at different levels of explanation. Closer attention must be paid to the dynamic linkages between gangs, gang members, and their physical and social environments.

Dealing with Causation

Confusion in public discourse and in scholarly analysis concerning widely varied youth groups has consequences both for understanding delinquent and criminal behavior and for their control, as Sullivan's chapter suggests. But we approach *causation* with well-deserved caution, given both the theoretical and empirical weakness of the field (Katz and Jackson-Jacobs 2004). Andrew Abbott charges that, by neglecting study of the "recurrent patterns of action in recurrent structures" that constitute social life, sociologists' approaches to causality are "so much reification" (Abbott 1999, 220). Traditional variables-oriented research isolates "snapshots" of situations and of behavior and, by relating them statistically, infers causal relationships. A great deal has been learned from such studies, as evidenced by chapters 4 and 5 in this volume (see also Hughes 2005a). Clearly, however, causality cannot be fully understood without greater attention to the contexts of those snapshots, and of processes associated with their recurrence. This is the theme of chapter 3, by Lorine Hughes. Only by *contextualizing* behaviors of interest in time and place can we understand *how* gangs "facilitate" delinquent behavior by gang members (Hall, Thornberry, and Lizotte, chapter 4 in this volume; Thornberry et al. 2003), for example, or *why* violence in communities and gang homicides are statistically associated with "collective efficacy" (Papachristos and Kirk, chapter 5 in this volume; Sampson, Morenoff, and Earls 1999; Sampson, Raudenbush, and Earls 1997).

Hughes also briefly discusses the work that she and I have been doing while revisiting those old Chicago gang data, one goal of which is to more systematically contextualize the behavior that was observed, a theme to which we return in the final chapter.

As we note in the preface, these first three chapters are in some sense "diagnostic" of the state of gang research. The next several chapters exemplify many of the problems of traditional and emerging gang research and some possible approaches to their solution.

Conclusion

My intellectual journey is not ended, as this book attests. As Hughes's chapter notes, more systematic analysis of the Chicago gang data that my colleagues and I gathered more than forty years ago now add to our earlier discoveries. With support from the National Consortium of Violence Research (NCOVR), nearly 17,000 pages of transcribed detached worker interviews and field observer reports have been digitalized (see Hughes 2005b).[20] The first paper based on these data, "Disputes Involving Youth Street Gang Members: Micro-social Contexts" (Hughes and Short 2005), contextualizes such disputes in ways that were not possible in the early years of the research program. The new analysis of the data confirms the role of status considerations in disputes involving gang members but reveals other considerations that enter into the resolution of such disputes, such as dispute pretexts, relationships among disputants, interactional processes, peer backup, and audience intervention. Escalation of disputes into violence results less often than we had expected. Further analyses of the data will permit more in-depth examination of group and individual participation in such collective behaviors as the "wolf-packing" type of guerrilla warfare that so often characterizes gangs even today, as well as gang violence that takes place in large crowd situations. Many other aspects of these gang members' lives can be studied with these data, individually and collectively. We are also exploring possibilities of accessing other, more recent, data sets for comparative analyses, and we hope to expand our inquiries into such mainstream concerns as Donald Black's "pure sociology" paradigm as it may apply to our data (Black 1993; Cooney 1998).

Although gangs and life in general have changed since our Chicago observations were made, documentation of both changes and continuities is important if knowledge is to be cumulative. We begin with the idea that some aspects of group processes and individual and group decision making transcend social change. We want to formulate and study hypotheses related to this idea to the extent possible with both old and new gang data. As noted in the preface, the amazing diversity of gangs demands that they be studied, as does their relevance to issues of crime control. Gangs in their myriad forms, composition, and behavioral repertoires provide virtually unlimited opportunities for learning about human behavior. That, above all, is why they must be studied.

Notes

1. Criminology and studies of deviance have also become more specialized and isolated from their parent disciplines, especially sociology (see Short forthcoming-a).

2. The precise number of Thrasher's gangs will never be known. Gilbert Geis relays the story, told to him by Solomon Kobrin, longtime Shaw and McKay associate at the Illinois Institute for Juvenile Research, that the 1,313 number was a joke played by graduate students who were working on the book. The number was the address of a local brothel! (Geis and Dodge 2000.)

3. The National Commission on Law Observance and Enforcement is commonly referred to as the Wickersham Commission, after its chairman, George W. Wickersham.

4. William F. Whyte's *Street Corner Society* (1943) briefly describes the age-graded gang structure of "Cornerville." Doc and his mates had belonged to gangs when they were younger, but were now young adults. Whyte's book is primarily about the social structure of the community rather than the gangs to which they once belonged. His painstaking fieldwork documented organizational aspects of a slum community that some had overlooked in their enthusiasm for social disorganization.

5. Thrasher acknowledged Shaw's cooperation and referred to several of Shaw's books and documents, but except for the references in *Social Factors in Juvenile Delinquency* (Shaw and McKay 1931, 134, 193), Thrasher's classic book appears to have been ignored by Shaw and his colleagues.

6. I had read portions of Cohen's Harvard thesis before publication of the book, when Henry McKay and others at the Illinois Institute for Juvenile Research brought them to my attention. Not long afterward, Al Cohen and I met, became friends, and began to share our mutual interests in both delinquent subcultures and self-reported delinquent behavior.

7. Harold Finestone also participated in this discussion. "Cats, Kicks, and Color" (Finestone 1957) had not yet appeared, but the ideas set forth in that article were discussed, and the manuscript was sent to us.

8. A paper with this title was presented at the 1958 ASA meetings. The issue of *The Journal of Social Issues* in which the paper was published also included Walter Miller's influential paper "Lower Class Culture as a Generating Milieu of Gang Delinquency" (1958).

9. I served as director of this team and the Youth Studies Program.

10. It is personally embarrassing to me that, as a Chicago-trained sociologist, more systematic analysis of these data was not an integral part of our original research plans. The explanation, I think, is twofold. My major professor was William F. Ogburn, and my dissertation concerned business cycles as a social force affecting crime. Collaboration with Andrew Henry, whose dissertation focused on the influence of business cycles on suicide, included psychological aspects of aggression in the Harvard tradition. *Suicide and Homicide* (Henry and Short 1954) was much influenced by Andy's postdoctoral experience at Harvard. The Chicago gang project was a collaborative effort with Harvard-trained social psychologist Fred Strodtbeck; and Albert Cohen's work, and Al personally, were major influences on the project.

11. This paper was read originally at the annual meeting of the Society for Social Research at the University of Chicago in the spring of 1961.

12. The 1974 edition of *Group Process and Gang Delinquency* added a preface (v–xiv) and a "Bibliography of publications since 1964 based on data collected with National Institutes of Research Grant M-3301" (285–86; see also Cartwright, Tomson, and Schwartz 1975; Short 1997).

13. A third tradition of particular importance for criminology emerged at the University of Pennsylvania, under the leadership of Thorsten Sellin and later Marvin Wolfgang. Sellin's classic monograph *Culture Conflict and Crime* (1938) elaborated on what Edwin Sutherland once called "the basic principle in the explanation of crime" (see Cohen, Lindesmith, and Schuessler 1956, 20). Sutherland and Sellin knew each other well and coedited the September 1931 issue of *The Annals of the American Academy of Political and Social Science*, which was devoted to "Prisons of Tomorrow."

14. The University of Chicago's mainframe computer in 1959 was, I believe, a Univac I, which was housed in the Administration Building. Computation of even rudimentary measures such as factor analysis was a long and tedious process, and not always reliable!

15. Keiser's chapter on the development of the Vice Lords is an excellent description of Chicago's shifting gang scene, especially in near west side black neighborhoods during the mid- to late 1960s, after we had left the field. It is important to note that Keiser's aim is explicitly "not to describe what happened, but what Vice Lords believe happened." (Keiser 1969, 1).

16. We began to study the Nobles in 1959. The Vice Lords were added in 1960, when a worker assigned to them by another agency transferred to the YMCA program.

17. Although the language seems arcane, compared to images of gangs projected by media and held by many in the public, we need to remember that most street gangs, at least in the embryonic stages of their delinquent behavior, are kids. We must guard against possible blind spots in our research, as well as those in media and other public images.

18. Drug use and crime, so far as gangs were concerned, were not the main problem, and neither criminal nor drug-oriented gangs were identified in police files.

19. Buried somewhere in my files is a sheaf of papers compiled by a prominent member of the Vice Lords, consisting primarily of newspaper articles about the gang, its violence, and criminal activity. As I recall, the "brochure" has a cover featuring crossed pool cues, with an icon in each corner depicting a bloody knife, a smoking gun, a wad of money, and dice with "craps" up.

20. Lori Hughes's need for a Ph.D. dissertation topic and NCOVR support were a happy coincidence for both of us.

2

Are "Gang" Studies Dangerous? Youth Violence, Local Context, and the Problem of Reification

Mercer L. Sullivan

G ANGS ARE ALWAYS WITH US, it seems, along with gang studies. Gangs are a perennial phenomenon of modern life, documented in American cities for more than a century (Asbury 1927) and now increasingly in suburban and ex-urban communities as well (Miller 2001). Gangs, the phenomenon, also holds a perennial fascination for journalists and social scientists, periodically inspiring research and writing that reliably finds an audience. As a result, "gangs," the cultural category, is firmly ensconced in the vocabularies of ordinary life and academic discourse. Everyone knows what gangs are. They are violent and they are bad. That is why we study them and take steps to control them and prevent young people from joining them.

Perhaps there is something mistaken in all this. In this chapter, I raise the possibility that this focus on gangs as objects of study and official action is, in some fundamental ways, a flawed enterprise. Not because gangs do not exist, but because the label is too vague and the focus on gangs distracts us from an object of study that is broader and more intrinsically problematic. That object is youth violence. If young people choose to associate and call themselves gangs, that may be more or less problematic. When they engage in violence, however, whether that violence is labeled gang violence, as it often is, or not, as is also often the case, that is always problematic. Youth violence takes many organizational forms. Lumping these together as "gang" phenomena carries distracting baggage. The perennial fascination with gangs is partly romantic.

15

It can, and sometimes does, cloud our view of what we should be placing front and center, the problem of youth violence.

Much of what youth gangs do is expressive activity, the construction of systems of cultural symbolism and performance. The complex intertwining of cultural symbolism and on-the-ground patterns of behavior poses a serious problem for research. If we mistake symbols for behavior, we commit errors of reification. Mass society and mass media feed on and reinforce the tendency to reify youth gangs. Because youth gangs can be such potentially colorful phenomena, they are good candidates for inciting moral panic, as existing research has shown (Shelden, Tracy, and Brown 2001; Zatz 1987). Youth gangs are always good for a story, not just in the mass media but among adolescents themselves, as they try to make sense of their lives to one another.

The danger for research is that of imposing an archetypal narrative on a wide variety of experiences embedded in very different local ecological contexts. I argue here that studying these local contexts should be the primary aim of research, because it is within these contexts that youth violence is generated and controlled. To the extent that we wash out the differences among these contexts in the way we do research, we risk mistaking a colorful archetype for the real and varied problems that require attention.

One case in point is the relationship of the prevalence of gang membership to aggregate rates of youth violence. Here, we find an odd, and oddly little noticed, contradiction that points out the dangers of identifying youth violence too closely with youth gangs. During the 1990s, youth gangs were widely reported to be increasing in numbers and membership throughout the United States (Miller 2001). Yet, during the latter part of the decade, youth violence decreased sharply (Butts and Travis 2002), while gang membership underwent but a slight decline and remained at historically unprecedented levels. If gang membership becomes far more prevalent and gang membership is strongly related to youth violence, how can youth violence decline while gang membership remains at historically high levels? Given the choice, who would not prefer more gangs and less youth violence to the opposite combination?

To unravel this apparent contradiction, it is first necessary to take a closer look at the methods and findings associated with research on gangs at the separate levels of society and individual. I then address some definitional issues at the heart of operational measures at these different levels of analysis. Then I propose an analytic typology of forms of association and apply that typology to an analysis of gang membership and youth violence in New York City during the latter 1990s, a period when New York experienced a perceived emergence of a new generation of gangs, along with a steep decrease in serious youth violence.

Gangs and Violence: Societal and Individual Levels of Analysis

From 1975 through the present, a number of surveys of increasing sophistication have sought to document the prevalence of youth gangs and youth gang membership in the United States (Curry, Ball, and Decker 1996; Klein 1995a; Miller 2001; National Youth Gang Center 1997; Spergel and Curry 1988). Although these surveys are not directly comparable because of varying methods of data collection and continually expanded jurisdictional coverage, their cumulative results have been widely interpreted as showing steady and widespread proliferation of gangs over a period of more than two decades, peaking in 1995. This phenomenon has been described as "an almost incredible proliferation" (Thornberry et al. 2003, 1). Miller estimates the national increase in the number of youth gangs over the twenty-five-year period prior to 1995 at 250 percent. Since 1995, annual surveys by the National Youth Gang Center conducted by more uniform methods have continued to track prevalence rates, recording a decrease between 1996 and 2002 of 14 percent (Egley and Major 2004), most of which occurred in smaller cities and rural areas.

Yet, during this latter period, serious youth crime, concentrated in urban areas, decreased far more rapidly. Between 1994 and 2000, juvenile arrests for violent felony offenses decreased by 34 percent (Butts and Travis 2002). Arrests for violent crimes among adults also decreased during this period, although less sharply (Blumstein and Wallman 2000). Disentangling these age-specific trends is complex, especially in light of evidence that much of the youth violence epidemic of the late 1980s and early 1990s involved victimization, in both directions, across the age divide between adolescents and young adults (Cook and Laub 1998). Nonetheless, taken together, these patterns indicate considerable divergence between trends in youth gang reports and trends in youth violence during the latter 1990s, in contrast to the decade before 1995, when gangs and youth violence increased rapidly in tandem. For the latter period, it appears dubious that gangs were the driving force behind changes in rates of youth violence, because gangs remained at historically high levels, while juvenile violent crime in 2000 had receded to rates not seen since 1980 (Butts and Travis 2002).

In contrast to this body of research on aggregate trends at the societal level, research on individual-level associations between self-reported gang affiliation and violent and other illegal behavior has demonstrated robust positive relationships over a series of studies. Those who report some level of involvement in gangs in these surveys consistently report more illegal behavior than those who report no such involvement. The earlier of these individual-level studies reported differences between individuals who did and did not report gang involvement (Battin et al. 1998; Esbensen and Huizinga 1993; Esbensen et al. 2001). The most recent research reports both between-individual and intra-individual changes in levels of violent and other illegal behavior associated with being involved with a gang. Even those who have been in a gang at some point report less crime during periods when they were not actively involved (Thornberry et al. 2003).

Problems of Definitional Ambiguity

What are youth gangs? Who decides, and how? These questions have been around for some time, and a number of answers have been proposed (Ball and Curry 1995; Bursik and Grasmick 1993; Decker and Kempf-Leonard 1991; Horowitz 1990; Maxson and Klein 1990). Unresolved issues include the following: Do we include illegal behavior in the definition of a gang, in which case the association between gangs and crime becomes tautological (Ball and Curry)? Do we include groups such as motorcycle gangs, skinheads, or, crucially, drug-dealing networks and organizations (Klein 1995a, 1995b)? What, if any, age distribution distinguishes gangs from adult crime organizations (Klein)? How do we distinguish between crimes by gang members and crime as collective behavior of gangs (Maxson 1999)? How do we bound the units we refer to as gangs, in terms of including or excluding individuals classified by their degree of association (e.g., core, peripheral, wannabe; Battin et al. 1998; Esbensen et al. 2001; Winfree et al. 1992)? It is not surprising that some experts in the field agree with Esbensen and colleagues' recent assertion that "there is little, if any, consensus as to what constitutes a gang and who is a gang member, let alone what gangs do either inside or outside the law" (106).

Without trying to resolve these issues, let us distinguish for present purposes three broad definitional approaches. The simplest is equating youth gangs with group delinquency, eliminating any distinction between the two. Another alternative is to establish a set of definitional criteria that distinguish youth gangs from other forms of youthful association and group delinquency. A third approach, favored in much recent research, is to turn over the task of deciding what youth gangs are to the people being studied. Comparing the advantages and disadvantages of these approaches helps us identify some possible ways in which the paradox of the late 1990s—simultaneous gang proliferation and declining serious youth violence—may have come about.

Equating youth gangs and group delinquency ignores the fact that only some forms of group delinquency are identified by various parties—youths themselves, the mass media, police, community members—as being gang delinquency. These distinctions between gang and nongang delinquency are meaningful to many people and thus are social facts that legitimately claim the attention of social scientists. Once we admit the existence of these meaningful distinctions, however, we are faced with the problem that they do not make up a single, universally accepted package.

Perhaps in reaction to this quandary, recent criminological research has tended to sidestep many of these definitional issues. Recent researchers have tended to let research subjects themselves decide what gang phenomena are, without imposing definitions on them. For example, the National Youth Gang Survey, from which the best aggregate estimates of the national prevalence of gangs and gang membership are derived, is based on the reports of law enforcement officials (Egley and Major 2004; Miller 2001). In contrast, the individual-level studies discussed earlier are based on youths' own self-reports, including self-nominated status as gang members.

This may be an important clue to the paradox of the late 1990s, namely, that very different sources of information are supplying the data for estimates of gang prevalence trends and assessments of individual-level effects of gang membership on illegal activity. A number of issues complicate attempts to reconcile these data sources. The aggregated law enforcement estimates, for example, may have increased in part as a result of a wave of moral panic over gangs, as is suggested by some detailed local-level case studies (McCorkle and Miethe 2002; Zatz 1987).

One reading of the current state of knowledge is that we do not know what gangs are but we do know who belongs to them. In sharp contrast to those who point out the lack of agreement of definitions of what represents a gang, Thornberry and colleagues and others defend the robustness of self-nomination as an indicator of gang involvement by pointing to the congruence of results using different measures and the consistent power of these measures in predicting illegal and other antisocial behavior (Esbensen et al. 2001; Thornberry et al. 2003). At a more fundamental level, however, individual-level studies do not count, classify, or take gangs as their basic units of analysis. The more basic issue is that individual-level studies tell us about individuals, not about the characteristics of the groups in which they claim membership.

A Heuristic Typology of Groups

I first became uneasy about the multiple meanings of the term *gang* in earlier research that I conducted in Brooklyn during the 1980s (Sullivan 1989). I discovered that the criminally active youths we were studying did not consider themselves to be gang members, even though they committed crimes with others. They had definite conceptions of what youth gangs were. Some reported that they had once been gang members. Those days, however, were in the past, both for them as individuals and for their social areas. For the young males I studied in the 1980s, gangs were something they were involved in "when they were kids." Gangs had faded not just from their individual lives but also from the fabric of their neighborhoods at that time. New York City, in contrast to cities such as Chicago and Los Angeles, has experienced more pronounced cycles of youth gang activity over the years, going back to the nineteenth century (Asbury 1927; Klein 1995b; Schneider 1999).

To describe these phenomena, I borrowed terminology from social network theory and referred to the criminally active groups I was studying as cliques rather than gangs. Using a more neutral, analytic term was a deliberate gesture intended to recognize the research subjects' own distinction between group criminal activities that were related to gang membership and those that were not. Continuing this approach and drawing on the heuristic terminology developed by social anthropologist Jeremy Boissevain (1974), I distinguish here three analytic categories of association: action-sets, cliques, and named gangs. The emphasis here is not on defining gangs but rather on distinguishing types of association in terms of joint activity, enduring association, publicly acknowledged criteria of membership and identity, and law-violating behavior.

An *action-set* is simply an aggregation of individuals cooperating together in a coordinated line of activity. They need not continue their coordinated activity over any specified period of time or share any explicit recognition among themselves or in the view of others that they are associated on any permanent basis.

A *clique* is an aggregation of individuals with some form of diffuse and enduring bonds of solidarity, at least for the near term. They engage in a variety of activities together on some kind of regular basis. They need not have a name or leader or share ritual symbols of group membership.

A *named gang* has the properties of a clique, along with a name and explicit criteria of membership recognized by members and others. Gangs are far more likely than cliques to have designated leadership, formalized rules and codes of conduct, and ritualized symbols of membership, but they do not have to have all or any particular combination of these. Despite controversy among criminologists on this issue (Ball and Curry 1995), the term *named gang* will be used here with the explicit implication that its members engage in some illegal activities together. There are, of course, nondelinquent, named groups of youths who do not engage in delinquency (e.g., sports teams and clubs).

These terms are not mutually exclusive. A clique might become a gang over time, or vice versa. An action-set could be made up of some or all members of a clique or a gang. Using one or another term, however, adds precision to statements about particular instances of social action, such as an episode of criminal activity.

This typology is purely heuristic, introduced here for the purpose of allowing us to analyze the relationship between perceptions of youth gang emergence in New York City in the late 1990s and comparative ethnographic case studies of actual behavior on the ground during that period.

These comparative case studies examine the complex interplay of cultural symbolism with the actual social organization of youth violence in different and specific neighborhood contexts. The wide variation revealed here between different ecological areas of the same city goes to the heart of the problem of reification by demonstrating the local embeddedness of patterns of youth violence and the inadequacy of the rubric *youth gangs* for describing these patterns. First, however, we look at some of the things these different neighborhoods do share: local media and a municipal police force.

Gang Emergence in New York City in the 1990s

Three sources of data—media reports, police statistics, and field observations and interviews—are used here to examine the extent, nature, and perceptions of a period of gang emergence in one city.

Media Reports

The first source of data we examine is newspaper reports of youth gang activity in New York City. We gathered data by performing an online search through Lexis-Nexis of a standard package of New York City area newspapers, using the search term "youth gang*" to capture single and plural references. That search, covering the decade from 1990 through 1999, returned 937 references. We then culled that list to exclude all reports that did not refer specifically to recent youth gang activity in New York City. Excluded reports primarily included references to other cities and to films and books. The remaining 342 reports are plotted by year in figure 2.1.

The trend line shows cyclical variation, with three peaks. The steepest of the three occurs in 1989–1990 and reflects one sensational incident of violence in April 1989: the rape and nearly fatal assault of a female jogger in Central Park during an evening of violence, when a crowd of several dozen teenagers ran amok, assaulting and robbing multiple victims. The second peak, flatter and lower, occurs between 1992 and 1996. Most of these stories are about Chinatown youth gang members and a series of incidents and subsequent prosecutions involving them. The third peak is the one that is most closely

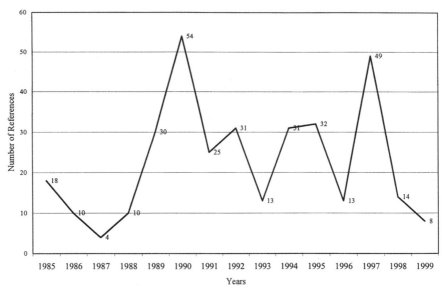

FIGURE 2.1
New York Media References to Youth Gangs in New York City

related to the national gang emergence phenomenon reflected in the National Youth Gang Survey. These stories are about large gangs with names that are also found in other cities, such as Los Angeles and Chicago: Bloods, Crips, Latin Kings, Nietas. The nationally famous gangs finally came to New York City in 1997, at least in name.[1]

The focal events underlying figure 2.1 can be usefully compared using our heuristic typology. Extensive documentation of the events of April 19, 1989, make it clear that the youth violence that occurred on that evening was perpetrated by spontaneous action-sets, in a manner similar to Canetti's (1984/1960) well-known descriptions of mob behavior. Although five youths were convicted of raping and assaulting the jogger, these convictions were overturned in December 2002, after a lone adult male confessed to the crime. No one, however, has disputed that violent crowd behavior occurred that day. Media attention to the event was so intense that it contributed a new term to the English language, *wilding*. Whether or not *wilding* was ever a term in common usage before reporters picked it up from one of the youths involved, neither the term nor the behavior in the park to which it gave rise is related to named gangs.

Chinatown youth gangs are another matter. As careful research by Chin (1996) has shown, these gangs were highly organized and responsible for systematic extortion and violence over a period of nearly twenty years, from the mid-1970s through the mid-1990s. These were named gangs with highly defined structures of leadership and criteria of membership. Extensive crack-downs by local and federal law enforcement effectively ended this pattern of gang organization.

The putative coming of the national gangs to New York City in 1997, in comparison, was a more nebulous matter, as indicated by the sharp peak and immediate decline in media reports. In 1997 stories about the Bloods and the Crips and Latin Kings surged. By 1998 they had fallen off. National-level research about reports of gang migration from cities like Los Angeles and Chicago to many other areas has concluded that, despite these reports, massive gang migration did not occur in the 1990s (Maxson, Woods, and Klein 1996). Something did happen in New York City during that time, and gangs with these names are still in the news as of this writing. However, the predicted massive crime wave resulting from the emergence of these gangs never happened. In fact, quite the opposite occurred.

Police Statistics

Figures 2.2 and 2.3 present trend lines for violent felony arrests and misde-meanor arrests, respectively, for the period 1985–1998. Separate trend lines are indicated for the city as a whole and for the three neighborhood areas in which we collected field data.

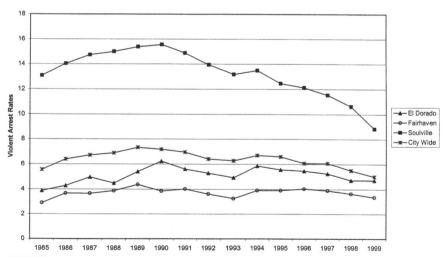

FIGURE 2.2
Total Violent Felony Arrest per 1,000 Population by El Dorado, Fairhaven, Soulville, and Citywide by Year, 1985–1999

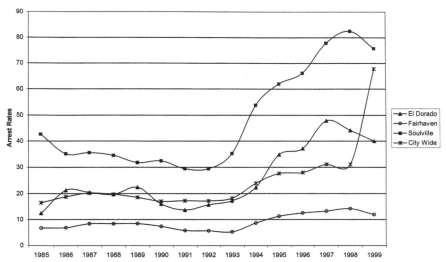

FIGURE 2.3
Total Misdemeanor Arrests per 1,000 Population by Neighborhood and Citywide by Year,
1985–1999

The two figures show opposite trends during the 1990s: a general decrease in violent felony arrests and a sharp increase in misdemeanor arrests. Much of this apparent contradiction is easily resolved. When comparing police statistics with other forms of crime data, criminologists generally attribute greater validity and reliability to police reports of serious violent crimes than to police reports of less serious crimes. More serious crimes are far more likely to be reported, and police have far less discretion in making arrests for serious crimes. The declines in serious violent crime in New York City are consistent with nationwide trends from the mid-1990s through the present, as documented in criminal victimization surveys as well as police reports (Blumstein and Wallman 2000; Catalano 2004).

The rise in misdemeanor arrests portrayed in figure 2.3, in contrast, is not only logically consistent with what we know generally about greater police discretion in making misdemeanor arrests. It is also consistent with the stated policies of the New York Police Department during this period (Bratton and Knobler 1998). Massive misdemeanor arrests were part of an explicit policy to reduce serious crime by getting tough on less serious crime, a policy referred to as "fixing broken windows" (Kelling and Coles 1996). The issue of the true causal relationship of the trends in figures 2.1 and 2.2 has been a matter of some controversy (Eck and Maguire 2000), but not one that is relevant to the matter at hand. Whatever contribution the crackdown on less serious crime made to the reduction in serious crime (most agree that it did contribute; the disputes are over how much), there is broad agreement that serious violent crime was declining in New York City both before and after the 1997 spike in media reports of a new generation of violent gangs (Karmen 2000; Silverman 1999).

Comparative Ethnographic Data on Gang Emergence and Youth Violence

Comparative ethnographic field studies provide a third source of data on the relationship between youth gangs and youth violence in New York City during the latter 1990s. The data were collected from 1995 through 1999 in three different neighborhoods, referred to here as El Dorado, Fairhaven, and Soulville. Observations and interviews focused on samples of approximately twenty-five students recruited in middle schools in each of these neighborhoods. We contacted them while they were in the seventh grade, followed them through the transition into high school during the ninth grade, and then did follow-up interviews with five sample members from each area again in 1999 (Sullivan et al. 1999). The focus of the study from the beginning was on school and community violence, not on gangs per se. However, the topic of gangs surfaced repeatedly. As the following data make clear, the meanings of the term *gang* were contested throughout.

The field data are used here first to describe the social ecology of youth violence in each of these three areas and then to trace the evolution over a five-year period in local perceptions of youth gangs. The symbolic representation of youthful violent behavior as having to do with gangs, as variously understood and as signified by the explicit use of the term *gang*, is thus grounded in an ecological analysis of changing patterns of youth violence based on interviews and observations with young people, parents, teachers, social workers, police officers, and other residents of these areas. Grounding the study of gang phenomena in this way allows us to situate multiple and shifting meanings of the term in a more comprehensive analysis of youth violence. This procedure then leads to some plausible resolutions of how gang emergence can occur during a time of overall declining youth violence.

Common features of behavior and language appear across the three sites in the ways that young people talked about the social organization of youth violence. Two key terms are *backup* and *represent*. *Backup* means having a network of friends to protect a person from attack, with force if necessary. Having backup was the most commonly cited way to insure personal safety while traveling to and from school or anywhere else without adult companionship. To *represent* means to assert a social claim to a social group or a very specific local area, such as a city block or a housing project, with the clear implication that the members of the group or the youthful residents of the area would provide backup. These terms refer explicitly to youth violence and collective organization. They differ from the term *gang* in that they refer to social processes, not to reified groups. Three site-specific case studies follow.[2]

Each case begins with a description of the physical and social ecology of the site, followed by a description of the pattern of youth violence that unfolded within that ecological context during the period of our observations. During this period, youth gang reports in the local media both mushroomed and subsided, a process evident within each case. The comparative analysis of the three cases then examines similarities and differences in the ways that the cultural symbolism of youth gangs is intertwined with actual patterns of youth violence.

El Dorado: Blocks and Bloods

El Dorado is a neighborhood in which most families are made up of first- and second-generation immigrants to the United States. Most of this immigration is from the Dominican Republic. Poverty rates in the neighborhood are high. Crime rates are also high compared to other areas of the city, although they are understated in the local area statistics presented in figures 2.2 and 2.3 because the police precinct in which they are located also includes lower-crime areas with higher proportions of higher-income, non-Latino whites. One side of El Dorado also borders a high-poverty, high-crime, predominantly African American neighborhood.

The school that we studied drew all of its students from the immediate ethnic enclave area. The physical ecology of the area consisted of a grid pattern of streets on which most of the residential buildings were low- to moderate-density multifamily dwellings, either row houses or small apartment buildings. High-rise, public housing superblocks were largely missing.

In combination, these various aspects of the physical and social ecology contributed to an organization of adolescent social life in which the single block-face area became an important source of social identity (Perkins, Meeks, and Taylor 1992). Adolescents identified strongly with their blocks, which they represented and which provided them with backup. Group violence tended to occur between groups from different blocks. Some blocks were known for delinquent groups who engaged in systematic criminal activity, including extortion and drug dealing. These groups were sometimes called block-gangs by local residents and school officials, but not all blocks were dominated by delinquent groups. Some, but not all, relationships between groups and individuals from different blocks were polarized. When they were polarized, it was said that the respective blocks "have beef."

One highly delinquent group was associated with a block adjacent to the school. They were known as the Redwood boys, after the name of their street. During the fieldwork period, this group engaged in many beefs, primarily with a group from another street, Castle. Local youths had ideas about what youth gangs were, but they tended to distinguish these from their block-group loyalties:

> *Interviewer*: What gangs do you know?
> *Ali*: Nieta, Zulu, the Dominican Power, Puerto Rican Power. The Latin Kings. The Panthers . . .

These groups were "all over the place" and distinguished not by where they lived but rather by their attire, particularly their "beads." The interviewer then asked Ali to compare these groups to groups in his local area, which elicited an ambivalent opinion about whether Redwood and Castle were or were not "gangs":

> *Interviewer*: So tell me because I don't understand something and maybe you can help . . . like, you are from Castle, right?
> *Ali*: Yes.
> *Interviewer*: And you might have beef or might not have beef . . . That's not a gang, is it?
> *Ali*: No. Well, yes—
> *Interviewer*: What's the difference?
> *Ali*: Not a gang, but the crew. It's like people you know.

Although most beefs within this immigrant enclave area were confined to the area, sometimes hostilities also broke out between Latino youths in El Dorado and African Americans in the adjacent neighborhood who lived in a large, superblock public housing project. Youths in El Dorado called this area the Desert, because the interior courtyards were often vacant, in contrast to their own usually bustling streets.

In the early period of fieldwork, 1995–1996, beefs between these groups were described in terms of these place-based identifications, as, for example, "between Redwood and Desert." By the end of the fieldwork, following the spike in newspaper gang reports of 1997 portrayed in figure 2.1, these conflicts had been redefined. We heard at one point that Redwood and Castle had joined together to fight the Bloods from the Desert who were trying to "take over the neighborhood."

By the time of the final field interviews, this beef too was over. The Redwood boys were no longer a presence. Targeted police action involving close cooperation with school officials had led to the arrest and incarceration of the Redwood leaders. Reports of Bloods from the Desert had also lessened. Local residents noted that crime in general had become far less serious since the highly violent years of the earlier 1990s.

In the context of the history and social ecology of El Dorado, there was a gang emergence phenomenon in this area in the late 1990s. The Bloods came to the Desert and made beef. Yet this conflict appears to have been primarily a relabeling of local rivalries that already existed. It was significant enough to cause two opposed factions, Redwood and Castle, to join together briefly. The whole thing, however, was ephemeral and took place during a period of general decline in violence in this area.

Fairhaven: Not in This Neighborhood

In contrast to the other two areas, the residential composition of Fairhaven was far more middle-class and white. Many residential blocks were lined with one- or two-family homes. Crime rates, as shown in figures 2.2 and 2.3, were below those of the other two areas and the city as a whole. The major exception to this pattern was a small area of public housing where many of the residents were poor and African American.

The social ecology of youth violence here was structured by public systems of public housing, parks, and school assignment. The local middle and high schools drew in many students from outside the neighborhood because of school overcrowding in surrounding areas that were poorer and whose residents were more likely to be African American and Afro-Caribbean in origin. Many of the incidents of youth violence that we recorded occurred around the bus routes carrying students to and from the Fairhaven schools. The fights along the bus routes came about in part because the school zoning patterns mixed adolescents from different areas together, scrambling patterns of backup and representing based on affiliation with local areas of residence. An additional locus of delinquent activity was a local park dominated by youths, almost all non-Hispanic whites, who sometimes drank alcohol and sold and used drugs.

One incident during the fieldwork period that caused local concern leading to public meetings occurred on a commercial strip during the immediate after-school hours. A local newspaper reported it as a gang incident. Interviews that we conducted raised questions about whether any blows were actually struck, but the presence of groups of teenagers jeering at each other in broad daylight was sufficiently unusual to unnerve many residents of this usually peaceful area (Sullivan and Miller 1999).

In most of the bus route confrontations and in this purported gang incident, however, there is little indication of the presence of a named gang. The structure of association underlying these incidents is that of action-sets or cliques. One partial exception indicates the transitory and marginal importance of gang ideology to youth confrontations in this area. Maxina, a seventh-grade student whom we followed closely, described a brief period when she and her friends toyed with calling themselves a girl gang:

> She want to come up in my face and talk how she wants to fight me and only reason why she want to fight me, 'cause we have this thing called Phat Phive. You know, it's just a name for the group of kids, like me and Marilyn, all of us hang out together. So we gave our group a name and . . . the only reason why she wants to fight me 'cause she wants to pick on the people Phat Phive. So that's why we, there's no such thing as a Phat Phive no more. It's just considered friends . . . because if there's Phat Phive, then they're just going to use that as a beef, to come and fight us, because we're a group and we give our group a name.

The closest thing to a named gang we recorded in Fairhaven was the group of youths who hung out in a Fairhaven park. One youth, who never got into fights, called it the "the Haven gang" and avoided the park. Kevin, who did hang out and sometimes got into fights, disputed the label:

> *Kevin*: It's just a bunch of kids that hang out. . . . They play handball in the park, basketball.
> *Interviewer*: But they call themselves a gang?
> *Kevin*: It's not a gang; it's a crew.

Most of the delinquent acts committed by the group associated with the park consisted of underage drinking and illegal drug use, along with some associated rowdiness among members of the group. However, we also heard of occasions when youths from outside the neighborhood tried to sweep in and ride off with bicycles, provoking collective responses from those in the neighborhood. As the invaders were youths of color and, with a couple of exceptions, the locals were not, these tales of defending the neighborhood from outsiders had clear overtones of racial conflict. One such incident was described by Bobby. Bobby himself had a history of abuse by his father and got into a lot of fights at school but did not consider himself a gang member.

> *Bobby*: There was like fifty kids on, all kids on bikes, there's like two on each bike looking to steal bikes and they were all on [street name] and this kid. . . . rides by and they're like, "Yo, give me your bike," and he's like, "Yeah get out of here," and they all started chasing him, so he called me out and like we got like five cars to come down by my house.

There are one or two references to the Bloods in the Fairhaven materials, but they refer to things happening outside the neighborhood. Fairhaven residents, like most residents of New York City who paid any attention to the newspapers, heard about the coming of the Bloods in 1997, but it had very little to do with them.

Soulville: Bloods in the Streets

Soulville is a predominantly African American neighborhood. Many residents are poor, although there are also some more middle-class areas. Crime rates have been high for years, as indicated in figures 2.2 and 2.3. The phenomenon of the coming of the Bloods and Crips to New York City in 1997, reflected in news trend line reports in figure 2.1, was centered in a few neighborhoods of the city, including Soulville. Our field data also reflect a lot of activity and discussion about this phenomenon, along with many direct observations of youths wearing the red bandanas and other insignia associated with membership in the Bloods. The Bloods did come to Soulville, in some sense, but what happened is far more complex than any simple notion of gangs suddenly appearing where there were no gangs before. Our data suggest mutually reinforcing effects of media panic and street rumor, on the one hand, and some real changes in the amount and organization of youth violence on the other.

At the beginning of the fieldwork period, we documented high levels of fighting among students from the middle school we were studying. Many of these fights involved multiple participants, but they were not organized as named gangs. Some groups involved in fights could be associated with a particular block or housing project, but other fights involved essentially ad hoc groupings, time-limited action-sets rather than cliques, much less named gangs.

Beginning in 1996 and rapidly increasing in 1997, named gang affiliations swept through the area. Local youths began choosing to identify as either Bloods or Crips, mostly Bloods. These identifications, however, were ambiguous and highly contested. There was no single group leader or structure within either category, and there were many subsets of these categories. Rumors ran rife and mutated constantly. A favorite topic of conversation was the difference between "real Bloods" and "fake Bloods." Most individuals carrying the insignia of Blood membership were said to be "fake Bloods."

Many stories were told of the rituals supposedly associated with Blood membership. In order to be inducted into the Bloods, various accounts claimed that a person had to do something such as randomly slash the face of a total stranger with a razor. In other versions, the slashing victim had to be a family member, or one's own mother. The crescendo of this hysteria peaked on Halloween 1997. As the day approached, rumors circulated throughout New York City that Halloween would be a day of mass Blood initiation. The chancellor of the

New York City schools issued a public statement that schools would remain open despite widespread calls from parents and others that they be closed. The Soulville middle school we were studying remained open, but only a handful of students showed up.

The mass slashings never occurred. The hysteria subsided, and, as indicated in figure 2.1, the newspapers lost interest. The downside of the 1997 spike in figure 2.1 includes a number of stories debunking the Bloods and Crips panic. Yet there are still reports of police crackdowns on the Bloods as of this writing, both in New York City and throughout the New York region, especially in northern New Jersey. Some entity or loosely related group of entities called the Bloods did appear in New York, but the panic came and went as violent crime citywide continued to decline.

Our field data suggest some clues as to the nature of these entities and the actual relationship of Bloods and Crips identification to the social organization of youth violence. Here we examine two accounts from the field data. The first describes changing patterns of affiliation and fighting in one housing project. The second is drawn from a single life history of a highly violent youth from age twelve to sixteen.

In the following interview, a youth describes how his housing project includes both self-identified Bloods and self-identified Crips:

> *Interviewer*: How about around here? . . . Are the cops cracking down on the gangs around here, like Bloods and Crips?
> *Asa*: No, they don't act up over here; they don't act up at all. Like when there's beefin' right here, they come together. Everybody come together. When there's beefin' in one project everybody come together.
> *Interviewer*: So there's Bloods and Crips in the same project.
> *Asa*: Yeah, same project.
> *Interviewer*: But they're cool with each other?
> *Asa*: Cool.

Asa went on to describe how recently a group calling themselves Bloods had tried to come into their project to settle a beef between one its members and a resident of the projects. In the face of this invasion from outside the project, Bloods and Crips inside the project joined together to repulse them. In this case, identification with other residents of the housing project superseded identification with Bloods or Crips. Two sets of group identification are available, and one or the other may be salient in a given situation.

In a series of intensive interviews with a youth called Dion over several years, we documented his involvement in many serious violent incidents and his repeated confinement in a series of youth and adult institutions. (After he turned sixteen, he became a legal adult in New York state.) Dion's fighting group in the early days called themselves the Mobsta Kids (pseudonymous). After one period of confinement, however, he came back to the community, briefly, calling himself a Blood. He explained the relationship between the two:

> *Dion*: Yeah. Mobsta Kids we Bloods.
> *Interviewer*: Are you still the leader?
> *Dion*: I'm not the leader of Bloods. I'm just a leader of Mobsta Kids. We Mobsta Kids for life.
> *Interviewer*: So what is the difference? It's the Bloods and it's the Mobsta Kids. What is the difference?
> *Dion*: Mobsta Kids is a family. Bloods is brotherly love.

Here Dion distinguishes clearly between a tight-knit group of individuals who have an enduring association and an ideology of association spanning many different situations and subsets of individuals. His identification with the Bloods became particularly important in correctional institutions, where he adopted it. In the close quarters of these total institutions, African Americans found themselves for a time at a disadvantage at the hands of Latinos, who were better organized as Latin Kings. Taking on the identity of Bloods put them on more equal footing. Yet the meaning of being a Blood or a Latin King inside an institution was quite different than on the outside.

By the time of our last interviews with Dion, he was again in the community and no longer identifying with either Mobsta Kids or Bloods. He was still criminally active but now more as an individual in pursuit of income, selling drugs. He viewed fighting for personal and group honor as a phase of his immature past.

There is some indication in our data that the Bloods hysteria of the late 1990s was associated with specific, localized increases in violence. This is not visible in figure 2.2, because the Soulville trend line combines figures from four different precincts. In one of these, however, there was a slight increase in violent felonies in 1997, coinciding exactly with the spike in media reports of gang activity and also with the patterns of violence evident in our ethnographic data. These local increases, however, were not enough to affect the long-term citywide decline in serious violence that continues to this day.

Comparative Case Analysis

Comparing similarities and differences across the sites demonstrates the wide range of phenomena associated with youth gangs, the looseness of fit between cultural symbols and the behaviors they are taken to represent, and the rapid shifts, even within a single ecological area, in how youths enact violence and what they call it when they do.

To be sure, there are notable similarities. We have already noted a common language for talking about threats to physical safety and the social organization of adolescent life. In addition to the terms *representing* and *backup*, we could add the universally understood designation of someone thought to be a physical coward as an *herb*. This piece of New York City youth folklore apparently dates back to an old fast-food commercial on television. Another similarity is that youth in all three areas recognized a new kind of gang phenomenon around 1996 and 1997, the supposed coming to New York City of gangs with names like the gangs in Los Angeles portrayed in Hollywood movies and popular music. Indeed, something did happen that was widely noticed. The fact that it coincided with an overall citywide downturn in serious violence, however, was not much noticed at the time.

Other similarities include the transience and ambiguity of gang labels. Examples of this from each area have been presented. Who was a "gang member," a "Blood," or a "real Blood"? These were lively topics of conversation, marking salient symbolic categories with murky specific referents. Answers to these questions were ambiguous and changed rapidly.

Yet the way in which the gang panic of 1997 played out in each area was specific to the area, in ways that can be related to local social ecology. These relationships should be thought of as configurational and contingent rather than causal (Ragin 1987). The elements include physical ecology, sociodemographic characteristics of the population, patterns of municipal services, the history and traditions of an area, and a large element of collective agency through which people actively shape and reshape communities. Some specific comparisons illustrate the ways in which such elements produced such different patterns of youth violence and people's interpretations of that violence.

El Dorado's block-gang conflicts were clearly directly related to the area's physical layout of low-rise multifamily buildings arranged in a grid. Not every such physical area will give rise to block-gangs, but, in combination with the poverty and cultural isolation of this immigrant community, the result is not surprising. One may speculate that as members of a relatively recent Latino immigrant minority group, the youth who lived there were less prone to appropriate the symbolism of African American gangs in Los Angeles than their African American peers in Soulville.

Some Soulville youth, in contrast, did so appropriate, with gusto but without much organization or consistency. The large superblock public housing projects that were far more prevalent in their area did not encourage the formation of block-gangs. Loyalty to particular projects and buildings, however, was a primary source of social identity, one that could be more salient when the chips were down than were the newly appropriated LA-style identities.

Proximity could trump media-inspired symbolism, which is not to say that the latter had no effect. Collective acts of naming can have practical consequences. There is some indication that the widespread adoption of LA-style names and symbols was in fact associated with brief upsurges in violence in some areas of Soulville. A more isolated example of this can be seen in Maxina's account of the brief career of the Phat Phive in Fairhaven.

Fairhaven resembles in some ways what Suttles once described as the "defended neighborhood" (Suttles 1972). Such an area is surrounded by poorer areas in which residents must constantly exert themselves to protect their own identity and social reputation by defining, expelling, or surveilling outsiders. Both the local merchants' unease over rowdy youths from outside the area and local teenagers' accounts of fighting off outside invaders illustrate this process. Fairhaven, however, was far from sealed off from poor people of color, despite the fact that its population as a whole was predominantly white and mostly middle-income. Less affluent youth of color came into the area to attend school and also lived in a small, bounded area of public housing within the neighborhood. Anxiety over diversity and change in the neighborhood shaped local perceptions of youth violence. A more extended study of this area that grew out of the present study takes as its subject the active social construction of whiteness as an ethnic identity (Miller 2000).

Discussion

Triangulating among the three data sources and the three neighborhood research sites described here, some possible solutions to the puzzle of declining serious youth violence during a period of greatly expanded gang membership begin to emerge. The term *gang* is used in many different ways. Sometimes it is equivalent to all youth group violence, and at other times it describes something much more specific. When used in a more specific sense, it refers to ritual and symbolic aspects of group identification. The emergence of this kind of symbolic identification is a real cause for concern, but it takes many forms. At the same time, much youth violence, even though it is still group violence, is not gang violence in this more specific sense. When people hear that there are a lot more gangs than there used to be, that seems to imply that there are more groups of youths engaging in crime and violence. Yet gang emergence can be just as much a matter of putting new labels on continuing patterns of activity. That clearly happened in two of the areas we studied and may have happened on a broader scale nationally.

The problem with gang studies as a distinct category of criminological inquiry is that *gang studies*, by virtue of the very title, implies answers to questions that should remain open to inquiry. Short has warned against "blind spots and reification in our research" and has recommended that we take care to study "gangs and other youth collectivities as units of analysis" (Short 1998). The philosophical term *reification* is defined as "improperly treating something as if it were an object" (Kemerling 2002). The objectness of gangs in some times and places is real enough, as numerous classic studies have shown, but extrapolating from such studies is fraught with peril. Gangs and gang identification processes vary enormously, too much for us to assume some universal essence. Generic gang prevention programs that concentrate on the outward symbols of group membership at the expense of concentrating on the specific local contexts of youth violence can shortchange the development of effective, knowledge-based, problem-oriented solutions. Reifying youth gangs imperils the study of youth violence. It is time to move forward from gang studies as a bounded field of inquiry toward a broader concern with youth violence and the diverse forms of youthful collective behavior.

Notes

An earlier version of this chapter was published in the Journal of Contemporary Criminal Justice (2005, vol. 21:170–90). Copyright © by Sage Publications, Inc. Reprinted by permission of Sage Publications.

1. A national study of media "youth gang reports" finds a similar pattern, with a slightly earlier peak, in 1995, and subsequent decline (Shelden, Tracy, and Brown 2001).

2. Because of promises of confidentiality of data made during sample recruitment, all names of places and persons are pseudonymous.

3

Studying Youth Gangs: The Importance of Context

Lorine A. Hughes

THRASHER'S *THE GANG: A Study of 1,313 Gangs in Chicago* (1927) demonstrated long ago the value of studying gangs as they exist in the real world. Although Thrasher was less than clear about his data and methods (see Short 1963, xviii), a concern for the relationship between gangs and their physical and social surroundings is evident throughout his analysis. For Thrasher, and for all others associated with the "contextualist paradigm" advanced by the Chicago school, "no social fact [made] any sense abstracted from its context in social (and often geographic) space and social time" (Abbott 1997, 1152).[1]

The "Variables Paradigm"

Most recent studies of gangs have strayed considerably from the Chicago vision. Research and thinking about gangs today reflect, in many ways, the general disciplinary shift of sociology away from contextual analyses to a "variables paradigm," in which concern is with outcome rather than process, with effect rather than cause (see Abbott 1997, 1999; see also Sampson 2000). In the field of gang research, the Chicago school now seems little more than a bygone era to which tribute is paid in literature reviews but which is ignored in conceptualization, research design, and execution.

The variables paradigm undeniably has advanced knowledge concerning gangs. Recent developments in surveys of law enforcement, a major source of quantitative data, have resulted in increasingly rigorous and comprehensive estimates of the prevalence and characteristics of gangs, gang members, and "gang-related" crime (however gangs are defined). Repeated surveys of the same organizations, such as those conducted by the National Youth Gang Center (see Egley, Howell, and Major 2004), provide a measure of stability to such estimates and encourage greater confidence in them. Secondary analyses of official records offer insights into general patterns of participant and offense characteristics of officially defined gang incidents. Although official data have been criticized extensively (see Hughes 2005a), they continue to benefit from the development of increasingly sophisticated gang intelligence and other special units within law enforcement and court organizations. Systematic surveys of young people attempt to transcend the limitations of official data, and data obtained from officials, by asking questions directly from population samples. In addition to their ability to provide information about a broader range of correlates and consequences of gang membership and activity, such surveys produce estimates of gang prevalence and demographic composition that supplement, and in some respects are more reliable and valid than, those that depend on official detection and reporting. Their chief value, however, is their usefulness for etiological inquiry at the individual level of explanation.

Despite methodological limitations (see Hughes 2005a), all the major sources of quantitative data consistently show a disproportionate involvement of gang members in crime, drug use, and violence. Longitudinal analyses of self-report data indicate further that increases in such activities correspond directly to periods of active gang membership, compared to periods before and after membership (Esbensen and Huizinga 1993; Thornberry et al. 1993, 2003). In view of the recently documented spread of street gangs to perhaps eight hundred or more cities and towns in the United States (Klein 1995a, 90),[2] the implication of these findings is hardly trivial. Yet the causal significance of gangs has received little attention in quantitative research. Although the existence and patterns of a facilitative effect have been well established in survey research (see Hall, Thornberry, and Lizotte, chapter 4 in this volume; Thornberry et al. 2003), explanation of the processes within the gang that promote such facilitation are noticeably absent. Official data and data gathered from officials are likewise silent concerning this issue.

Instead, quantitative research is largely descriptive, focusing on the prevalence of gangs, the sociodemographic characteristics of individual gang members, and the extent and correlates of gang crime and violence. Although such research is useful for the identification of important risk factors as a basis for the management of gang problems, it fails to capture the complexity and dynamics of gangs and their influence on the behavior of individual gang members (Hagedorn 1990). Understanding these phenomena requires sensitivity to process and to interactional fields within social time and space. By their very nature, however, survey research and analyses of official records can reveal only general patterns to be found in data that are static and have been either stripped of such contexts or contextualized at broad macrolevels far removed from behaviors of interest.

Gangs in Time and Space

In his recent book, *Chaos of Disciplines*, Andrew Abbott (2001, 117) argues that "social process moves on many levels at once" and at differing speeds; "reality occurs not as time-bounded snapshots within which 'causes' affect one another . . . but as stories, cascades of events. And events in this sense are not single properties, or simple things, but complex conjunctures in which complex actors encounter complex structures." Gangs and the behavior of their members are no different; as human creations, they are embedded within multiple layers of complexity, amidst both social change and continuity. The long-term hegemony of the variables paradigm has discouraged gang researchers from attending to such complexities, however, and has left the field vulnerable to the very "blind spots" that Jim Short warned against in his 1998 presidential address to the American Society of Criminology.

Confronting this intellectual challenge requires that researchers adopt a multilevel conceptualization of gangs and employ methods and measures that counterbalance the emphasis on crude classifications of such macro- and individual-level variables as region of the country, city size, race and ethnicity, academic failure, troubled home and family life, antisocial attitudes, criminal involvement, and so on. The formation and evolution of gangs in time and space need to be examined, with special consideration of the immediate and long-term effects of varying social forces and processes, including changes in relationships among members of individual gangs and between gang members and others with whom they come into contact (e.g., police and members of both friendly and rival gangs). Behavioral responses to particular experiences—of individual gang members and cliques within gangs—as well as to developmental sequences and life course changes require documentation beyond identification of associated, correlated, and modeled variables. Moreover, criminal and violent activities of gang members must be located within larger sets of behaviors and related to specific situational characteristics and processes of interaction.

Although qualitative fieldwork permits examination of these issues, field researchers have not always capitalized on the strengths of their methods. With few exceptions (e.g., Brotherton and Barrios 2004; Fleisher 1998; Horowitz 1983; Sullivan 1989), temporal changes in the composition, structure, and activities of gangs and the behaviors of their members are ignored or only incompletely analyzed. Spatial dynamics also receive limited consideration. The immediate social contexts within which social interaction unfolds are rarely examined, much less treated as integral components of etiological understanding of why gangs and their members do what they do. Many field researchers provide detailed descriptions of the physical and social settings in which their subject gangs operate but set aside such information as background material rather than systematically incorporating it into their analyses.

The general neglect of contexts in field research has been exacerbated in recent years by the virtual abandonment of ethnographic studies in the participant-observation tradition. Field research now consists largely of in-depth interviews with former and/or currently active gang members. Analyses of data gathered in this way have yielded important insights into the attitudes and experiences of gangs and gang members, including those who are otherwise more difficult to locate for study (e.g., females and Asians). Because such data tend to be isolated from their spatial and temporal contexts, however, they are likely to reflect a different reality from the one that can be revealed through careful observation of gang phenomena (see Klein 1971). Misrepresentation is apt to be a particularly besetting problem in research that involves the use of narrative accounts to *illustrate* findings based on quantitative analyses of the data, rather than the utilization of statistical analysis to *confirm* or *modify* theoretical insights or generalizations derived from systematic study of narrative, qualitative data, that is, research in which qualitative data are used anecdotally to bolster quantitative analyses that lack sufficient contextualization of individual and collective social life (see Silverman 2001).

Consequences of Decontextualization

Decontextualization in gang research hinders theoretical progress. Separated from their spatial and temporal contexts, gang phenomena are treated as social facts to be described rather than explained. Although researchers have begun to document more diversity among gangs, and along more dimensions, aside from often uncritical references to underclass theory and levels of neighborhood disadvantage, little effort has been directed toward understanding the complex interplay between gangs and their physical and social environments. Gang researchers have been much more inclined to rely on findings from community studies in which production of knowledge about gangs is of secondary importance (e.g., Anderson 1992, 1999; Suttles 1968; Venkatesh 2000) than to examine these matters firsthand. Thus, research that focuses specifically on gangs offers few insights into the conditions under which these groupings emerge and take shape, expand, transform, wane, and dissolve.

Loose usage of such terms as *gang life* and *life in the gang* belies an equally limited understanding of what gangs and gang members do and why. Gangs and their members engage in a wide variety of behaviors, most of which are not criminal or violent. Too often, however, crime and violence are viewed as *the defining* characteristics of gangs and the only behaviors deserving of sustained empirical attention. Conventional behaviors and their role in the structuring and functioning of gangs tend to be ignored as though unworthy of scholarly inquiry (Katz and Jackson-Jacobs 2004). The end result is the development of an extensive body of literature that focuses too much on crime and violence and not enough on the location of such behaviors within broader interactional fields.

Preoccupation with crime and violence notwithstanding, the etiological significance of gangs for such behavior has not been adequately addressed (Katz and Jackson-Jacobs 2004). Ironically, it was the advent of much-needed longitudinal studies (Esbensen and Huizinga 1993; Thornberry et al. 1993) that provided momentum to the general neglect of causality. These studies found that delinquent behavior by both boys and girls increases during periods of active gang membership, compared to both prior and subsequent periods of reported nonmembership in gangs; hence, the well-established association between gang membership and participation in criminal and violent activities could not be attributed simply to birds of a feather flocking together. Clearly, if one accepts the reliability and validity of self-reported gang membership and delinquent behavior, something about gangs *causes* their members to behave badly.[3] With this information in hand, however, many researchers either regarded the causal issue as resolved or simply ignored it. Some turned their attention toward other matters, especially those representing the interest of government funding agencies in quantifiable issues with clear policy implications.[4] Thus, the focus of empirical research on gangs shifted increasingly to documentation of the scope and offense characteristics of gang-related crime and violence and the presence of gang members within the criminal justice system (see Coughlin and Venkatesh 2003). The background and personal problems of individual gang members were also catalogued in great detail, as were the signs of disorder that so often mark the neighborhoods in which these youth live.

Throughout this flurry of research activity, researchers continued to overlook the influence of the immediate social contexts in which criminal and violent behaviors develop or are avoided (Short 1998). Along with the failure to consider how social interaction is shaped by such situational characteristics as physical setting and the presence of weaponry and third parties, there has been a serious shortage of systematic investigations into group processes and their relationship to individual and collective behaviors. Indeed, except for the persistent prodding of venerable gang researchers such as Malcolm Klein, earlier insights into group cohesiveness (Jansyn 1966; Klein 1969) and status management (see Short and Strodtbeck 1965/1974; see also Horowitz 1983;

Sanders 1994) were put on hold, seemingly because they served little purpose for the decontextualized analyses favored by the prevailing research ethos. A major consequence of moving so far away from the Chicago model is that a satisfactory explanation of the causal effect of gangs on the behavior of their members has yet to be established.

A related problem is the conflation of activities that gang members undertake on behalf of the gang and those in which they engage as individuals or part of a clique. Although Maxson and Klein (1990, 1996) suggest that the distinction between "gang motive" and "gang member" definitions of violence makes little difference to descriptive event characteristics,[5] there is no reason to believe that the criminal and violent behaviors of gang members are in all cases a function of the group or that they necessarily characterize the gang.[6] Without proper contextualization, however, scholarly analyses run the risk of treating as conceptually similar behaviors that stem from differing causal processes.

A major consequence of such oversimplification is the tendency to draw conclusions about gangs (groups) by extrapolating from data on the behavior of gang members (individuals). This has been most evident in research concerning the relationship between gangs and drugs. Klein notes that "lumping together street gangs and drug gangs . . . is currently the worst error we make" (1995a, 103; but see Spergel 1995). As others (e.g., Decker and Van Winkle 1994; Klein, Maxson, and Cunningham 1991; but see Skolnick et al. 1990) report, most street gangs are not involved in drug distribution *as gangs*. Many gang members sell drugs, and many use them. Much variation is evident, however, and we know little of the significance of gang membership for either behavior. The latter point is especially important, inasmuch as it is often noted that, while many gang members sell drugs, they tend to do so on their own and not as members of their gangs (e.g., Hagedorn 1988). They may do so under protective arrangements associated with gangs, however, and gangs may be salient to drug activities in other ways, such as in recruitment of drug users, drug sellers, and "mules" for drug distribution. To understand such complexities, it is important for gang researchers to attend to the social relationships and interaction processes that frame the behaviors of gang members as individuals and as members of groups. Failure to do so encourages a confounding of the behavior of gang members and the nature of their gangs, rather than an interest in the conditions under which these phenomena intersect.

Contextualized Countertrends

Gangs and gangbanging are complex phenomena, requiring multifaceted research. Although surveys and analyses of official data permit broad assessments of the scope of gangs and the characteristics of gang members and their behaviors, such decontextualized data provide only partial and, at times, misleading representations of gang realities.[7] Qualitative methods offer the best hope for putting quantitative findings into perspective, but concern for spatial and temporal contexts has been notably lacking among contemporary field researchers. Stereotypical images of gangs thus persist, together with a deficiency of new theoretical ideas concerning the causes and consequences of gangs, gang membership, and gang member behaviors.

Despite such problems, there is reason for optimism. New perspectives and analytic strategies that permit detailed examination of relationships among gang members and between gang members and others are emerging. Insights gained from social network analyses, for example, are adding precision to the measurement of such relationships and challenging stereotypes of gangs. Mark Fleisher (chapter 6 in this volume; see also Fleisher 2002a, 2005) documents networks of female gang members that extend far beyond gang boundaries, networks which, based on his field observations and interviews, help to provide resources for resource-deprived gang members. In chapter 7 of this volume, Andrew Papachristos makes more precise the nature of relationships among the Erls, one of the gangs introduced in Gerald Suttles's classic treatise *The Social Order of the Slum* (1968). The public health perspective discussed by Bill Sanders and Steve Lankenau in chapter 8 expands the range of such network analyses to data concerning the influence of social relationships on those behaviors previously neglected by gang researchers.

My own work with Jim Short (Hughes and Short 2005) examines more systematically earlier insights concerning the importance of status in gang life (Short and Strodtbeck 1965/1974). By combining quantitative and qualitative analyses—more precisely, by employing quantitative analyses of carefully coded field observations to inform theoretical insights derived from the qualitative, narrative data—previous insights concerning the nature of status management in dispute-related incidents involving youth street gang members are modified. In these data, the majority of disputes were resolved nonviolently, and by taking into account the influence of such microsocial contexts as relationships between disputants and dispute pretexts on dispute outcomes, the gang facilitation effect on the behavior of gang members is clarified and causal understanding is advanced.

Less evident in this work and in the small number of network analyses, however, is a concern for temporal contexts and the different forms that gangs take in response to varying external and internal influences. Given the ubiquity and rapidity of social change, this clearly is an important lacuna and one that must be addressed. Understanding the linkages between modern-day gangs and their historical contexts, of course, requires comparative research. The importance of comparisons is a major theme throughout this book (see, especially, chapters by Malcolm Klein, Pete Simi, Rob White, and John Hagedorn).

Conclusion

Although the importance of studying gangs and the behavior of their members as they exist in time and space cannot be denied, few seem to recognize how far gang research has strayed from the contextualist ideal. With the ascendance of the variables paradigm, studies of gangs mirror larger trends in sociology, in that they now rely primarily on "decontextualized facts with only a tenuous connection to process, relationship, and action" (Abbott 1997, 1158). Instead of being conceived of as groupings of real people who construct their realities through social interaction in the real world, gangs are often reified in the research literature (Short 1998; Sullivan 2005, chapter 2 in this volume). The popularity of this approach is no surprise, as it eases methodological and conceptual burdens while facilitating the development of general descriptions. Gang researchers thus are able to provide answers to a wide range of "what" questions. Although this type of research is clearly needed, problems arise when the tendency to treat gangs as though they exist in a social vacuum is as widespread as it is among contemporary gang researchers.

The general neglect of contexts has resulted in oversimplified representations of gangs and gang life, none of which adequately addresses the questions of how and why. References to underclass theory and neighborhood disadvantage notwithstanding, few researchers take seriously the processes by which gangs influence and are influenced by their physical and social environment. As a result, we know very little about the causes and consequences of gang formation, diversity, and change. Knowledge of the relationship between gangs and the behavior of their individual members is equally limited. Analyses of group processes, and how they shape gang member behaviors and are shaped by them, are notably absent in recent gang research literature. Much of the contemporary research on gangs focuses, instead, on static—and more easily measured— characteristics of gang members. The criminal and violent behaviors in which a gang member engages are then said to be undertaken *because* he or she is a gang member, an identity that is conceptualized as bounded and therefore impervious to influences related to the many other statuses and roles that gang members assume. A more astute explanation would relate such behaviors to the larger interactional fields in which they take place. To do this, gang researchers must first rekindle their interest in the human element that was so evident in the work of Thrasher and other Chicago school scholars. This is the essence of the contextualist paradigm.

Notes

1. An important qualification is suggested by Howard S. Becker (1999, 3), eminent sociologist and former student of Everett C. Hughes at the University of Chicago. Becker describes the Chicago school legacy as an "eclectic" mix of sociological approaches rather than a truly "unified school of thought."

2. Due in part to differing definitions of gangs and sampling frames, national prevalence estimates vary widely (see Curry, Ball, and Decker 1996).

3. Katz and Jackson-Jacobs (2004, 91) suspect that such "insider reports" are "unreliable if not downright delusional."

4. See Savelsberg, Cleveland, and King (2004) for a discussion of the effects of government funding on criminological scholarship.

5. Based on their analysis of homicide case files maintained by the St. Louis Metropolitan Police Department between 1985 and 1995, however, Rosenfeld, Bray, and Egley (1999, 513) report that "compared to the gang-affiliated events, the gang-motivated homicides involve more participants who are closer to one another in age, are more likely to take place in public, exhibit a somewhat distinctive spatial distribution, and are less likely to involve drugs." In addition, gang-motivated and gang-affiliated homicides were found to have peaked at different times.

6. The "gang-motive" definition of criminal violence employed by law enforcement in Chicago and in other jurisdictions (see Maxson and Klein 1996) represents an attempt to differentiate between incidents that are influenced by gang membership and those that are not. As is true of all official data, however, primary concern is with outcome rather than process.

7. In gang research, quantitative data and methods have not been combined with the type of "social systems" approach envisioned by sociologist James Coleman (1994).

4

The Gang Facilitation Effect and Neighborhood Risk: Do Gangs Have a Stronger Influence on Delinquency in Disadvantaged Areas?

Gina Penly Hall, Terence P. Thornberry, and Alan J. Lizotte

THE DELINQUENT AND VIOLENT NATURE of many youth gangs is a well-known but not yet fully understood phenomenon. Gang members have exceptionally high levels of involvement in criminal behavior, especially more serious and violent types of offending. This finding has been reported in studies based on observational data (Hagedorn 1998a; Klein 1971; Miller 1966; Moore 1978; Taylor 1990b), survey data (Fagan 1989, 1990; Fagan, Piper, and Moore 1986; Short and Strodtbeck 1965/1974; Tracy 1979), and official records (Cohen 1969; Klein, Gordon, and Maxson 1986; Maxson and Klein 1990). Indeed, recent longitudinal research has shown that gang members are responsible for the lion's share of these behaviors (Battin et al. 1998; Thornberry et al. 2003). Given both the strength of this association and the rapid proliferation of gangs to more and more communities in this (Howell 2003) and other developed countries (Klein et al. 2001), understanding the association between gang membership and criminal involvement is an increasingly important issue.

Using data from the Rochester Youth Development Study, Thornberry and colleagues (2003) examine the causal role of gang membership in eliciting delinquent behavior. Tests of three competing hypotheses supported the notion that gangs provide a facilitating context for youth to commit violent and delinquent acts, findings similar to those of other longitudinal studies (Battin et al. 1998; Esbensen and Huizinga 1993; Gatti et al. 2002; Thornberry et al. 1993). Gang membership has a strong impact on delinquent behavior, even when individual characteristics and tendencies are held constant. The pattern of these longitudinal findings of within-individual change is strongly suggestive of a causal impact of gangs on offending—an impact that occurs within a variety of social contexts such as residential areas or neighborhoods.

Area characteristics, especially levels of disadvantage, have been linked to both the presence of gangs and levels of crime. Although gangs have become more widespread, they are not equally present in all neighborhoods. A substantial body of research suggests that they are more likely to originate and thrive in disadvantaged neighborhoods. Thrasher's early work (1927) found that gangs occupied areas in the "poverty belt," which were characterized by shifting populations, business encroachment, and deteriorating neighborhoods. Throughout the course of the twentieth century, research continued to demonstrate this association. Cartwright and Howard (1966) and Short and Strodtbeck (1965/1974) found that gangs were more likely to flourish in neighborhoods characterized by low-income, female-headed households, and working-class residents. More recent studies also link neighborhood disadvantage, gangs (Fagan 1996; Vigil 1988), and gang members (Bowker and Klein 1983; Curry and Spergel 1992; Moore 1978, 1991; Short 1990).

In addition, disadvantaged neighborhoods have higher levels of crime and delinquency, as established by Shaw and McKay (1942) and subsequent researchers (Elliott et al. 1996; Sampson 1997; Sampson and Groves 1989; Sampson and Laub 1994). This research generally tests an indirect causal effect of neighborhood characteristics on delinquency, suggesting the importance of such contextual effects in models predicting delinquency.

Even though prior research indicates that both the presence of gangs and levels of delinquency are higher in more disadvantaged neighborhoods, this research has not examined whether the facilitating effect of gang membership on delinquency varies by neighborhood context. This study uses longitudinal data from the Rochester study to examine the extent to which the level of neighborhood disadvantage interacts with gang membership in facilitating an individual's involvement in violence, delinquency, drug use, and drug sales. We begin with a brief discussion of conceptual models for understanding the joint impact of area disadvantage and gang membership on these problem behaviors.

Conceptual Approaches

We know that during periods of active membership, an individual's rate of involvement in problem behaviors increases significantly compared to periods preceding or following gang membership. Within-individual change scores

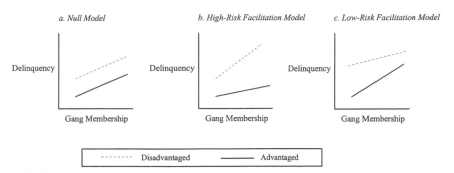

FIGURE 4.1
Alternate Conceptual Models for Understanding the Interaction between Gang Membership and Neighborhood Risk

are suggestive of a causal impact of gang membership on antisocial behavior, as each individual acts as his or her own control (Farrington 1988). Using this approach, Thornberry and others (2003) tested multivariate models that controlled for major risk factors for antisocial behavior, as well as random effects models that, in addition, controlled for unobserved heterogeneity. In all cases they found a strong effect of current gang membership on antisocial outcomes. The present study builds on these findings by examining whether this effect interacts with neighborhood context. That is, we examine whether the magnitude of the effect differs between more-advantaged and less-advantaged neighborhoods. We model three logical possibilities concerning this interaction, as depicted in figure 4.1.

Null Model

One possibility is that the gang facilitation effect operates approximately the same way regardless of the level of neighborhood disadvantage. In the null model, the powerful impact of the more immediate social environment of the gang network would exceed, indeed swamp, the impact of the broader social environment of the neighborhood. That is, we would expect that, regardless of the level of disadvantage, youth who join gangs will be more delinquent during their period of membership. This expectation is consistent with prior research showing a pronounced impact of gang membership on behavior (e.g., Thornberry et al. 2003) and a modest impact of area characteristics on individual rates of offending (e.g., Elliott et al. 1996; Lizotte et al. 1994; Simcha-Fagan and Schwartz 1986). If this model is correct, area characteristics will not moderate the impact of gang membership on delinquency. In figure 4.1a, we see that the slope depicting the impact of gang membership on delinquency is the same for youth residing in disadvantaged areas as for those residing in advantaged areas.

High-Risk Facilitation Model

A second model suggests that the gang facilitation effect will be stronger in the high-risk environment of disadvantaged areas. Because these areas have low levels of social control and collective efficacy compared to more advantaged areas (Kornhauser 1978; Sampson, Raudenbush, and Earls 1997), they may be less able to ward off the corrosive impact of street gangs on individual behavior. In disadvantaged areas, individual adolescents also have access to fewer protective factors to counteract the criminogenic influence of street gangs; in contrast, in more advantaged areas, protective factors such as stronger parental supervision and higher levels of collective efficacy are likely to counteract these influences. If this model is correct, we would expect a positive interaction between the level of disadvantage and gang membership in predicting individual involvement in delinquency. Accordingly, in figure 4.1b we see that the slope is steeper in disadvantaged compared to advantaged areas.

Low-Risk Facilitation Model

A third model leads to the opposite expectation, that is, that the impact of gang membership on delinquency will be smaller in disadvantaged, as compared to advantaged, areas. Individuals growing up in disadvantaged areas are exposed to a greater density of individual, family, and structural risk factors for delinquency and violence (Beyers et al. 2001; Stern and Smith 1995; Wikström and Loeber 2000). Gang membership is only one of many influences that could lead to delinquency, and, within this broader context of risk, it may not have a particularly salient impact on behavior. The level of risk in these areas is so high that delinquency is likely, whether or not the adolescent joins a gang. On the other hand, risk factors are less abundant and less extreme in more-advantaged areas. In this more benign atmosphere, exposure to street gangs may be particularly facilitative of delinquency. If this model is correct, we would expect the impact of gang membership on delinquency to be larger in advantaged areas, even though the overall level of delinquency is higher in disadvantaged than advantaged areas because of the density of risk factors in the former. In figure 4.1c, therefore, the slope representing the impact of gang membership on delinquency is steeper in advantaged areas.

Methods

We use data from the Rochester Youth Development Study (RYDS), an ongoing longitudinal study investigating the causes and consequences of serious, violent, and chronic delinquency. The Rochester study has followed a panel of juveniles from their early teenage years through age thirty, completing a total of thirteen interviews with respondents. The present analysis uses only the adolescent data (waves 1 through 9), as this is the developmental stage when gang membership is most prevalent (Thornberry et al. 2003). The study began in 1988, at which time 1,000 seventh- and eighth-grade students were sampled from public schools in Rochester, New York. Subjects and a primary caregiver (most often the biological mother) were interviewed every six months from the spring of 1988 until the spring of 1992.

Youth at high risk for serious delinquency and drug use were oversampled because the base rates for these behaviors are relatively low (Elliott, Huizinga, and Menard 1989; Wolfgang, Thornberry, and Figlio 1987). Males were over-sampled (75 percent versus 25 percent) because they are more likely than females to be chronic offenders and to engage in serious and violent delinquency (Blumstein et al. 1986; Huizinga, Morse, and Elliott 1992). Students from high-crime-rate areas of the city were oversampled, based on the assumption that adolescents who live in such areas are at greater risk for offending than are those living in low-crime-rate areas. In order to identify these areas, each census tract in Rochester was assigned a resident arrest rate, reflecting the proportion of the tract's total population arrested by the Rochester police in 1986.[1] Since the probability of selection into the study is known for all the students, we can weight the data to represent the target population—the total cohort of seventh and eighth graders in the Rochester public schools in 1988. All data are weighted in the analysis presented here.

The current analysis is very similar to that conducted by Thornberry and colleagues (2003, chapter 6) but focuses on the conditional effect of neighborhood disadvantage on the gang facilitation effect. Again, we group data from waves 2 through 9 into four annual time periods. Data from waves 2 and 3 comprise year 1, data from waves 4 and 5 comprise year 2, waves 6 and 7 comprise year 3, and waves 8 and 9 comprise year 4. These annual periods coincide with academic years. The average age of respondents at year 1 is approximately fourteen, and by year 4 it is seventeen. Due to the limited number of female gang members, the present analysis is restricted to the 577 males who completed interviews at waves 2 through 9.

Measures

Table 4.1 summarizes the measures used in the present analysis. The dependent variable is the frequency of involvement in various forms of antisocial behavior. At each wave, respondents were asked if they committed each of thirty-six delinquent acts and, if they had, how often they had done so. The General Delinquency index includes thirty-two nonoverlapping items measuring behaviors ranging from status offenses, vandalism, and minor property crimes to serious violent and property crimes. The Violent Delinquency

TABLE 4.1
Descriptive Statistics for Variables Used in Analysis

Variable Name	Source	Year 1 Mean	Year 1 S.D.	Year 2 Mean	Year 2 S.D.	Year 3 Mean	Year 3 S.D.	Year 4 Mean	Year 4 S.D.
Dependent Variables									
General Delinquency (Logged)	Adolescent	1.41	1.57	1.48	1.65	1.55	1.74	1.57	1.89
Violent Delinquency (Logged)	Adolescent	0.61	0.89	0.46	0.71	0.38	0.70	0.35	0.71
Drug Use (Logged)	Adolescent	0.31	0.93	0.35	1.00	0.44	1.14	0.76	1.51
Drug Sales (Logged)	Adolescent	0.14	0.65	0.18	0.73	0.26	0.89	0.31	1.07
Gang Membership Status									
Current Gang Member	Adolescent	0.18	0.39	0.14	0.35	0.12	0.32	0.07	0.26
Not Current Gang Member	Adolescent	0.11	0.31	0.15	0.35	0.17	0.38	0.21	0.41
Neighborhood Effects									
Neighborhood Disadvantage	1990 Census	1.31	0.84	1.29	0.85	1.22	0.87	1.20	0.88
Interactions									
Gang Member × Disadvantage		0.25	0.63	0.20	0.58	0.15	0.49	0.10	0.41
Not Gang Member × Disadvantage		0.15	0.49	0.20	0.57	0.21	0.57	0.25	0.63
Risk Factors									
Family Poverty	Parent	0.34	0.48	0.34	0.47	0.30	0.46	0.33	0.47
Parental Supervision	Adolescent	3.60	0.40	3.57	0.40	3.55	0.43	3.54	0.46
Commitment to School	Adolescent	3.09	0.35	3.09	0.38	3.07	0.36	3.06	0.39
Delinquent Peers	Adolescent	1.39	0.47	1.43	0.56	1.43	0.55	1.43	0.55
Negative Life Events	Adolescent	1.34	0.22	1.31	0.22	1.31	0.22	1.26	0.20
Prior General Delinquency	Adolescent	5.93	17.48	10.43	34.34	9.20	26.57	11.31	30.50
Prior Violent Delinquency	Adolescent	1.56	5.36	1.07	3.94	0.63	2.46	0.50	1.60
Prior Drug Use	Adolescent	0.71	6.08	1.89	12.98	2.20	14.86	3.50	19.78
Prior Drug Sales	Adolescent	0.02	0.25	0.96	7.33	0.81	7.48	1.33	9.18

index includes six items, such as throwing objects at a person and physically attacking someone with a weapon. In addition to self-reports of delinquency, we also asked about involvement with illicit drugs. The Drug Use index measures the respondent's use of ten different substances, ranging from marijuana to harder drugs like heroin and cocaine. Last, two items measuring the sale of marijuana and the sale of hard drugs make up the Drug Sales index. All the dependent variables are logged because of the skewness toward high values of self-reported delinquency data.

Gang membership status is based on the respondent's self-reported involvement in gangs during the six-month period since the previous interview. Responses at two consecutive waves were combined to form a single response for the relevant year. For each year, a three-category variable measures gang membership: Current Gang Member includes all respondents who were gang members during a particular year for the analysis; Not Current Gang Member includes all respondents who were gang members in some other year but not during the current year;[2] and Never Gang Member includes respondents who were never involved in street gangs across the four years of data collection. The last group is the omitted category in all equations in this analysis. As table 4.1 shows, 18 percent of boys were gang members in year 1, while the percentage drops in subsequent years (14 percent, 12 percent, and 7 percent respectively). Not surprisingly, the percentage in the Not Current Gang Member group increases from year 1 to 4 (11 percent, 15 percent, 17 percent, and 21 percent respectively).

An index of fifteen variables based on 1990 census tract data for Monroe County (U.S. Census Bureau 1992) is used to measure area social and structural disadvantage (see appendix). Using tracts as the unit of analysis, an index was created using principal components analysis with one factor (eigenvalue = 11.11; factor loadings are all above 0.5; Cronbach's alpha for the variables in the index = 0.83). Index scores for tracts range from −1.24 to 2.52, and individuals were assigned index scores based on tract of residence at the beginning of each of the four years.

Interaction terms were created for each year by multiplying the index score by gang membership status. In some cases, the calculation of these variables resulted in problems with collinearity between the interaction term and the gang membership term. The area disadvantage term and the gang membership term were mean-centered prior to the calculation of the interaction term in those cases.[3]

Control Variables

The literature on risk factors for gang membership (see Hill et al. 1999) and for delinquency and violence (e.g., Farrington 1987; Hawkins et al. 1998) suggests that risk is generated in multiple domains. These include social class position, family, school, peers, individual characteristics, and prior delinquent behavior. We include one central indicator from each of these domains in this analysis. Family Poverty is a dichotomous variable indicating whether family income falls below the federally defined poverty level for a given family size. Parental Supervision is a four-item scale indicating the extent to which the youth feels that his parents are aware of his whereabouts, friends, and activities. Values on the scale items range from "never" (1) to "often" (4) ($\alpha = 0.56$). Commitment to School is a ten-item self-report scale assessing the youth's agreement with questions about the importance of schoolwork, with four response choices, ranging from "strongly agree" to "strongly disagree" ($\alpha = 0.81$). Delinquent Peers is based on the subject's report of how many of his friends were involved in eight types of delinquent activity (a four-point response scale, ranging from "none of them" to "most of them"; $\alpha = 0.88$). Negative Life Events is a count of the number of life stressors (0–8) experienced by the adolescent, such as breaking up with a girlfriend, being suspended from school, or being seriously ill. Finally, Prior General Delinquency, Prior Violent Delinquency, Prior Drug Use, and Prior Drug Sales constitute four measures of prior problem behavior. These variables were constructed in the same way as the corresponding dependent variable, measured in the year immediately preceding the dependent variable, as are all the risk factors described above. Because in each equation we control for the same type of prior delinquency that corresponds to the dependent variable, the reported equations predict change in delinquency from one year to the next.

Results

Bivariate correlations between neighborhood disadvantage and the outcome variables for each of the four years are presented in table 4.2. As expected, delinquency is positively associated with area disadvantage in all cases, and the correlations are statistically significant for both general and violent delinquency

TABLE 4.2
Bivariate Correlations between Neighborhood Disadvantage and Self-reported Delinquency (Logged)

	Year 1	Year 2	Year 3	Year 4
General Delinquency	.09*	.09*	.08*	.12**
Violent Delinquency	.12**	.09*	.12**	.12**
Drug Use	.09*	.06	.04	.04
Drug Sales	.07	.08	.02	.04

*p < .05 (two-tailed); **p < .01 (two-tailed).

for each year. For drug use and sales, only the correlation for year 1 drug use reaches statistical significance.

Tables 4.3 through 4.6 present the results of multivariate ordinary least squares regression for general and violent delinquency, drug use, and drug sales for years 1 through 4. Looking at overall patterns across the tables, it is evident that the variables in the models are explaining a reasonable amount of variance in delinquency (R^2 estimates range between 0.11 and 0.56).

Table 4.3 presents the results for the full model predicting general delinquency for years 1 through 4. At each of the four years, current gang membership exerts a positive and statistically significant effect on delinquency. This effect is relatively steady across the four time periods, indicating the stability of the gang's influence in facilitating such delinquent behavior regardless of the age of the subjects. These findings replicate those reported in Thornberry and

TABLE 4.3

The Impact of the Interaction between Gang Membership Status and Neighborhood Disadvantage on General Delinquency, Males Only (Unstandardized Regression Coefficients in Parentheses)

	Self-reported General Delinquency (Logged)			
	Year 1 (n = 504)	Year 2 (n = 506)	Year 3 (n = 460)	Year 4 (n = 405)
Gang Membership Status				
Current Gang Member	.34** (1.38)	.26** (1.27)	.25** (1.47)	.21** (1.62)
Not Current Gang Member	.09** (0.48)	.11** (0.56)	.21** (1.02)	.01 (.07)
Neighborhood Effects				
Neighborhood Disadvantage	.03 (.05)	.01 (.01)	.06 (.12)	.08 (.15)
Interactions				
Gang Member × Disadvantage	−.11* (−.30)	.04 (.13)	.04 (.16)	.02 (.25)
Not Gang Member × Disadvantage	−.05 (−.31)	−.08* (−.48)	−.11* (−.41)	.01 (.03)
Risk Factors				
Family Poverty	.02 (.06)	−.01 (−.05)	−.04 (−.18)	−.04 (−.14)
Parental Supervision	−.07* (−.26)	−.01 (−.04)	.00 (−.01)	−.09* (−.38)
Commitment to School	−.12** (−.52)	−.16** (−.68)	−.23** (−1.05)	−.05 (−.22)
Delinquent Peers	.31** (1.06)	.09 (.28)	.13** (.45)	.20** (.72)
Negative Life Events	.15** (1.06)	.14** (1.03)	.18** (1.45)	.16** (1.52)
Prior General Delinquency	.23** (.02)	.17** (.01)	.13** (.01)	.14** (.01)
Adjusted R^2	.56	.34	.38	.26

*p < .05 (two-tailed); **p < .01 (two-tailed).

TABLE 4.4

The Impact of the Interaction between Gang Membership Status and Neighborhood Disadvantage on Violent Delinquency, Males Only (Unstandardized Regression Coefficients in Parentheses)[a]

	Self-reported Violent Delinquency (Logged)			
	Year 1 (n = 504)	Year 2 (n = 506)	Year 3 (n = 460)	Year 4 (n = 405)
Gang Membership Status				
Current Gang Member	.32** (.72)	.29** (.59)	.31** (.69)	.31** (.82)
Not Current Gang Member	.12** (.34)	.07 (.14)	.10 (.17)	.20** (.32)
Neighborhood Effects				
Neighborhood Disadvantage	.02 (.01)	.03 (.02)	.05 (.03)	.08 (.05)
Interactions				
Gang Member × Disadvantage	−.08 (−.12)	.07 (.09)	.04 (.06)	.02 (.08)
Not Gang Member × Disadvantage	−.07 (−.27)	−.03 (−.08)	.02 (.03)	−.11 (−.13)
Adjusted R^2	.42	.28	.28	.27

*p < .05 (two-tailed); **p < .01 (two-tailed).
[a]Each equation also includes the six risk factors listed in table 4.3, with the comparable prior delinquency variable substituted. Coefficients are available upon request.

TABLE 4.5

The Impact of the Interaction between Gang Membership Status and Neighborhood Disadvantage on Drug Use, Males Only (Unstandardized Regression Coefficients in Parentheses)[a]

	Self-reported Drug Use (Logged)			
	Year 1 (n = 504)	Year 2 (n = 506)	Year 3 (n = 460)	Year 4 (n = 405)
Gang Membership Status				
Current Gang Member	.03 (.07)	.05 (.15)	.15* (.55)	.24** (1.32)
Not Current Gang Member	.03 (.09)	.01 (.03)	−.10 (−.30)	.12* (.41)
Neighborhood Effects				
Neighborhood Disadvantage	.01 (.01)	−.05 (−.06)	−.03 (−.04)	−.07 (−.08)
Interactions				
Gang Member × Disadvantage	.13 (.19)	.23** (.45)	.05 (.13)	.08 (.60)
Not Gang Member × Disadvantage	.02 (.06)	−.02 (−.08)	.07 (.15)	.00 (.00)
Adjusted R^2	.19	.24	.22	.26

*p < .05 (two-tailed); **p < .01 (two-tailed).
[a]Each equation also includes the six risk factors listed in table 4.3, with the comparable prior delinquency variable substituted. Coefficients are available upon request.

TABLE 4.6
The Impact of the Interaction between Gang Membership Status and Neighborhood Disadvantage on Drug Sales, Males Only (Unstandardized Regression Coefficients in Parentheses)[a]

	Self-reported Drug Sales (Logged)			
	Year 1 (n = 504)	Year 2 (n = 506)	Year 3 (n = 460)	Year 4 (n = 405)
Gang Membership Status				
Current Gang Member	.08 (.12)	.21** (.44)	.15 (.40)	.13* (.59)
Not Current Gang Member	.00 (.00)	−.02 (−.05)	−.04 (−.09)	−.01 (−.03)
Neighborhood Effects				
Neighborhood Disadvantage	.00 (.00)	−.02 (−.02)	−.07 (−.06)	.04 (.04)
Interactions				
Gang Member × Disadvantage	.19** (.17)	.16* (.23)	.11 (.19)	.08 (.48)
Not Gang Member × Disadvantage	−.01 (−.03)	−.04 (−.10)	.03 (.05)	.00 (−.01)
Adjusted R^2	.28	.22	.11	.21

*p < .05 (two-tailed); **p < .01 (two-tailed).
[a] Each equation also includes the six risk factors listed in table 4.3, with the comparable prior delinquency variable substituted. Coefficients are available upon request.

colleagues (2003); controlling for each of the risk factors and, in this case, neighborhood effects as well, active gang membership facilitates increased involvement in delinquent behavior. Parental supervision, commitment to school, delinquent peers, negative life events, and prior general delinquency are all statistically significant predictors of general delinquency. The findings for prior delinquency indicate that we are in fact predicting the change in delinquency from one year to the next. Controlling for the other variables in the model, however, neighborhood disadvantage exerts no statistically significant effect on levels of general delinquency across the four time periods.

The results for the interaction terms are most consistent with the null model.[4] At years 2 through 4, the interaction between gang membership and area disadvantage is not statistically significant, indicating that the facilitating effect of gang membership on general delinquency is approximately the same in more- and in less-disadvantaged areas. In year 1, however, consistent with the low-risk facilitation model, the gang facilitation effect on general delinquency is significantly less in disadvantaged areas. This model suggests that youth living in disadvantaged areas are at such risk for delinquency that the influence of the gang has little effect on their behavior. Positive bivariate correlations between neighborhood disadvantage and delinquency (see table 4.2) and between disadvantage and the risk factors used as controls (not shown) indicate that these risks are more abundant in disadvantaged areas, supporting the plausibility of this explanation.

Tables 4.4 through 4.6 present findings for the other types of problem behavior studied—violence, drug use, and drug sales. These tables have been abridged for ease of discussion. Significant coefficients for the risk factors are of the same magnitude and direction as those reported in Thornberry and others (2003).

Controlling for risk factors and area disadvantage, gangs facilitate violent delinquency across all four time periods (table 4.4). As was the case for general delinquency, the statistically significant bivariate associations found between neighborhood disadvantage and violent delinquency become insignificant when entered into the multivariate model. In addition, none of the interaction terms is statistically significant. Again the null model is supported, indicating that the facilitating effect of gang membership on violent delinquency is the same regardless of the level of neighborhood disadvantage.

Turning to the drug measures, gang membership only facilitates drug use among older boys (table 4.5), and for drug sales it is statistically significant for years 2 and 4 (table 4.6). These results for drug use and sales differ from models that do not include neighborhood disadvantage and interaction terms (see Thornberry et al. 2003). In those models, there is a clear gang facilitation effect across time for both types of delinquency.

For drug use, coefficients for neighborhood disadvantage are not statistically significant. The results for the interaction terms are most consistent with the null model, as three of the terms are not statistically significant. The one significant interaction, for year 2, is positive, which is consistent with the high-risk facilitation model. The direction of this effect is opposite to the one significant interaction found for general delinquency.

Finally, we examine involvement in drug sales (table 4.6). At the earliest ages, years 1 and 2, the interaction terms are positive and significant. The gang facilitation effect has a significantly greater influence on drug sales among youth living in disadvantaged areas compared to those living in more-advantaged areas. This finding, coupled with the finding for drug use, suggests that gangs may influence younger adolescents in disadvantaged areas to both sell and use drugs. Following the logic of the high-risk facilitation model, it is possible that gangs have a greater influence on youth in these areas because of the low levels of social control. It is also possible that the gang has a greater influence on drug-related delinquency in these areas because drugs are a source of income for impoverished youth.

Discussion

The findings reported in this chapter are most consistent with the null model; in most cases, the gang facilitation effect has a similar impact on levels of delinquency, regardless of the magnitude of neighborhood disadvantage. Indeed, twelve of the sixteen interaction terms do not reach conventional levels of statistical significance. Moreover, among the four statistically significant findings, one supports the low-risk facilitation model and three support the high-risk model. Thus, consistent support for either of these models is lacking. Overall, gang membership facilitates problem behaviors in both neighborhood contexts and does so at a similar magnitude.

We next discuss possible implications of the four significant interactions, starting with general delinquency. Consistent with the low-risk facilitation model, the ability of the gang to facilitate delinquency is stronger in advantaged neighborhoods only for young gang members (year 1). Perhaps because these boys live in areas characterized by low levels of risk factors for delinquency, the influence of the gang may be particularly salient. Conversely, because risk factors for delinquency are higher in disadvantaged areas, youth living in such areas are at greater risk for delinquency regardless of gang membership.

In contrast, for drug-related behaviors, the significant neighborhood-by-gang-membership interactions that are observed are consistent with the high-risk facilitation model. This may be because youth in disadvantaged areas have fewer protective factors to ward off the risk generated by gang membership. Moreover, the significant interactions occur only at younger ages, suggesting that the conditioning effect of neighborhood context weakens among older boys. We speculate that this pattern, especially the findings for drug sales, may be related to age and New York state drug laws for adults (sixteen and older). Disadvantaged areas support open drug markets more often than privileged areas. This increases the visibility of drug sales and thus the likelihood of getting caught. As others have suggested, it is possible that gangs are more likely to use younger members for drug transactions since they are not subjected to the level of penalty imposed on adults.

These four interactions notwithstanding, the overall pattern in these data is most consistent with the null model. The impact of gang membership on adolescent involvement in delinquency and drugs does not vary substantially by neighborhood disadvantage in this time and place.

Zero-order correlations show that neighborhood disadvantage is positively related to the outcome variables at each year and that it is statistically significant half of the time. In the multivariate models, however, the main effect of neighborhood disadvantage is inconsistent in direction across types of crimes and fails to reach statistical significance. This is expected, as the control variables entered into this model represent mediating risk factors that are more abundant in disadvantaged areas. Therefore, the absence of a main effect for disadvantage does not indicate no association between neighborhood context and delinquency; instead, it reflects its indirect effect.

Also of interest are the differences between the main effects of gang membership found by Thornberry and others (2003) and those found in this analysis with respect to the drug measures. In Thornberry and colleagues' analysis, gang membership consistently facilitates drug-related behaviors across time. When neighborhood disadvantage and interactions are added to the models, however, four of the eight main effects of gang membership on drug use and sales are not statistically significant. Also, significant interaction effects are somewhat more likely to be found for the drug measures. This suggests the importance of including levels of neighborhood disadvantage in any examination of the gang facilitation effect on drug involvement. This may not be necessary for delinquency or violence, however.

Overall, we find little support for the notion that levels of neighborhood disadvantage influence the gang facilitation effect. Even though disadvantaged neighborhoods are home to more gang members and present more risk factors for delinquency, the gang's capacity to encourage delinquent behavior is not remarkably stronger in these areas. As gangs continue to form and spread throughout the United States, all types of communities are at increased risk for delinquency and crime. Within gang research, further exploration of how environmental contexts influence gang formation, membership, and activity will no doubt enhance our ability to prevent and reduce their negative impact on society.

APPENDIX
Variables Included in the Index of Area Social and Structural Disadvantage

Percent Total Families in Poverty
Percent Persons in Household on Public Assistance
Percent Persons Sixteen Years and Older Unemployed
Percent Males Sixteen Years and Older Unemployed
Percent Persons Twenty-five Years and Older with Less than a High School Diploma
Percent Persons Twenty-five Years and Older with Some College Education
Percent African American
Percent Hispanic
Coefficient of Racial/Ethnic Homogeneity[a]
Median Household Income
Percent Single-Parent Households
Percent Female-Headed Households
Percent Total Units Vacant
Percent Occupied Units Renter-Occupied
Percent Specified Owner-Occupied Units below Median Value

[a]This variable was created by summing the squared values of the percent total persons of Hispanic origin, African American, white, and "other" racial/ethnic groups. The value of this coefficient ranges from .25 to 1, with a score of 0.25 indicating that the tract is 100 percent racially/ethnically heterogeneous and a score of 1 indicating that the tract is 100 percent racially/ethnically homogeneous.

Notes

Support for the Rochester Youth Development Study was provided by the Office of Juvenile Justice and Delinquency Prevention (86-JN-CX-0007, 95-JD-FX-0015, 96-MU-FX-0014), the National Institute on Drug Abuse (5-R01-DA05512), the National Science Foundation (SBR-9123299, SES-9123299), and the National Institute of Mental Health (5-R01-MH56486, 5-R01-MH63386). Work on this project was also aided by grants to the Center for Social and Demographic Analysis at the University at Albany from NICHD (P30-HD32041) and NSF (SBR-9512290). Points of view or opinions in this document are those of the authors and do not necessarily represent the official positions or policies of the funding agencies.

1. Each tract's resident arrest rate—not its crime rate—was used because there is a substantial gap between where crimes occur and where offenders live. Indeed, the correlation between 1986 arrest rates and crime rates across all of Rochester's census tracts was only 0.26. We assume that risk for being an offender is more highly related to coming from a neighborhood with a high rate of active offenders than to coming from an area with a large number of crimes.

2. Some were gang members in prior years, some in later years, and some in both prior and later years.

3. Variables that were centered include Not Current Gang Member and its interaction term for years 1 and 2, and Current Gang Member and its interaction term for year 4.

4. Considering the purpose of the current chapter—to examine the possible conditioning effect of neighborhood disadvantage on the gang facilitation effect—we will not discuss the findings about interaction effects involving those who are not currently in a gang.

5

Neighborhood Effects on Street Gang Behavior

Andrew V. Papachristos and David S. Kirk

SOCIAL DISORGANIZATION THEORIES and systemic reformulations provide some of the most compelling and enduring explanations for the development, persistence, and geographic distribution of gang behaviors. Since Thrasher's (1927) seminal study, generations of researchers have conceived of gangs and gang behaviors as the product of social dislocations associated with urban life, including poverty, social immobility, ethnic conflict, and economic isolation. The systemic model of gang behavior offered by Bursik (2002; Bursik and Grasmick 1993) extends these theories by focusing on the regulatory capacities found in the social networks of neighborhood residents—that is, neighborhood social disorganization disrupts resident networks that would otherwise provide the capacity for the social control of street gang behaviors. Unfortunately, as applied to gangs, these theories remain to be empirically tested—less because of theoretical rigor than because of the lack of appropriate data.

Despite the strong theoretical tendency to attribute gang behaviors to neighborhood characteristics and processes, few studies have systematically measured or tested such claims. The present study seeks to rectify this shortcoming by combining neighborhood-level survey data from the Project on Human Development in Chicago Neighborhoods with detailed homicide records to test some of the central hypotheses concerning the influence of neighborhood-level processes on gang behaviors, in this case homicide. By integrating theoretical advancements made in the neighborhood-effects literature with research on street gang behavior, this study focuses on how neighborhood-level processes

63

like social control and collective efficacy are related to gang versus nongang homicide.

Social Disorganization and Street Gangs

Sociological research generally offers structural explanations of the etiology, persistence, and geographic distribution of gangs, the most compelling of which are social disorganization theory and its various manifestations.[1] Work by early Chicago school scholars established this tradition by defining the gang in relation to the ecological processes of disorganization and reorganization: The gang is a geographically, temporally, and socially "interstitial" group that forms in response to the disintegration of norms and customs and the consequential weakening of social institutions and mechanisms of social control (Park and Burgess 1924; Shaw and McKay 1942; Thrasher 1927). Thrasher's view still provides the bedrock of much of our theoretical understanding of gangs:

> Gangs represent the spontaneous effort of boys to create a society for themselves where none adequate to their needs exist. . . . The failure of normally directing and controlling customs and institutions to function efficiently in the boy's experience is indicated by disintegration of family life, inefficiency of schools, formalism and externality of religion. . . . All these factors enter into the picture of the moral and economic frontier, and, coupled with deterioration in housing, sanitation, and other conditions of life in the slum, give the impression of general disorganization and decay. The gang functions with reference to these conditions in two ways: It offers a substitute for what society fails to give. . . . It fills a gap and affords an escape. . . . Thus the gang, itself a natural and spontaneous type of organization arising through conflict, is a symptom of disorganization in the larger social framework. (12–13)

The work of Shaw and McKay advances the social disorganization understanding of gangs by formalizing the argument that gangs are a product of social immobility, ethnic heterogeneity, and low economic status (Shaw and McKay 1942). These factors disrupt the normative foundation that permits effective social control, thereby fostering a state of "social disorganization," or the inability of a community structure to realize common values of its residents and maintain effective social control (Bursik 1988; Kornhauser 1978; Sampson and Groves 1989). The extension of social disorganization theory to gang behaviors is straightforward: Gangs arise either to take the place of weak social institutions in socially disorganized areas, or because weak institutions fail to thwart the advent of unconventional value systems that often characterize street gangs.

William Julius Wilson's (1987) "underclass" perspective of gang research coincides with its social disorganization predecessor by focusing on structural aspects of the city, but it differs by asserting that unique changes in the post-Fordist economy have increased the importance of gangs in underclass neighborhoods (e.g., Hagedorn 1988; Venkatesh 1997). Venkatesh aptly summarizes this perspective:

> These [underclass] researchers argue that the contemporary street gang is a product of postwar systemic factors that have deleteriously affected the economic and institutional fabric of inner cities. Specifically, the gang partially fills the void left by other community-based institutions. *Adaptation* is the central trope . . . for underclass researchers to explain a range of phenomena: for example, the gang can be a substitute for poorly functioning familial structures; its value orientation offers a moral chart for those youths excluded from mainstream cultural systems. (89, emphasis in original)

The main critique of social disorganization is that these theories were largely developed at a time when an abundant supply of manufacturing jobs permitted social mobility among the lower classes and the ensuing aging-out of gang behaviors in favor of prosocial life course outcomes, such as marriage, blue-collar employment, or military service (Bursik and Grasmick 1993; Fagan 1996). The decimation of the manufacturing and industrial labor sectors of the economy generated new gang forms, particularly "drug" and "corporate" gangs, which arise as quasi-permanent social institutions to mitigate some of the social dislocations associated with underclass neighborhoods.[2]

Bursik and Grasmick's (1993) systemic model emphasizes the importance of relational networks to facilitate social control (see, e.g., Kasarda and Janowitz 1974). Rather than simply focusing on neighborhood characteristics such as social-economic status or ethnic heterogeneity, the systemic model stresses the *mechanisms* of social control, in particular the "regulatory capacities that are embedded in the affiliational, interactional, and communication ties of neighborhood residents" (Bursik 2002, 73–74). Accordingly, gang activity is likely to arise in neighborhoods, regardless of social class, where networks of private, parochial, and public control cannot effectively provide services to the neighborhood or regulate undesirable behaviors.

For all their theoretical appeal, social disorganization and underclass theories of gangs have received little empirical support, mainly because of data limitations. Qualitatively, most of the research on the relationship between street gangs and neighborhoods is descriptive in nature, relying largely on one-gang, one-neighborhood studies.[3] From Whyte (1943) to Venkatesh (1997), ethnographic studies chronicle numerous examples of the dynamic relationship between neighborhood context and gang behaviors. Studies report that gang-neighborhood dynamics both *hinder* and *foster* various levels of social control (e.g., Anderson 1999; Jankowski 1991; Keiser 1969; Pattillo 1998; Suttles 1968; Venkatesh; Whyte). Anderson reports that the presence of gang members and drug dealers on public streets generates fear among residents, thereby weakening informal control (see also Lane and Meeker 2003; Skogan 1990). Whyte, Jankowski, Pattillo, and Venkatesh, however, all find that gangs and gang members are integrated into other neighborhood institutions, often providing useful, if only de facto, forms of social control, support, or economic opportunities. Such discrepancies are most often explained by temporal or contextual differences, which make it difficult to generalize theoretically. For example, the hyperorganized "corporate" and "drug" gangs described by Padilla (1992), Papachristos (2001), Taylor (1990a), and Venkatesh are attributed to the unique gang history and culture of the research site. In particular, gang research based on Chicago gangs is most often criticized for the city's unique gang history.[4] The dearth of multisite or multigang qualitative research further confounds the issue.

Although quantitative studies lend support for the general social disorganization model (e.g., Sampson and Groves 1989), application to gangs has not sparked the same methodological rigor or empirical testing. Studies consistently demonstrate that gangs and gang behaviors are more likely to be concentrated in poor and disorganized neighborhoods (Curry and Spergel 1988; Rosenfeld, Bray, and Egley 1999; Short and Strodtbeck 1965/1974; Spergel 1984). Unlike the more general tests of social disorganization theory, however, these studies do not directly measure any of the mechanisms of social control that are hypothesized to mediate gang behaviors. Rather, they rely on aggregate census data to describe neighborhood characteristics (e.g., Curry and Spergel; Rosenfeld, Bray, and Egley) or on samples of gang-involved youth to analyze patterns of offending (e.g., Esbensen, Huizinga, and Weiher 1993; Thornberry et al. 2003). The former attributes mechanisms of social control to the social-demographic characteristics of the neighborhood but lacks actual measures, survey or otherwise, of the informal networks that serve as means of control. The latter, by focusing on the gang member as the unit of analysis, ignores the neighborhood factors, or else fails to measure the mechanisms of neighborhood social control. The neighborhood-effects literature provides a set of clear and testable hypotheses of social control mechanisms and processes that are consistent with the social disorganization and underclass theories of gang behaviors.

Neighborhood Effects, Collective Efficacy, and Gang Homicide

"Neighborhood-effects" research, where a neighborhood effect is defined as an emergent property of neighborhoods, net of neighborhood differences in population composition (Cook, Shagle, and Degirmencioglu 1997; Leventhal and Brooks-Gunn 2000; Sampson, Morenoff, and Gannon-Rowley 2002), has its roots in early Chicago school theorizing on the influence of urban environments, but it stresses the social processes or mechanisms that act as engines for *how* neighborhoods influence a given phenomenon or behavior (Sampson, Morenoff, and Gannon-Rowley, 447). The common thread throughout this literature is that key dimensions—including social disorganization, concentrated disadvantage, and social inequality—affect a host of outcomes, including crime, school dropout, social disorder, and public health. The backdrop for much of this research is Coleman's (1988) assertion that social capital is a form of social organization in which the structure of ties and relations between individuals makes possible certain actions, including social control. While the phrase *social capital* has come to take many meanings, the neighborhood-effects literature holds that these forms of social capital are situated in *structures of social organization* and are not simply the sum of individual or neighborhood characteristics (Coleman 1990, 302).

Sampson and colleagues (Sampson, Raudenbush, and Earls 1997) suggest that "collective efficacy" is a crucial mediating process that explains the relation between neighborhood structures and behavioral outcomes. Collective efficacy is a concept based on a combined measure of neighborhood informal social control, social cohesion, and trust. Sampson and colleagues (Sampson, Morenoff, and Earls 1999) argue that researchers must move beyond a reliance on social capital and density of social ties when examining the determinants of crime and social control. They describe social capital as a "resource potential," but one that must be activated and utilized. Thus, collective efficacy refers to the process of activating or converting social ties to achieve any number of collective goals, such as public order or the control of crime.

Figure 5.1 outlines a basic theoretical model of the systemic social disorganization theory, with collective efficacy as the key mediating variable and gang behaviors as an outcome. This model is an extension and application of previous research demonstrating that collective efficacy mediates the structural effects of neighborhood disorganization on delinquency, crime, criminal victimization, observed disorder, and homicide (Morenoff, Sampson, and Raudenbush 2001; Sampson, Raudenbush, and Earls 1997). We hypothesize that collective efficacy operates similarly with respect to gang behaviors.

Through the use of neighborhood-level data that captures the mechanisms in figure 5.1, the goal of this chapter is to provide an empirical test of the general systemic social disorganization theory as it applies to gang behaviors, in this case gang-related homicide.

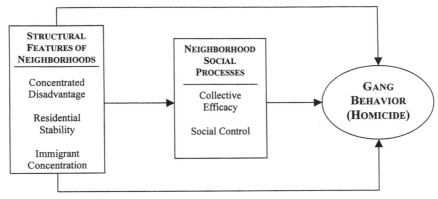

FIGURE 5.1
Causal Model of Systemic Social Disorganization Theory Applied to Gang Behavior (Gang Homicide)

Data and Methodology

Data on neighborhood social processes come from the Project on Human Development in Chicago Neighborhoods (PHDCN) 1994–1995 Community Survey of 8,782 Chicago residents. There were 847 census tracts combined into 343 neighborhood clusters (NC) constructed to be "as ecologically meaningful as possible, composed of geographically contiguous census tracts, and internally homogeneous on key census indicators" (Sampson, Raudenbush, and Earls 1997, 919). Investigators surveyed respondents on neighborhood measures focused on levels of social organization (i.e., formal and informal social control, relationships and trust among neighbors) and criminal activity. Of particular importance is the measure of *collective efficacy.* Our measure of neighborhood collective efficacy replicates methods employed by Sampson, Raudenbush, and Earls and Morenoff, Sampson, and Raudenbush (2001) which combine a total of ten survey items that tap the constructs of social control and social cohesion/trust. Following Morenoff, Sampson, and Raudenbush, we also utilize empirical Bayes residuals of collective efficacy as an explanatory variable as a means of correcting for bias resulting from measurement error.

We utilize three measures of neighborhood structure: concentrated disadvantage, immigrant concentration, and residential stability. We hypothesize that concentrated disadvantage is positively associated with homicide because of the lack of institutional resources in disadvantaged communities and the lack of middle-class neighbors to serve as a "buffer" against poverty (Wilson 1987). In accordance with the social disorganization perspective, we hypothesize that immigration concentration is positively associated with homicide because of its influence on weakening social ties and institutions. Finally, we hypothesize that residential stability is negatively related to crime, in that stability is conducive to the formation and maintenance of social networks. A total of ten indicators were combined via factor analysis to create these three measures (see appendix A for a list of items used to construct the various measures utilized in this analysis). Items used to construct factors scores are weighted by their factor loading (see appendix B for a table of the factor loadings).

Homicide data were obtained from records of all homicides in the city of Chicago.[5] Data recorded at the incident level include demographic, geographic, motive, and gang information on both the offender and victim. Address information from each incident was used to geocode the location of the homicide to the corresponding neighborhood cluster. We rely upon the Chicago Police Department's designation of gang motivation to determine if a homicide is gang-related. Definitions of gang-related homicide vary drastically across municipalities but can generally be categorized as "member-based" and "motive-based" definitions (for a review, see Maxson and Klein 1996). Member-based definitions, such as those used in Los Angeles, more broadly classify any homicide involving a gang member as gang-related. In contrast, more conservative motive-based definitions, such as those used in Chicago, classify a homicide as gang-related only if the crime itself was *motivated* by gang activity and, therefore, would be more commonly associated with group-level actions such as turf defense, drug dealing, or existing gang conflicts. So a homicide of one gang member by another gang member because of a personal dispute (e.g., the infidelity of a lover, intoxication) would be classified as gang-related by the former definition but not by the latter. The Chicago data used here adhere strictly to the conservative definition of *gang-related.*[6]

The use of a conservative definition has a crucial advantage: It ensures that the actual reason for the homicide is a *group* reason, even though the actual event may simply entail the interaction between two individuals. That is, the homicide is motivated, and often preceded, by an extra-individual (gang) circumstance. The unit of analysis is the *gang* and not the gang member, as would be the case in the member-based definition. The drawback, however, is that the conservative definition tends to underestimate the total number of interactions.[7] For the sake of precise definition of the interaction, we err on the side of conservatism.

Statistical Models

We model the number of homicides per neighborhood during 1995 as sampled from an overdispersed Poisson distribution. In all models, a random intercept term is included in order to examine the variability across neighborhoods in the homicide rate.

Three sets of covariates are utilized in analyses, starting with a baseline model and moving toward a more inclusive model with the addition of relevant covariates. Three different dependent variables are examined with each set of covariates, thus producing a total of nine statistical models. The three dependent variables are (1) total homicides per neighborhood in 1995, (2) gang-related homicides per neighborhood in 1995, and (3) non-gang-related homicides in 1995. Model 1 is the baseline model, with homicide as the outcome and three neighborhood structural characteristics (Concentrated Disadvantage, Immigrant Concentration, and Residential Stability) as covariates. Models 2 and 3 expand upon the baseline model with the addition of Collective Efficacy, and then a control for prior homicide in each neighborhood (pooled from 1991 to 1993). Similar to previous studies, it is hypothesized that collective efficacy is negatively related to homicide.

Results

Tables 5.1 and 5.2 present a descriptive summary of homicides in Chicago during 1995, with table 5.1 illustrating the racial distribution of homicide. In table 5.1, it can be seen that a vast majority of 1995 homicides had black victims. It is also noteworthy that 21 percent of homicides with black victims were gang-related, while 46 percent of Hispanic homicides were gang-related. Furthermore, while there were roughly twice as many black gang homicides as Hispanic gang homicides (130 versus 65), there were nearly six times as many black nongang homicides as Hispanic.

Table 5.2 presents the average characteristics of the neighborhoods in which these homicides occurred. At least one homicide was reported in 244 of Chicago's 343 neighborhoods. At least one gang homicide occurred in 121 neighborhoods, and at least one nongang homicide occurred in 223 neighborhoods. Compared to neighborhoods with no homicides reported, on average, homicides occurred in neighborhoods with greater levels of concentrated disadvantage, less immigrant concentration, less residential stability, and greater

TABLE 5.1
1995 Gang Homicides by Race and Ethnicity (percentages in parentheses)

	All Homicides 1995	Black Homicides	Hispanic Homicides	Other Race/Ethnic Homicides
Total	815	611	141	63
Gang	205 (25.2)	130 (21.3)	65 (46.1)	10 (15.9)
Nongang	610 (74.8)	481 (78.7)	76 (53.9)	53 (84.1)

TABLE 5.2

Means of Neighborhood Correlates by Gang Motivation for Homicide (1995)

	All of Chicago	No Homicides	Total Homicides	All Gang Related	Top 50 Gang Related	All Nongang Related	Top 50 Nongang Related
			By Prevalence of Homicide in Neighborhood				
N (# of Neighborhoods)	343	99	244	121	50	223	50
Sum of Homicides, 1995	815	0	815	205	134	610	309
Concentrated Disadvantage	0	−0.581	0.236	0.358	0.470	0.294	1.058
Immigrant Concentration	0	0.146	−0.059	0.016	1.097	−0.116	0.778
Residential Stability	0	0.030	−0.015	−0.119	−0.100	0.009	0.154
Collective Efficacy	3.889	4.034	3.830	3.791	3.755	3.818	3.708
Proportion Black	41.1	13.2	52.4	53.5	57.0	56.1	93.5
Proportion White	35.3	63.5	23.8	19.8	13.0	21.5	2.1
Proportion Hispanic	19.8	17.4	20.8	24.1	28.3	19.5	4.1

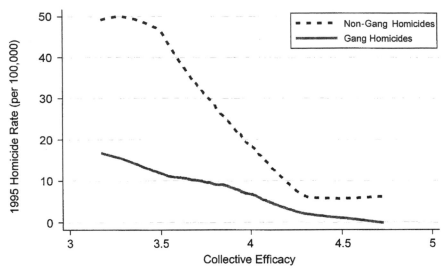

FIGURE 5.2
Homicides in Chicago by Neighborhood Collective Efficacy, 1995

concentrations of black residents. Homicides also occurred, on average, in neighborhoods with relatively lower levels of collective efficacy. Rank correlations (Spearman's rho), which rank Chicago neighborhoods according to their homicide count, provide one means of examining the association between collective efficacy and the different types of homicides. The correlation between gang homicide and collective efficacy equals −0.273, while correlation between nongang homicide and collective efficacy equals −0.455. As another means of examining the relation between collective efficacy and homicide, figure 5.2 plots the pattern of association in the raw data with a smoothed line graph. This figure again illustrates that the association between collective and homicide is negative, albeit a flatter association for gang homicide.[8]

Table 5.2 also displays the average neighborhood characteristics of those neighborhoods in Chicago with any gang and nongang homicides in 1995, and the characteristics of neighborhoods where gang and nongang homicides are heavily concentrated. Fifty neighborhoods account for 134 out of the 205 gang homicides (approximately 65 percent), and fifty neighborhoods account for 309 out of the 610 nongang homicides (approximately 51 percent). Fifteen of the top fifty neighborhoods of gang homicides also ranked in the top forty neighborhoods in the number of nongang homicides. This relationship holds in the ecological patterning of neighborhoods as well.

Figure 5.3 displays maps of nongang homicides compared with gang homicides at the police beat level. While nongang homicides are experienced over a large number of police beats, the heaviest concentration occurs on the south

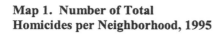

Map 1. Number of Total
Homicides per Neighborhood, 1995

Map 2. Number of Gang-Related
Homicides per Neighborhood, 1995

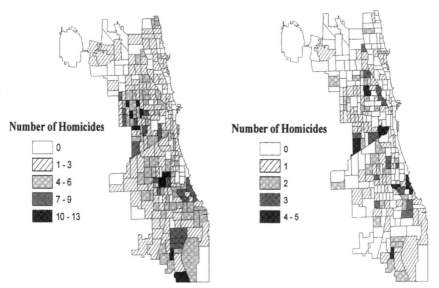

FIGURE 5.3
Number of Nongang and Gang Homicides by Police Beat, Chicago, 1995

and west sides of the city. Gang homicides are much more sparsely distributed throughout the city but are also heavily concentrated on the south and west sides. Neighborhoods highest in gang homicides are not always the same as those highest in nongang homicides, however. It is not the case that all high homicide areas experience a gang problem. Also, several neighborhoods experienced a gang homicide but not a nongang homicide; gang homicides almost entirely drive the murder rate in these neighborhoods.

The association between the police beat count of gang and nongang homicides in 1995, as measured by Spearman's rho, equals 0.309. Using the homicide rate per 100,000 neighborhood residents in the correlation instead of counts, rho equals 0.291. These findings suggest that there may be differences in structural characteristics and social processes such as collective efficacy between neighborhoods with gang homicides and those with nongang homicides. Disentangling these differences is one central objective of our regression models.

Table 5.3a attempts to replicate Sampson, Raudenbush, and Earls (1997), and finds very similar results. Comparing models 1 and 2 in table 5.3a, it can be seen that the addition of collective efficacy partially mediates the effect of concentrated disadvantage on homicide. In model 3, results show that concentrated disadvantage and residential stability are positively associated with the

TABLE 5.3a
CPD Total Homicide, 1995

	Model 1		Model 2		Model 3	
	Coeff	*Std Err*	*Coeff*	*Std Err*	*Coeff*	*Std Err*
Constant	3.220***	0.043	3.195***	0.047	3.184***	0.045
Concentrated Disadvantage	0.696***	0.047	0.520***	0.063	0.322***	0.076
Immigrant Concentration	−0.063	0.052	−0.101**	0.050	−0.057	0.051
Residential Stability	0.056	0.040	0.138**	0.045	0.149***	0.044
Collective Efficacy			−1.059***	0.252	−1.053***	0.241
Total Homicide Rate, 1991–1993					0.006**	0.002

* = .05; ** = .01; *** = .001

expected homicide rate, and that immigrant concentration is unrelated to the total homicide rate. Collective efficacy is negatively related to homicide, even after controlling for prior homicide.

Table 5.3b displays results of analyses of nongang homicides. Here the strength and direction of association between covariates and nongang homicide are similar to those found with total homicides. Whereas homicides and immigrant concentration are unrelated to total homicides, however, nongang homicides are strongly negatively related to immigrant concentration. Recall that the immigrant concentration variable is based on the percentage of Latino and the percentage of foreign-born residents in a given neighborhood, and that it is expected that greater heterogeneity of ethnic groups make more problematic the maintenance of informal neighborhood social control, thus leading to greater levels of crime. In this case however, empirical results point to the opposite.

Moving to results in table 5.3c, similar to nongang homicide, results show that the strength and direction of association between covariates and gang homicide are largely similar to those found for total homicides. However, now there is a weak positive relation between immigrant concentration and gang homicide (p-value = 0.073 in model 2 and 0.107 in model 3). What seems to be happening when aggregating to total homicides is that the positive association between gang homicides and immigrant concentration is offset by the strong negative association between nongang homicides and immigrant concentration.

That said, we find that collective efficacy mediates the effect of concentrated disadvantage on each of the three dependent variables, as well as the effect of immigrant concentration, particularly for nongang homicides.

Discussion

As hypothesized, we found that neighborhood social processes, in this case collective efficacy, mediate the effects of some of the structural features of neighborhoods. Furthermore, we conclude that collective efficacy operates similarly on violent gang behavior as it does on other forms of violent behavior.

We hypothesized that greater immigration and heterogeneity of ethnic groups would make it more problematic to maintain informal neighborhood social control and lead to greater levels of crime, but found the opposite for nongang homicides. Martinez (2002) offers one explanation for the benefit of immigration, arguing that immigration may actually strengthen communities by replacing population loss and because strong ties to the family and labor market offset negative consequences associated with poverty and disruption of ties.

Another explanation that diverges from social disorganization accounts of violence is that immigrant concentration may be disruptive of homicide in certain urban areas but positively related to homicide in still other areas. As

TABLE 5.3b
CPD Nongang Homicide, 1995

	Model 1		Model 2		Model 3	
	Coeff	Std Err	Coeff	Std Err	Coeff	Std Err
Constant	2.885***	0.048	2.856***	0.052	2.844***	0.051
Concentrated Disadvantage	0.687***	0.050	0.511***	0.065	0.78***	0.077
Immigrant Concentration	−0.199***	0.052	−0.233***	0.051	−0.163**	0.057
Residential Stability	0.085**	0.043	0.169***	0.048	0.196***	0.047
Collective Efficacy			−1.098***	0.263	−1.133***	0.245
Nongang Homicide Rate, 1991–1993					0.009**	0.003

* = .05; ** = .01; *** = .001

TABLE 5.3c
CPD Gang Homicide, 1995

	Model 1		Model 2		Model 3	
	Coeff	Std Err	Coeff	Std Err	Coeff	Std Err
Constant	1.928***	0.071	1.904***	0.075	1.898***	0.075
Concentrated Disadvantage	0.561***	0.055	0.402***	0.083	0.345***	0.088
Immigrant Concentration	0.186*	0.088	0.150	0.083	0.128	0.079
Residential Stability	−0.003	0.075	0.073	0.082	0.055	0.083
Collective Efficacy			−0.994**	0.389	−0.884**	0.384
Gang Homicide Rate, 1991–1993					0.014**	0.007

* = .05; ** = .01; *** = .001

Lee and colleagues (Lee, Martinez, and Rosenfeld 2001) suggest, immigrants residing in predominately black neighborhoods may be too few to provide the positive benefit from immigration noted above and therefore are consistent with the potentially negative consequences suggested by early social disorganization theorists (e.g., Long 1974; Shaw and McKay 1942).

Table 5.1 indicates that almost half of Hispanic homicides were gang-related, while less than one-quarter of black homicides were gang-related. Table 5.1 also shows that the ratio of black to Hispanic gang homicides is roughly two to one, but the ratio for nongang homicides is roughly six to one. Because most nongang homicides involve black victims and occur in areas heavily populated by blacks, nongang homicides in table 5.3b reflect the overall nature of black homicide. Blacks in Chicago typically live in areas with few immigrants, and this is particularly true in areas susceptible to high levels of homicide involving black victims. Areas of Chicago with the greatest number of immigrants, correspondingly, have comparatively low levels of black violence. This may account for the negative correlation between homicide and immigrant concentration in our analysis of nongang homicides.[9] In other words, because homicide victimization of blacks dwarfs that of all other ethnic groups, and black victimization occurs in areas with few Hispanics and foreign-born individuals, it appears that there is a negative relation between black violence and immigrant concentration.

However, the influence of immigrant concentration operates differently in Hispanic neighborhoods. Figures 5.4 and 5.5 graphically illustrate these points,

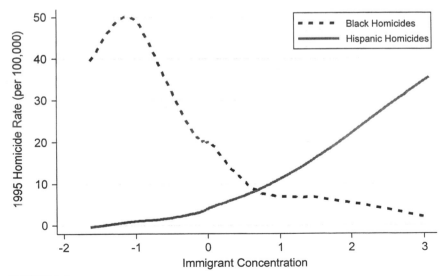

FIGURE 5.4
Homicides in Chicago by Immigrant Concentration and Gang Race/Ethnicity, 1995

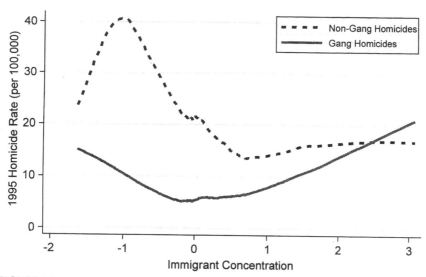

FIGURE 5.5
Homicides in Chicago by Immigrant Concentration and Gang Motivation, 1995

with plots of the relationship between homicide and immigrant concentration. Figure 5.4 shows a positive association between Hispanic homicide and immigrant concentration, as suggested by social disorganization theorists. For black homicides, there is a rise and a sharp decline in the relationship between homicide and immigrant concentration. However, there are very few black homicides in neighborhoods with high levels of immigrant concentration. This finding occurs because there are actually very few blacks, and therefore very few potential black homicide victims, in areas with high immigrant concentration. Figure 5.5 confirms the point suggested before, that most nongang homicides involve black victims, and the association between nongang homicide and immigrant concentration actually reflects the nature of the relationship between black homicide and immigrant concentration. Thus, the original hypothesis concerning the negative repercussions of ethnic heterogeneity may still hold some value, but the effect may not be uniform across differing neighborhood types. Further research is needed to explore this particular hypothesis and the similarity of neighborhood effects across ethnic groups more generally.

One important caveat is worth noting. Our present models, unfortunately, do not include any measure of the spatial effects of homicide (e.g., Morenoff, Sampson, and Raudenbush 2001; Rosenfeld, Bray, and Egley 1999). Such factors should be seriously considered in future research on gangs and neighborhood effects, especially given the geographic concentration of gang violence.

Preliminary analyses by the authors using spatial econometric models suggest that the findings presented here hold when considering the spatial dependency of homicide (Kirk and Papachristos 2005).[10]

Conclusion

Seventy-five years after Thrasher's (1927) seminal work, critical questions remain: How do gangs facilitate social behaviors? How do gangs react to and influence their social contexts? And how do different neighborhood contexts produce gang behaviors? One way to address such a research agenda, as with the advancement of social science in general, is to apply a methodological or theoretical approach found in other areas of social research to the phenomena in question to discover similarities, differences, or other intriguing patterns. The recent developments in the neighborhood-effects literature provide one such avenue of inquiry. The present study finds general support for the systemic model of gang behavior, in that informal mechanisms of social control significantly lower the level of lethal gang violence. However, disaggregating analyses by gang versus nongang homicides clarify some of these processes, revealing relevant issues for future research on gangs and neighborhoods.

Neighborhoods with high levels of violence are not necessarily the same neighborhoods that have high levels of gang violence. Both types of neighborhoods are similar in regards to structural characteristics, such as concentrated disadvantage and residential mobility, as well as their levels of collective efficacy and informal social control. But what, then, predicts why a particular neighborhood experiences a gang problem? If social disorganization theory operates the same with respect to gang behavior as it does for deviance more generally, what factors explain why some disorganized neighborhoods give rise to gang violence, while others with similar structural features do not? Immigrant concentration appears to be one such factor; neighborhoods that have a high rate of gang homicide without a corresponding high rate of nongang homicide are characterized by high levels of immigrant concentration.

Analyses disaggregated by gang motivation show that concentrated immigration is a more complex factor in social disorganization models than previously suggested in either the gang or the neighborhood-effects literature. The effect of immigrant concentration on nongang homicides is negative, essentially yielding the opposite result of that predicted by the social disorganization model. However, the effect of immigrant concentration *is* positive for gang homicides, in large part because of the large portion of Hispanic homicides that are gang-related. Thus, gang homicide more closely follows the classic social disorganization predictions than do nongang homicides, due to the larger number of gang homicides committed in neighborhoods with high immigrant concentration. This finding is consistent with Curry and Spergel's (1988) analysis, which shows that black gang homicides tend to follow the "underclass" hypotheses, while Hispanic gang homicides follow more traditional social disorganization hypotheses.

Perhaps the most important question that follows from this discussion is why neighborhoods with high levels of immigrant concentration tend to have high levels of lethal gang violence but not high levels of nongang lethal violence? What is it about neighborhoods with concentrated immigration that leads to specific types of violence? Future research, especially comparative studies, should try to better understand what it is about immigrant neighborhoods that generate gang violence and how such factors are different in nonimmigrant neighborhoods that also experience gang problems. Analyses disaggregated by race and gang motivation seem clearly to be necessary for this purpose.

These findings provide direction for future research on gangs and neighborhoods. On the one hand, gang research would be well served by integrating methodological and theoretical developments of neighborhood research, specifically focusing on structure and process rather than merely on outcomes. As decades of qualitative research has demonstrated, gangs are and continue to be key actors in (and not just outcomes of) processes of control. Gang research should try to better understand how gangs are integrated into neighborhood-level social networks, using multiple methods of investigation and theoretical perspectives. Conversely, neighborhood research can benefit greatly by giving more consideration to the role of gangs in neighborhood-level processes. Analyses here show that while collective efficacy mediates gang violence, it does not fully explain why some neighborhoods experience a gang problem, while similar neighborhoods do not. Thus, ignoring gangs in the study of neighborhood social control overlooks not only significant deviant behaviors in many neighborhoods but also potential actors in networks of social control. Integrating the study of gangs with the study of neighborhoods may explain some of these differences, especially with respects to mechanisms of social control.

Appendix A: Construction of Neighborhood Measures

Aggregate measure I is developed from individual responses to the 1994–1995 PHDCN Community Survey, and measures II–IV are developed from responses to the 1990 decennial census.

I. Collective Efficacy
   A. Social Cohesion and Trust: "Strongly agree, agree, neither agree nor disagree, disagree, strongly disagree."
      i. This is a close-knit neighborhood.
      ii. People around here are willing to help their neighbors.
      iii. People in this neighborhood can be trusted.
      iv. People in this neighborhood generally don't get along with each other (reverse coded).
      v. People in this neighborhood do not share the same values (reverse coded).
   B. Informal Social Control: "Would you say it is very likely, likely, neither likely nor unlikely, unlikely, or very unlikely" that people in neighborhood would intervene:
      i. If a group of neighborhood children were skipping school and hanging out on a street corner.
      ii. If some children were spray painting graffiti on a local building.
      iii. If a child was showing disrespect to an adult.
      iv. If there was a fight in front of your house and someone was being beaten or threatened.
      v. Suppose that because of budget cuts the fire station closest to your home was going to be closed down by the city. How likely is it that neighborhood residents would organize to try do something to keep the fire station open?
II. Concentrated Disadvantage: Proportion of Population in Neighborhood Cluster
   A. Below poverty line
   B. On public assistance
   C. Female-headed families
   D. Unemployed
   E. Less than age 18
   F. Black
III. Immigrant Concentration: Proportion of Population in Neighborhood Cluster
   A. Latino
   B. Foreign-born
IV. Residential Stability: Proportion of Population in Neighborhood Cluster
   A. Same house as in 1985
   B. Owner-occupied house

APPENDIX B
Oblique Rotation Factor Loadings, Neighborhood
Structure Measures

Variable	Factor Loading
Concentrated Disadvantage	
Below poverty line	0.93
On public assistance	0.94
Female-headed families	0.93
Unemployed	0.86
Less than age 18	0.94
Black	0.60
Immigrant Concentration	
Latino	0.88
Foreign-born	0.70
Residential Stability	
Same house as in 1985	0.77
Owner-occupied house	0.86

Source: Data from the 1990 census.

Notes

This research was supported in part by National Science Foundation grant SES-021551 to the National Consortium on Violence Research (NCOVR). The Project on Human Development in Chicago Neighborhoods was conducted with support of the John D. and Catherine T. MacArthur Foundation, the National Institute of Justice, and the National Institute of Mental Health. We thank the editors, Bob Bursik, Jeff Fagan, Tracey Meares, and Rob Sampson for helpful comments on earlier drafts of this chapter. Any findings or conclusions expressed are those solely of the authors.

1. For a review, see Bursik and Grasmick (1993) or Kornhauser (1978). Subcultural approaches to gang behaviors (e.g., Cohen 1955; Miller 1958) are not discussed here, due to space limitations.

2. Both the social disorganization and underclass approaches focus mainly on the lower echelons of the stratification system, thus ignoring the development of gangs in stable, middle-class neighborhoods, let alone the recent proliferation of gang problems in suburban and rural areas (see Bursik and Grasmick 1993; Klein 1995a). The systemic model discussed below is one approach to solving this problem.

3. Short and Strodtbeck (1965/1974), Jankowski (1991), and Hagedorn (1988) are the most striking exceptions to the one-gang, one-neighborhood ethnographic standard.

4. As Maxson and Klein (2001, 247) note, "The danger in evaluating any research emanating from Chicago lies in understanding the uniqueness of its context."

5. Data were provided by the Chicago Police Department's Division of Research and Development. The analysis of the data reflects the findings and opinions of the authors and in no way represents the views of the Chicago Police Department or the city of Chicago.

6. Ultimately, the investigating detectives make the decision as to whether a homicide is gang-related. While homicide data are not the most ideal source of gang data, to the best of our knowledge there exists no systematic neighborhood-level survey of gangs or gang members comparable to the PHDCN. Arguably homicide data are the most reliable sources of crime data, especially given the resources used to investigate each case and maintain records.

7. This underestimation is relative. With an average of 182 gang-related homicides a year over the past ten years, the conservative definition in Chicago provides an adequate sample size for most statistical methods.

8. The visual differences in the slopes in figure 5.2 are a matter of scale—there are simply more nongang homicides. No statistically significant difference in the slopes exists.

9. One of the comments we received on an earlier version of this paper is that this finding might reflect how we have measured immigrant concentration. To assess the validity of this critique, we performed analyses using an alternative specification of immigrant concentration, based on the census measure of percent foreign-born in 1990, as opposed to a combined measure of percent foreign-born and percent Latino. Inferences are the same regardless of which measure of immigrant concentration is used.

10. These preliminary models are available directly from the authors.

6

Youth Gang Social Dynamics and Social Network Analysis: Applying Degree Centrality Measures to Assess the Nature of Gang Boundaries

Mark S. Fleisher

THAT YOUTH GANGS ARE SOCIAL GROUPS whose members are bound by common affiliation (a bounded group) and that boundaries (of some sort) separate gangs are fundamental to the history of gang research and are now common ways of conceptualizing youth gangs. This chapter argues that research design not only can but does have a significant effect on these (and perhaps other) widely accepted descriptive concepts of youth gangs. I gathered participant observation (PO) and social network (SN) data in the same neighborhood and use these data to assess the nature of gang boundaries and gangs as social groups. PO data will support our standard concepts of youth gangs. Social network analysis (SNA) will not. I do not argue that SNA is better than PO, or vice versa. I argue that SNA and PO can complement one another, together creating a more nuanced analysis of adolescent life in a specific ecological niche.

Crime is the single most significant act uniquely defining youth gangs (versus delinquents). Ethnographic and survey research has shown that gang groups have the transformational power to encourage youth to commit more crime or more serious crime or both. Thus we can reasonably expect to find in geographically disconnected gangs similar group-level structural patterns, which are absent in nongang delinquent and nondelinquent groups. We should then be able to measure gangs' structural uniqueness and posit how structural uniqueness exacerbates mutual (perpetrator/victim) risk (versus nongang delinquents).

Social network analysis in this chapter has three main points. The first point is that gang affiliation is a demographic variable—an attribute—and has no necessary relational and social structural properties. The second point is that the gang-group level of analysis does not denote unique structural features (versus delinquent groups) that might be called "gang structure." The third point is that gang youth interact independent of gang affiliation.

On Groups and Boundaries

A central theoretical assumption is that a youth gang is a bounded social group. Leading from this assumption, we further assume that mutual interactions bond members in a more or less equal way. The final assumption is that such bonds are fostered by symbols (gang colors, gang territory, and hanging out together) and common need (protection, power, and solidarity).

Participant observation reinforces the gang-as-group notion. Fieldworkers commonly use snowball samples. If a snowball sample has twenty youths, they nominate one another in a continuous series, and their links are apparent. Likely as well is that these youths share multiple relations. A small sample would show many intragroup ties. Expanding a sample beyond twenty informants finds them in a more expansive social scene. A standard snowball sample sends a researcher from youth A to B, B nominates C, and C nominates D, and so on, until the researcher has run out of nominations (or time or money or both). Looking beyond the snowball, we find that A, B, C, D . . . X have ties beyond those to one other. Informant A may be linked to (F, G, and H) and B to (X, Y, and Z); however, A <> B friendship is the only link joining (F, G, and H) and (X, Y, and Z). Without too many steps, (F, G, and H) and (X, Y, and Z) are now able to reach one another.

If we accept the above three assumptions, gang teens gathered in a snowball sample form a mutually exclusive bounded gang group.[1] Data inclusive to this sample could lead to a misinterpretation of group size, the nature of intra- and intergroup relations, and the group's demographic composition. On those misinterpretations may be generated a faulty assessment of risk enhancement and risk reduction factors. By virtue of the sampling design, data on individual teens, actors in their personal networks, and the type and level of risk as a function of whole network structure are excluded. Being out of sight (youth excluded from a snowball) may not mean out of reach.

George Homans (1950, 84) argues that group members interact more among themselves than they do with outsiders. Extending this group concept into gang research, we have assumed that gang groups meet Homans's condition. This is not, however, an intuitively rational assumption. A poverty adaptation would require the ability to extend one's reach beyond intragroup ties, in an effort to acquire material and social resources. Symbolic restrictions imposed on group size and composition would restrict potential access to resources in a resource-depleted context. Such a sociocultural maladaptation would not, it would seem, be self-perpetuating over time or space.

If Homans's group definition were expanded to a gang neighborhood, inter-gang boundaries and gang groups would be observable to fieldworkers. Observations of street corner behavior and interviews may likely reinforce a gang's mutual exclusiveness. Gang members say they have boundaries. Fieldworkers and police see graffiti, colors, and gang names, and assume group distinctiveness. Gang nomenclature supports mutual exclusiveness. Gang members call one another brothers, sisters, and "homies"; they say they "ride" and hang together. A boundary seems to make sense if we accept the above three assumptions. A boundary would maintain gang-group stability (a group is more stable if people have known one another a long time), enhance group closeness (improve degree of friendship), and decrease intragroup conflicts (inhibit intragroup squabbling and fights). Examples of ethnographically defined groups and boundaries are noted below.

Achieving an Ethnographic Definition of a Study Group

James Spradley's 1970 ethnography *You Owe Yourself a Drunk: An Ethnography of Urban Nomads* is a replicable, linguistic anthropological study that develops a cognitive linguistic model of "hobo" knowledge of street survival. Spradley carefully defines his hobo population. Hobos are visible; they have sleeping spots; they hop trains; more abstractly, hobos share a common knowledge of survival generated by a finite set of survival rules; and hobo jargon expresses shared knowledge. Hobo knowledge is mutually exclusive of other categories of knowledge; it takes effort and time to learn to be a hobo.

Twenty years later, Spradley's train-hopping hobos were gone. Nevertheless, the culture of the street was marked by drug dealers, drug addicts, beggars, pimps, prostitutes, cardsharps, petty hustlers, and adolescents proclaiming in riotous color their identity as Crips and Bloods. In the late 1980s and early 1990s, these gangs were appearing in Seattle's central district (Fleisher 1995). Distinct behavioral, linguistic, or cultural rules clearly separating Crips and Bloods were blurred. There were Bloods who hung out with Blood friends in Blood territory, but there were Crips and Bloods who hung out together.

Fremont Hustlers were a coed, multiracial gang on Kansas City's northeast side (Fleisher 1998). Given the way the police talked about their criminal involvement in drug distribution, burglary, armed and unarmed assaults, and homicide, Fremont Hustlers seemed to be a well-bounded, somewhat co-herent group of gang youth. It would be reasonable to assume that a high level of criminal activity might result in egocentric networks that included few if any outsiders and in a sociocentric structure that, reinforced by atti-tudes and group norms, would block information flow to parties outside the group.

PO found that the Fremont Hustlers were a bunch of adolescent males and females hanging around a girl's house, usually doing nothing but listening to the radio and smoking cigarettes or blunts. When asked about the gang's name, Fremont Hustlers, common responses were, for instance, "That's just the name we gave ourselves because other kids were doing it too."

Fremont kids would disappear. No one would know where they were for weeks or months. Some Fremont youth went to jail or juvenile detention; some went to visit relatives in Alabama and Mississippi; some stayed with rival gang members; and some simply found housing elsewhere and visited Fremont on occasion. No one cared where they were. These observations were counterarguments to the increasing sentiment that was supposed to typify a group of gang members.

Fremont adolescents shared the list of personal and family problems with Seattle Crips and Bloods: family violence, parental drug addiction, estrange-ment from parents, and literal or episodic homelessness caused by poor parental relations. City and gang name notwithstanding, Seattle's Crips and Bloods were virtually indistinguishable from Kansas City's Fremont Hustlers.

Putting Social Network Analysis in the Field

Social network analysis focuses on individuals' personal networks and struc-tural properties of sociocentric (whole) networks (Wasserman and Faust 1994). A social network is a set of actors and a relation measured across those actors. Relations link actors. Relational data are contacts, ties, and attachments that link one actor to another. Fundamental to SNA is the assumption that network actors' interactions create persistent social patterns of interaction (social struc-ture) that influence individual behavior.[2] A system of network relations is not the property of actors but of the systems actors create.

Champaign, Illinois

The U.S. Department of Justice, Office of Juvenile Justice and Delinquency Prevention issued a two-year grant (2000-JR-VX-0006) that supported data collection and analysis of egocentric network, sociological (education, drug use history, employment, and so on), sociosexual, and public health data on gang women on the north side of Champaign. Locals call the area the north end.

North end gang women identified themselves as members of Vice Lords, Gangster Disciples, and Black P. Stones. Participant observation showed that north end gang affiliation had no necessary criminal or social obligations. There were no gang meetings, no script to memorize, no need to sell drugs, and no need to hang out with or feel personal closeness to fellow gang members. There were no fights supporting gang pride. Violence was personal and usually instigated by love relations gone awry. Most importantly, a gang affiliation did not impede social, economic, or personal relationships among north end gang women.

Egocentric Network Analysis

The Seattle and Kansas City studies are not easily replicable, but the north end study can (and should) be replicated. The research uses SNA, sociological, and public health structured instruments, a replicable sampling design, and common SNA procedures (Fleisher 2002b, 22–28). Table 6.1 shows descriptive statistics on informants' personal social networks.

Inactive networks were some 25 percent smaller than active networks (9.0 versus 12.7 members) and had half as many males per network (1.7 versus 3.5 males). Active and inactive gang women's self-reported crime had varying levels of property, economic, and violent crimes. Active women self-reported that, over the previous ninety days, they had committed 240 property, 572 economic, and 359 violent crimes. Inactive women self-reported 110 property, 466 economic, and 169 violent crimes (Fleisher 2002b, 87–105). The mean age of active informants is 18.8; for inactive women it is 22.5. The mean age of all women in active networks is 20.0 (n = 284); in inactive networks it is 22.75 (n = 309). The mean age of all men in active networks is 20.0 (n = 115); in

TABLE 6.1
Descriptive Statistics on Egocentric Networks

Network Characteristic	Active Gang Women	Inactive Gang Women
Mean age (years)	18.8	22.5
Mean number of members in ego networks	12.2	9.0
Percent of same-gang alters in ego networks	48.7	49.4
Percent of different-gang alters in ego networks	51.3	50.6
Percent of males per ego network	29.0	18.8
Mean number of males per ego network	3.5	1.7

inactive networks it is 22.67 (n = 66). Active network alters' mean age is 20.0 (n = 398); in inactive it is 22.74 (n = 375).

Shifting Perceptions of Crime and Aggression

Youths' lives are not static; neither is the composition of personal networks. The microsocial dynamics inferred in the "birds of a feather" argument accounts for shifting social ties and recomposition of egocentric networks. When youth share access to others' personal networks, they are exposed, in a real sense, to teenagers and adults who exhibit a range of risky behavior (no-risk or minimal-risk to high-risk behavior). They may find the behavior of their fellows distasteful (or not) and adjust their social ties to fit their preferences.

Teens form homophilous networks (McPherson, Smith-Lovin, and Cook 2001), shuffling and reshuffling friendship ties. Friends of similar temperament, preferences, and dysfunctions, such as excessive drug use or a propensity for violence, hang out.[3] A cohort of nonviolent-to-violent teens would reshuffle themselves into homophilous networks of, say, drug users, drug sellers, and violent youth. Research has shown that people who share similar interpersonal profiles are similar on salient sociodemographic variables (Wasserman and Faust 1994).

To help understand how recomposition of personal networks are linked to crime, the Champaign study's social network instrument asked informants to rate their perceptions[4] of the aggressiveness and crime frequency of each alter on a scale of 0 (not aggressive/no crime or fighting) to 5 (will shoot someone/ deeply involved in economic and violent crime and gets arrested often). Possible effects of personal network recomposition are expressed as informants' perception of crime involvement and aggression in table 6.2; n is the total number of males and females nominated in the aggregate of seventy-four friendship networks.

Males and females in active networks are perceived to be more crime involved. Men are 29 percent (n = 3.5 per network) of friendship nominations in active networks, and their perceived crime involvement is high.[5] Men are

TABLE 6.2
Perceptions of Crime Involvement and Aggression

Actor	Active Networks		Inactive Networks	
	Crime	Aggression	Crime	Aggression
Women	2.43 (n = 284)	3.50 (n = 284)	1.81 (n = 309)	3.15 (n = 309)
Men	4.15 (n = 115)	4.55 (n = 115)	3.17 (n = 66)	3.88 (n = 66)
Network Aggregate	2.93 (n = 399)	3.77 (n = 399)	2.05 (n = 375)	3.27 (n = 375)

18.8 percent (n = 1.7 per network) of friendship nominations in inactive networks, but their perception of crime involvement remains relatively high.

Men are perceived to be highly aggressive in active networks. Quite interesting is the high level of perceived aggression among active and inactive women. The level of inactive women's aggression is relatively close to men's. A reduction in women's self-reported violence (359 incidents by active women to 169 incidents by inactive women) is somewhat ironic. These data indicate that gang women's networks are low on self-reported crime but relatively high on aggression. Such aggression may include fights with and without weapons, and domestic violence. Perhaps informants do not perceive fights and domestic disputes to be criminal conduct.

Gang Boundaries

Gang boundaries on the north end are invisible. Blue does not claim one block, red another, and black yet another. Egocentric networks tend to be partitioned by gang, but a Vice Lord's and a Gangster Disciple's egocentric networks are not mutually exclusive. Sharing a gang or nongang attribute (affiliation), however, may be inconsequential if such ties do not give ego an advantage over alters, such as access to influential people or to social and material resources or both.

Figure 6.1 visualizes two key informants' (A and H) personal friendship ties on friendship, friendship direction, gang affiliation, and residential locale. Each line has an arrow indicating a one-way or two-way direction. A line with a direction is an arc. Such a visualization of a directed friendship network (graph) is a digraph. An arc shows the direction of relationship in a dyad. A dyad consists of two nodes (actors) and the possible arcs between them.

Figure 6.1 has three types of dyads: null dyads (B and D did not nominate each other); asymmetric dyads (A > D; B > C; C > D); and mutual or reciprocal dyads, A <> B. The digraph shows the interconnections among women in different gangs. These data show that friendship is not a necessary result of same-gang affiliation. Intragang dyads may be null, asymmetric, and mutual. Dyads between different-gang women may be mutual and indicate strong friendships (Granovetter 1973, 1361).

Actors' residential locations are also indicated: E and H reside on the west side of the north end; F, G, I, J, and K reside in Urbana, Champaign's adjacent neighboring community; and A, B, C, and D reside on different blocks in the north end. There is no obvious way to draw gang boundaries without losing data (arcs).

Field observations show that intergang interactions over a considerable geographic distance are persistent among different gang members, and that such

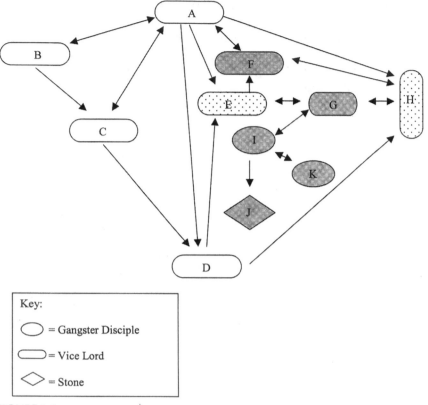

FIGURE 6.1
Friendship Digraph of Two Sociocentric Networks

ties offer mutual social and emotional support (Fleisher 2002a). Sociogeo-
graphic ties expand actors' access to social and material resources over geographic areas (see Sampson 2003, 165). From the perspective of a single actor,
if someone to whom she is linked drops out (moves away, gets a job and stops
hanging out, goes to prison), her replacement or rearrangement to other actors
may be more beneficial than a previous tie or arrangement.

Intergang Connections

Ethnographic observation, field interviews, and compositional measures of
egocentric networks show that these gangs are not mutually exclusive. This
means that gang affiliation itself is not a constraint on women's interactions.
Gang affiliation does not necessarily foster emotional bonds. PO may (partially)

support the assumption that if gang members hang out together long enough, group cohesion as well as enduring and stronger relationships automatically result.

The Champaign study did not assume that friendship and sentiment were synonymous. PO showed that same-gang women hung out together and were congenial; however, many said (paradoxically) that they disliked one or more of their nominated gang friends. Social interaction can be absent of sentiment and therefore cannot be used as a proxy of a gang boundary (A likes B more than C and therefore never hangs with C), nor can sentiment be used to make assumptions about intragang affective ties ("We're brothers for life"; "We'll die for one another").

Figure 6.2 is a digraph of informants' friendship nominations. The digraph shows that some teens have more friends than others, that some ties are symmetric, that others are asymmetric, and that others are null. The graph illustrates friend clusters, one in the center, one in the upper left, and one in the lower right.

A visual inspection shows that some teens receive more ties than they give. We can get empirical measures on tie giving and tie receiving and garner a detailed empirical description of inter- and intragroup network structure.

Degree Centrality

Sociocentric network analysis examines patterns of relations in a group. In this case, a gang attribute (name) is used to form the groups: All women, for instance, who say they are Vice Lords are a group, and so on. The analysis assumes that women make an equal contribution to their group. We are assuming group homogeneity on gang affiliation.

Degree centrality is a structural measure[6] of network activity.[7] There is a balance between being nominated as friend and nominating others. In a graph, nodes are measured in terms of degree, or nodes adjacent to it. In a directed graph, a node can be adjacent to or from another node, depending on the direction of an arc. A node's indegree is the number of nodes adjacent *to* it; a node's outdegree is the number of nodes adjacent *from* it. Indegree refers to the number of nominations received; outdegree, the number of nominations given. Each node has a measure of indegree and outdegree. These measures do not denote how well gang women know one another but are structural data about the digraph's dyads. An actor is highly degree central if she is in direct contact or is adjacent to many other actors. Actors with low degree centrality are peripheral.

A graph has a group degree centralization index. This index is a measure of the variability of actor degree centralization indices. It reaches its maximum value of 1 when one actor chooses all other actors in a group, and they interact only with her.

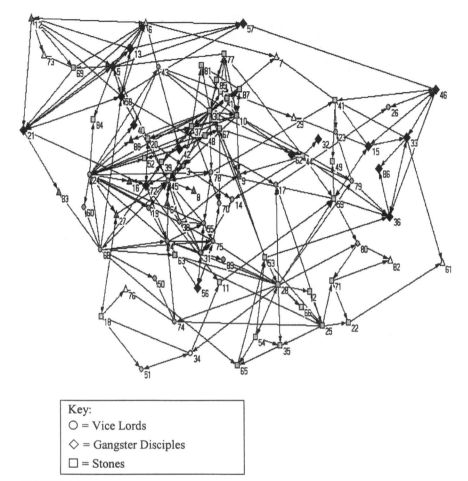

Key:
○ = Vice Lords
◇ = Gangster Disciples
□ = Stones

FIGURE 6.2
Digraph of Vice Lord, Gangster Disciple, and Black P. Stones Egocentric Friendship Networks

Seventy-four interviews generated a list of 456 alters, or a total of 530 (informants plus alters). Among them, eighty-nine received two or more friend nominations. The seventy-four informants each had an opportunity to name one or more of the other seventy-three women as some degree of friend. The two-plus friend nomination data set is used to compute degree centrality measure. Of the eighty-nine people, fifty-six were informants: twenty-six active, thirty inactive. Thirty-three more were alters: fourteen were males; nineteen were females. Gang affiliations were thirty-three Gangster Disciples, twenty-five Vice Lords, sixteen Stones, seven Black Disciples, three Mickey Cobras, one

TABLE 6.3
Number of Intra- and Intergang Ties of Gangs in Figure 6.2

Gang	N	Between Members	To Other Gangs	From Other Gangs
No affiliation	4	0	0	8
VL	25	46	36	43
GD	33	69	56	27
Stones	16	25	32	27
MC	3	1	3	10
BD	7	0	11	18
4CH	1	0	0	2

Four-Corner Hustlers, and four unaffiliated. (Small gang groups are included for the sake of completeness.)

Table 6.3 shows indegree/outdegree,[8] measured on eighty-nine two-plus friendship nominations.[9] This analysis was designed to create no indegree isolates (a node with zero indegree). The eighty-nine actors each had by design at least two nominations; however, 37.8 percent of the actors (thirty-three out of eighty-nine) in the analysis did not nominate as a friend anyone on the analyzed list of eighty-nine.[10]

Table 6.3 shows that there is a tendency for stronger within-gang choice effect. Same-gang ties are more likely than different-gang ties. Ties originating from other gangs to members of the three gangs (Vice Lords, Gangster Disciples, and Stones) are less likely to be present.

Friend selection has little to do with gang "loyalty," and is explained by the interaction of social and physical distance. The north end's four main sub-neighborhoods are geographically distant from one another. Physical distance is visualized in social space, and constrains social interaction (Latane et al. 1995; Wellman 1996).

Gang blocks correspond to physical space, but a clear analysis of physical and social space is difficult now that employment, cars and buses, Section 8 housing, imprisonment and relocation, and other social forces have altered the physical location of gang women's parents and grandparents over many decades. Such physical relocation accounts for the dispersion of geographically distributed ego-gang networks. Social distance is a function of shared needs, similar inter-personal interaction patterns, and similar sociodemographic histories. North end's same-gang women are more likely to have same-gang friends because they are nearby; subgroupings would be teenagers and young adults who share similar life burdens.

Table 6.4 shows gang-group centrality in normalized values. Everett and Borgatti (1999) define group degree centrality as the number of nongroup nodes that are connected to group members, where multiple ties to the same

TABLE 6.4
Degree Centrality Statistics

Statistic	Outdegree	Indegree	Normalized Outdegree	Normalized Indegree
Mean	3.15	3.15	3.58	3.58
S.D.	3.78	1.75	4.30	1.99
Sum	280.00	280.00	318.18	318.18
Variance	14.30	3.07	18.47	3.96

Network Centralization (outdegree) = 19.592%
Network Centralization (indegree) = 10.293%

node count only once. Expressed another way, group degree centrality is degree counts expressed as the percentage of the largest degree count in the data set.

We can generalize this definition to group indegree and outdegree centrality. Let group indegree centrality be the number of arcs coming into the group; group outdegree centrality is the number of arcs that are originating from the group. In both measures, arcs originating from the same person are counted only once. Table 6.4 shows that the variance of outdegree is four times as large as indegree.[11] Outdegree values have a larger range.

Normalized group degree centrality is defined as the group degree centrality divided by the number of nongroup actors. Normalized values are affected by the group size. A measure assessing group homogeneity or heterogeneity in structural positions is the coefficient of variation (CV), computed as (SD/mean)*100. The eighty-nine-member network is heterogeneous in structural positions of outdegrees (CV = 120) (influence) and somewhat homogeneous in structural positions of indegrees (CV = 56) (prominence). There is a mild centralization in the whole network. Positional advantages are distributed somewhat unequally (network centralization is 20 percent for the outdegree and 10 percent for the indegree).

These statistics indicate that this network is structurally best suited for influence (reaching out). I interpret this statistic to mean that the gang women's neighborhood network is structurally geared toward resource distribution and redistribution.

Summary

North end social dynamics occur in egocentric networks; these are gang women's operational social units. There are no structurally larger units; there are no hierarchies of friendship ties. Self-reported data and field observation show that same-gang members do not meet to discuss crime or have picnics and parties. Structural features of gang friendship networks would make such collective activity extremely unlikely.

Personal networks have flexible composition, and this flexibility is a response to and supportive of life course events (Fleisher and Krienert 2004). Intergroup connectedness adds to the pool of potential social ties, independent of gang affiliation; it strengthens the ability to create support networks; and it opens the possibility of geographic mobility (Fleisher 2001). Outdegree and normalized outdegree values show the whole network to be geared toward reaching deeply into the neighborhood social system of relations. Reach creates opportunities.

The north end neighborhood is depleted of economic opportunities; however, friendship ties are a highly valued "commodity." Shifting composition of personal networks and a whole network geared toward reach may be a systematic sociocultural adaptation to poverty. To be sure, the overt signs of poverty and physical dishevelment of the north end mask its social intricacies. Champaign research is replicable; additional studies in impoverished gang neighborhoods in similar communities may discover similar findings.

Notes

The analysis and opinions expressed in this article are mine and do not represent the policies or opinions of federal or private funding agencies. I would like to thank Dr. Stanley Wasserman (formerly at the University of Illinois, Urbana/Champaign), Rudy Professor of Sociology, Psychology, and Statistics, Indiana University, and Svetlana Shinkareva, University of Illinois, for their invaluable assistance on my north end gang research.

An earlier version of this chapter was published in the *Journal of Contemporary Criminal Justice* (2005, vol. 21:120–34). Copyright © by Sage Publications, Inc. Reprinted by permission of Sage Publications.

1. Law enforcement uses exclusivity as a defining criterion. During fieldwork on the north end, a CPD member said that the north end had gangs but does not now. There used to be more shootings, killings, and drug dealing, and gangs didn't mix. Today, s/he said, Vice Lords walk with Gangster Disciples and, therefore, are not gangs.

2. Fleisher (2002b, 173–75) uses p* models to express the probability of an overall multirelational network structure in terms of parameters associated with particular network substructures (Anderson, Wasserman, and Crouch 1999). *Substructure* refers to a specific hypothetical configuration of network ties linked to a small set of network members. The multivariate p* model allows for the exploration of interdependencies among different types of relations; p* analysis of these data shows a strong tendency for friendship ties to be reciprocated.

3. Fleisher's (1998) Fremont study focuses on the personal network formation and reformation over variable life circumstances.

4. McCarty (2002) argues for the value of perceptions in SNA.

5. Ennett, Bailey, and Federman's 1999 study of homeless youth reports a similar finding.

6. Structural analysis is not equivalent to social process. Observations of social process (field data) need to complement structural analysis, and vice versa. In gang

research this distinction is important: The most structurally central people in a gang network may not be gang leaders. Leaders could just as easily spring up on the network's structural margin, depending on personal traits of a potential leader and properties of the total network. There are no structural criteria defining gang social roles. The semantics of conventional gang terminology (core, peripheral) create a distorted structural picture of a gang group.

7. McCarty (2002) illustrates that egocentric networks can be analyzed as sociocentric networks and yield measures of group structure or descriptions of nodes relative to one another and the complete network. Sociocentric analysis measures networkwide structural properties, such as centrality and density, and links structural measures to social roles. Further analysis exceeds the scope of this chapter but can be found in Fleisher 2002b, chapter 5.

8. Indegree is a measure of prestige. Prestige is a structural measure and should not be confused with high status and/or being famous in a colloquial sense. Outdegree is a measure of influence. The person with the highest outdegree has the highest number of contacts to others in the network. Such a person would have access to a lot of people; however, high outdegree does not mean that person will be prestigious.

9. UCINET V is the software program used here for the social network statistical analysis (Borgatti, Everett, and Freeman 1999). Table 6.3 includes women who claimed association in Mickey Cobras, Black Disciples, and Four-Corner Hustlers; however, affiliation in these gangs was highly questionable and membership so low (Four-Corner Hustlers, n = 1; Mickey Cobras, n = 3; Black Disciples, n = 7) that their existence as gangs is highly questionable. Gang women who claimed these affiliations had boyfriends claiming the same affiliation.

10. This is likely to be a function of a five-wave sample. Had interviews continued, the network would have expanded, and egos would have nominated already nominated alters, increasing indegree and outdegree values. Fleisher and McCarty's (2004) analysis of network expansion illustrates that fifth-wave nominations of seventy-four informants, independent of nomination frequency, were connecting to already nominated alters. Self-reported crime data for the period six months prior to the field interview indicated that 60.9 percent of informants reported a property crime committed with one or more nominated alters, 60.6 percent reported an economic crime, and 54.9 percent reported a violent crime (Fleisher 2002b, 88). North end self-reported crime data and national gang crime data (National Youth Gang Center, forthcoming) find that a majority of crime incidents include one or two gang members. An analysis of twice (or more) nominated women, versus single nominations, is justified by the finding that most crime incidents are at least dyadic; given the gang affiliation composition of active and inactive personal networks, we can reasonably assume that crime was committed by mixed-gang, dyads, triads, and cliques. Alters' anonymity was ensured by not asking ego to report crime partners' sex, age, and gang affiliation.

11. Computational details appear in Wasserman and Faust (1994).

7

Social Network Analysis and Gang Research: Theory and Methods

Andrew V. Papachristos

Although a few studies have begun to explore the notion of applying social network analysis to the study of gangs, use of network theory and methodology is modest and selective at best.[1] In this chapter, I outline a broad and perhaps idealistic blueprint for the application of social network analysis in gang research. I begin by reviewing some basic theoretical and methodological principles of social network analysis and how it can be applied to the study of key ideas such as cohesion, power, status, conflict, and social capital among gangs and gang members. Throughout the discussion, I draw on extended examples using data from Gerald Suttles's (1968) classic, *The Social Order of the Slum*. Social network analysis provides a theoretical perspective and a methodological toolkit that not only coincides with the focus of much of gang research but also offers tentative solutions to many of its unanswered questions.

Social Network Analysis and Street Gangs

Social network analysis refers to both a theoretical perspective and a set of methodological techniques. As a theoretical perspective, it stresses the interdependence among social actors. This approach views the social world as patterns or regularities in relationships among interacting units and focuses on how such patterns affect the behavior of network units or actors (Marsden 1990; Wasserman and Faust 1994; Wellman 1983). A "structure" develops as a persistent pattern of interaction that can influence a multitude of behaviors, such as getting a job (Granovetter 1973), individual income attainment (Burt 1997), political decision making (Laumann and Pappi 1973), the diffusion of ideas (Coleman, Katz, and Menzel 1966), or social revolutions (Gould 1996).

As a methodological approach, social network analysis refers to a catalog of techniques steeped in mathematical graph theory and now extending to statistical, simulation, and algebraic models (see Carrington, Scott, and Wasserman 2005). A "social network" is defined as a set of social units and the ties among them. Social units can refer to a range of entities at multiple levels of analysis, such as students in a classroom, businesses in an industry, countries in an economic market, or members in a gang. The ties between them can refer to any type of linkage or interaction among units.

Network data can come from archival materials, survey questionnaires, or ethnographic observations (Marsden 2005). Network data is most commonly collected on relationships linking a set of g social units on a single type of relationship and is most often represented in a square matrix $X = \{x_{ij}\}$ where x_{ij} is the strength from unit i to unit j.[2] A data matrix is created, such that each cell represents the presence, absence, or strength of the tie between two social units (see appendix for an example).[3] This data matrix serves as the foundation for all computations of the various network measures discussed below. A directed graph, or digraph, provides a visual representation of the social network and consists of a set of nodes (units in social network) and a set of lines (the tie or relation) that link the nodes.

In addition to providing a highly visual and detailed way to describe a set of relations and actors, social network analysis facilitates the testing of structural hypotheses about patterns of relations, their properties, and their effect on social and individual behavior. Such hypotheses can range from the simple creation or existence of a group (Does a certain clique exist?) to more predictive aspects of relations (Does alliance formation influence trade patterns?). For example, Mark Granovetter's (1973) often-cited article "The Strength of Weak Ties" demonstrates that certain aspects of social networks, namely "weak ties" (those people with whom we have infrequent or peripheral contact) are the most useful in job attainment. Likewise, Ron Burt (2004) demonstrates that people occupying "structural holes," or brokerage positions in social networks, are more likely to generate and have access to "good ideas."

The gang is a social network consisting of members who interact at given points in time and space. The gang also acts as a group in various types of collective behavior, ranging from simply "hanging out" to gang warfare.[4] Such interactions help forge group identity and tradition, which in turn solidify the gang as a cohesive (or at least somewhat cohesive) social group (Decker

1996; Klein and Crawford 1967; Short and Strodtbeck 1965/1974; Thrasher 1927). These interactions and their consequences occupy the attention of most research—how particular gang or member interactions influence behavior, group processes, community levels of crime, and so on.

Theoretically, translating gang research into network analysis is straight-forward. The unit of analysis can either be the gang or the gang member. Ties between units can include a range of gang interactions, such as animosity, friendship, kinship, fighting, "hanging out with," going to school with, or living adjacent to. Methods of data collection can come from observation (Fleisher 2002a, 2005; Klein and Crawford 1967), surveys, focus groups (Kennedy, Braga, and Piehl 1997), or secondary data such as police records (Papachristos 2004a; Tita et al. 2005). Re-creating the gang as a social network entails linking each of the units, be they gang or gang member, by the type of relation being examined.

Hypotheses will vary according to both the unit of analysis and the type of relation. With the gang member as the unit of analysis, questions might focus on how relations between and among members structure other group processes or behaviors; for example, do friendship networks or subgroups within a larger gang mediate intergroup conflict? How does leadership and participation relate to behavioral patterns? Which types of ties predict social status, power, or influence within the gang, and how do these translate into collective action? Data on contacts outside the gang can be related to questions of how gang members are integrated into the larger community and, say, affect mechanisms of informal social control.

Complicating matters is the fact that gang membership is not an exclusive category. Gang members are not only gang members but are also siblings, parents, students, coworkers, churchgoers, and neighbors. As Simmel (1908/1955) pointed out nearly a century ago, individuals in modern society are best defined by a "web of group affiliation," the meshing of the various social roles and groups that define their existence. No single institution or group, even the family, completely defines the individual. While some categories may be more important than others, social network analysis can help untangle different levels and types of relations.

Using the gang as the unit of analysis permits examination of patterns of how inter- or intragroup relations influence other contextual factors such as neighborhood levels of violence, mechanisms of social control, fear of crime, and so on. How do gang wars or acts of retaliation unfold? How stable are gang conflicts or alliances? And do such interactions really influence group or member behaviors? Combining gang-level and gang member data reveals the portion of members that drive collective behavior—and free riders.

Gangs, like other corporate actors, face basic collective-action problems. Members need not participate in every action to gain benefits or feel consequences associated with the group, nor does participation in every action or every relationship mandate group membership. Most often, the group continues to exist despite the action or inaction of any individual member, be it deviant or otherwise. Like any social group, gangs must solve basic problems of order and control, through formal or informal mechanisms. The persistence of social groups, one of sociology's key problems, is already being addressed in network research on gangs.

In chapter 6 in this volume, Mark Fleisher questions the extent to which the female gangs represent true social groups, largely because of the presence of intergang friendships—that is, intergang friendships undermine the primary group nature of the gang.[5] Yet many of the gangs he identifies have well-documented and long-standing cultural identities that span nearly five decades and even appear in smaller cities, as those Fleisher examines—the Vice Lords and Gangster Disciples—have existed at least since the early 1960s and no doubt will continue to exist despite the actions of individual members. Such groups have, in a very real sense, become institutionalized in many Chicago neighborhoods. Elsewhere, I use various network techniques to demonstrate that patterns of *group* conflict net of any individual member action (a) are highly stable over time, (b) follow some normative precepts, and (c) play a significant role in the social contagion of gang violence (Papachristos 2004a, 2004b). Gang membership is not just another "attribute" variable as Fleisher suggests; belonging to a gang embeds members into real social networks that can influence individual and member behavior, including extreme acts such as homicide (Papachristos 2004a). As such, gangs qualify as "social groups," albeit not the monolithic groups the media and law enforcement accounts often portray (see also McGloin 2005).

An overarching assumption of a network approach to the study of gangs can be explicitly stated: *If gangs are important institutions or actors in specific contexts, patterns of interaction among groups or members should produce a structure that affects social behaviors of gang members, the corporate behavior of the group, and/or the communities they inhabit.* Network techniques provide tools with which to detect, describe, and analyze such structures.

Network Analysis and the Social Order of the Slum

In his classic study *The Social Order of the Slum*, Gerald Suttles (1968) augments field observations with secondary sources, semistructured interviews, and multiple statistical techniques; hence, many of the original arguments can now be reformulated under mathematical and statistical principles of social network analysis. In this section, I review[6] and apply three families of network measures to Suttles's data: (1) measures of density and centrality, (2) measures of cohesion and subgroups, and (3) measures of social capital. Social network analysis permits one to retest hypotheses about a highly detailed context more than thirty years after the original study. Although my findings describe some nuances undetected by Suttles, his conclusions remain remarkably resilient.[7]

The Social Order of the Slum

The Social Order of the Slum (Suttles 1968) provides one of the most detailed studies of the social organization of a Chicago ghetto. Suttles describes a process of "ordered segmentation," in which neighborhood actors negotiate and construct a moral and social order amidst dramatic ethnic, sex, age, and territorial segregation (10). Each of the neighborhood's four ethnic enclaves (Italian, black, Puerto Rican, and Mexican) possesses a unique communicative, situational, and interactional basis for order, which attempts to maintain ethnic solidarity and minimize intergroup conflict. These relational patterns—such as modes of dress, dating rituals, public interaction, and familial patterns—are re-created, maintained, and embodied in nearly all neighborhood institutions. The broad structure created by this ordered segmentation generates a "skeletal" frame within which young men create a world of "street corner groups" (155). The street corner groups are, in a sense, a microcosm of the larger neighborhood context—it is not a departure from the ordered segmentation of the adult order, but rather a replication of it.

Suttles dedicates three chapters to the thirty-two "named street corner groups" he identifies in the near west side. After cataloguing the age, race, and gender composition of these groups, Suttles discusses the primary group nature of the gang and its contribution to delinquency. His findings not only echo those of Thrasher (1927) but also those of modern gang research: Gangs in the Addams area have (a) little or no formal structure, (b) distinct age-graded subgroups, (c) an orientation toward territory, and (d) a basic core-periphery structure. When they are involved in conflict or delinquency, it is generally the "cafeteria style" described by Klein (1995a)—unorganized acts ranging from running away and truancy to theft and fighting. Most interaction, especially violence, is *intragang,* but intergang contests become events for displaying status or ethnic solidarity (Short and Strodtbeck 1965/1974). Suttles provides an extended example of one gang, the Erls, which he considers typical of the groups he observes.

The Erls

The Erls are a Mexican gang whose structure is created from a mishmash of friendship, kin, and conflict relations. Figure 7.1 depicts the ties among the gang's nineteen members using three types of relations—friendship ("cool with"), familial, and antagonistic.[8] The gang lacks any formal structure; rather, the social order is determined by each boy's frequency of interaction, type of relation to other members, commitment to "hanging out," fighting ability, and other interpersonal qualities. Yet, even without a formal structure, the boys generally recognize K-Man as the most influential member, followed closely by Tatters. Slight animosity exists between these two "leaders," and each has a base of constituents with whom they spend the majority of their time. Conflict between members is generally resolved by a third person to whom a positive

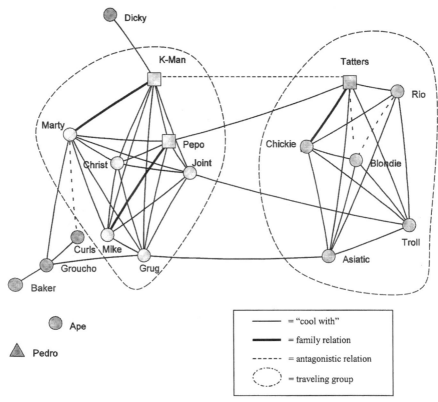

FIGURE 7.1
Patterns of Relationships among the Erls, 1963
Source: Suttles (1968, 189), figure 1.

relation exists. For example, Pepo often acts as a mediator between K-Man and Tatters, just as Groucho mediates between Curls and Marty.

Suttles asserts that the Erls are not very cohesive *except* when confronting gangs from other parts of the neighborhood. It is through external conflict that the group achieves a collective identity (Klein 1971; Short and Strodtbeck 1965/1974; Thrasher 1927). Otherwise, the majority of interaction, whether deviant or normative, occurs within two subgroupings, which Suttles calls "traveling groups." Traveling groups are composed of boys who, for friendship, kin, or residential reasons, spend more time with each other hanging out in various parts of the neighborhood. The two groups are centered on K-Man and Tatters, respectively. Several boys—Dicky, Curls, Groucho, Baker, Ape (the only non-Mexican boy), and Pedro—do not belong to any particular traveling group because of their infrequent presence on the street corner. As seen in figure 7.1, this creates a dual core-periphery structure within the larger gang. The traveling groups signify two distinct cores, areas with dense interaction and cohesion, and are only loosely connected to each other by three "cool with" relations. Four members (Dicky, Curls, Groucho, and Baker) are periphery members, as they do not spend sufficient time hanging out for reasons of age, work, or school. The remaining two members—Ape and Pedro—Suttles calls "hangers on" because their participation in gang activities is not consistent or reliable, even though the other boys cite them as "members."

Suttles's description of the Erls and its members raises questions about social status, solidarity, and cohesion, issues that occupy much of gang research. Network techniques can be used to address such issues.

Density and Centrality

Density is a basic network property that reflects the overall intensity of the connected actors: The more connected the network, the greater its density. A dense network is one where a lot of activity or a large number of strong ties exists among its members. A dense network of friendship ties among gang members, for instance, might signal a cohesive subgroup. Or a dense network of shootings among rival gangs might indicate a gang war. Density, Δ, of a network with g actors is measured as the sum of all entries in the matrix, divided by the possible number of entries:

$$\Delta = \frac{\sum_{i=1}^{g} \sum_{j=1}^{g} x_{ij}}{g(g-1)}$$

As a whole, interaction among the members of the Erls is not extremely dense; network density is approximately 26 percent ($\Delta = .26$). But Suttles states that the majority of interaction takes place within the two traveling groups. And indeed, relative to the whole network, interaction within traveling groups is considerably denser: K-Man's and Tatters's traveling groups have densities of 83 and 86 percent, respectively.

While density refers to the overall structure of the network, one might also be interested in the activity of any single unit, or in network terms, egocentric measures. The activity of any unit in a network is called its *degree*. The nodal degree, $d(n_i)$, refers to the number of lines adjacent to an actor, or simply the number of its direct ties. In an undirected graph, this is equal to the row (x_{i+}) or column (x_{+j}) totals. Or

$$d(n_i) = \sum_{j=1}^{g} x_{ij} = \sum_{j=1}^{g} x_{ji} = x_{i+} = x_{+j}$$

This is also referred to as *degree centrality*, in that actors with a higher degree are more "central" in the overall network. Centrality is often associated with the prominence, status, or prestige of an actor—that is, a greater number of ties make an actor particularly visible to other actors in the network (Friedkin 1991; Marsden 2002; Wasserman and Faust 1994).[9] A gang member with high centrality might be of a higher status, such as a leader, or the most active in some particular gang behavior, such as drug dealing. A gang with high centrality in a network of gang shootings might be of particular importance for law enforcement efforts—in this sense, prominence would have a negative interpretation.[10]

While many other centrality measures exist, one additional measure is worth mentioning: *betweenness centrality* (Freeman 1977). In contrast to degree centrality, which accounts for only direct ties, betweenness centrality considers *indirect* ties and thus refers to intermediaries in interactions. Formally, betweenness centrality, $C_b(n_i)$, of any node is measured as

$$C_B(n_i) = \sum_{j<k} g_{jk}(n_i)/g_{jk}$$

The probability that a "path" between actor j to actor k takes place through actor i and g_{jk} is the number of geodesics (shortest path between any two units) linking the two actors (Wasserman and Faust 1994, 190). Thus, $g_{jk}(n_i)$ is the number of geodesics that contain actor i and this index signals how "between" each of the actors is, as a sum of probabilities. An actor high in this measure occupies a position "in between" different parts of the network, a position of particular importance, as it connects those who would otherwise be unconnected.

Network measures of centrality for the members of the Erls are listed in table 7.1. These findings support much of Suttles's analysis but also offer some

TABLE 7.1
Selected Network Characteristics of the Erls

	Degree Centrality	Betweenness	Constraint
K-Man	6	20.333	0.309
Marty	6	15.833	0.34
Christ	5	3.317	0.445
Pepo	5	8.317	0.332
Mike	3	0.4	0.518
Joint	5	16.233	0.339
Grug	6	47.733	0.294
Dicky	1	0	1
Groucho	4	31	0.295
Curtis	1	0	1
Baker	1	0	1
Ape	0	0	0
Pedro	1	0	1
Asiatic	7	43	0.322
Troll	6	16.5	0.403
Chickie	4	0.333	0.629
Tatters	3	3	0.407
Rio	3	0	0.629
Blondie	3	0	0.629
Mean	3.68	10.8	0.52
SD	2.01	14.77	0.29

slight modifications. Considering only "cool with" relations, each member has an average of 3.7 ties. Although the boys cite K-Man as the most influential, several other members, including Marty, Grug, and Troll, all have the same degree centrality as K-Man ($d(n_i) = 6$); that is, in this sense they are just as prominent as K-Man. Tatters, the other "leader" mentioned by the boys, is considerably lower in degree centrality ($d(n_i) = 3$), not only for the entire gang but also for his traveling group. The most central actor is Asiatic ($d(n_i) = 7$), who is not identified by gang boys as occupying an important position. Consistent with other network research, this finding suggests that prominence as identified by the number of ties alone is not necessarily the most important factor determining leadership or status.[11]

With regards to betweenness centrality, Grug ($C_b(n_i) = 47.7$) and Asiatic ($C_b(n_i) = 43.0$) have scores more than double those of any other member and more than four times the network average ($C_b(n_i) = 10.8$). Looking at figure 7.1, it appears that not only do both Asiatic and Grug have dense ties *within* their respective subgroupings, but they also act as bridges between the two traveling groups. That is, the relation between them spans a "structural hole" (Burt 1992).

Cohesion and Equivalence

Suttles's designation of traveling groups is his method for describing cohesive subgroups within the Erls. The identification of cohesive subgroups is a chief concern of network analysis. Cohesive subgroups are subsets of actors among whom there are relatively strong, direct, intense, frequent, or positive ties (Wasserman and Faust 1994, 249). This concept is quite general and can be operationalized in a variety of ways and under a variety of conditions.

A *clique* is the most basic cohesive subgroup, one based on the complete mutuality of all actors. All actors are connected strongly with each other; those not strongly connected to each of the others are by definition not in the clique.

Within the Erls, there are fourteen distinct cliques:

1. Asiatic Troll Chickie Rio
2. Asiatic Troll Chickie Blondie
3. Asiatic Troll Tatters
4. Marty Christ Mike
5. Marty Christ Joint
6. Marty Christ Grug
7. Marty Pepo Joint
8. Marty Pepo Grug
9. Marty Grug Groucho
10. K-Man Christ Joint
11. K-Man Christ Grug
12. K-Man Christ Mike
13. K-Man Pepo Grug
14. K-Man Pepo Joint

The tremendous overlap among these cliques suggests that boundaries of some of these small groups may not be an all-or-nothing matter. Few, if any, social groups—baseball teams, businesses, families, religious institutions, or street gangs—fit the stringent clique criteria. Gang research that has focused specifically on this issue consistently shows that (a) gang boundaries are rather amorphous; (b) gang membership is a fleeting, if not transitory, experience; and (c) there exists a range of positive and negative inter- and intragang behaviors, ranging from the criminal to the mundane (e.g., Decker and Van Winkle 1996; Fleisher 1998, 2005; Klein and Crawford 1967; Short and Strodtbeck 1965/1974; Suttles 1968; Whyte 1943).

Relaxing the definition of cohesion allows one to define subgroups based on the social distance between actors and not simply on direct connections.

the absence of a tie between two parties, cliques, or subgroups. A person who fill such a hole can control the flow of information, resources, or action betwee the otherwise unconnected parts of the network. This person acts as a broke and is rich in social capital, insofar as his or her position permits for actio that would otherwise not be possible. When structural holes exist, an actor ca exert power by linking otherwise unconnected others. Social capital is define as this ability to provide brokerage over structural holes; it is the *type of tie tha* matters, not simply the number of ties.

Burt's (1992) measure of *network constraint* equates with the structural hol theory of social capital. Network constraint signals the extent to which a actor's ability to act is hindered by other densely connected, and therefor redundant, actors. In a network such as a clique, where all or most of the othe actors are connected, an actor is constrained by the fact that each member ha access to the same information and resources. Actors in this type of networ are said to be highly constrained because there are few structural holes an thus few brokerage opportunities or pathways to new information. In contras actors with low levels of constraint—that is, those that exist in networks whe contacts are nonredundant—are better situated to conduct entrepreneuria and innovative activities.

Network constraint, c_{ij}, is measured as

$$c_{ij} = (p_{ij} + \sum_q p_{iq} p_{qj})^2, q \neq i, j$$

where p_{ij} equals the amount of actor i's network time and energy that i invested in actor j, $p_{ij} = z_{ij}/\Sigma_q z_{iq}$, and z_{iq} refers to the strength of the con nection between i and j (Burt 1992, 55). The measure ranges from zero to on reaching its maximum when there is high redundancy among ego's alters. Th closer to the maximum, the more the network resembles a completely con nected network, the fewer structural holes, and the less opportunity to develo social capital. The most powerful actors—ipso facto those with the most soci capital—tend to be the least constrained.

Constraint scores for the members of the Erls are listed in table 7.1. Asiati and Grug have access to information that other members do not; accordingly they have the lowest constraint scores in the network ($c_{ij} = 0.32$ and 0.29, re spectively). They act, as do Pepo ($c_{ij} = 0.33$), Joint ($c_{ij} = 0.34$), and Grouch ($c_{ij} = 0.30$), as lynchpins holding together the larger group. If these member are removed from the network, as they are in figure 7.3, the structural hole become apparent—the Erls would cease to be anything resembling a cohesiv group. In short, although these members are not the most "central" in term of overall prominence, they are responsible for holding the gang together as

N-cliques are subgroups based on a specified distance among actors—that is, how far a path is between any two actors.[12] *N-cliques* allow the researcher to set the criteria based on the type of network studied, the nature of data, or a specific theoretical consideration. The all-inclusive cliques mentioned above are *n-cliques*, where n = 1, or in which every actor is connected by a distance of one relation. We can relax the definition of cohesive subgroups, allowing a subgroup to exist, say, if each person is connected by *at least* an indirect tie, in this case, n = 2. Under this condition, eight subgroups are found within the Erls:

1. K-Man Marty Pepo Joint Grug Asiatic Troll Tatters
2. Joint Grug Asiatic Troll Chickie Tatters Rio Blondie
3. K-Man Marty Christ Pepo Joint Grug Asiatic Troll
4. K-Man Marty Christ Pepo Joint Grug Groucho Asiatic
5. K-Man Marty Christ Pepo Mike Joint Grug Groucho
6. K-Man Christ Pepo Mike Joint Grug Dicky
7. Marty Grug Groucho Curtis Baker
8. Grug Pedro Asiatic Troll Chickie Tatters Rio Blondie

There is still significant crossover between cliques, however. This finding suggests that, while traveling groups are important, there are other cohesive subunits within and between traveling groups. Such cliques, as Suttles describes, are essential in resolving internal disputes and motivating various collective behavior, including intragang fights.

Whereas cohesion analyses identify subgroups within a larger network, an other major concern of network analysis is how specific roles or positions *within* the structure affect the larger network and its behavior, net of the individuals in such roles. In such cases, the concern is less with how person Q fits into the network and focuses instead on how people who occupy *positions* like that held by Q affect network behavior. One might consider how managers influence corporate production, how principals influence school test scores, or how gang leaders motivate subordinates to participate in group violence, for instance. Such analyses would reveal the extent to which any "gang structure" might exist based on a measured set of relations.

A common type of position analysis uses measures of *structural* or *role equivalence*. Two actors are *structurally equivalent* to the extent that they have identical relations with every other person in the network (Lorrain and White 1971).[13] Because *exact* structural equivalence is rare, it is best measured as the Euclidean distance between the relational patterns of two actors (Burt 1991, 126). Structural equivalence between actors i and j is the distance between rows i and j and columns i and j of the sociomatrix:

$$d_{ij} = \sqrt{\sum_{k=1}^{g} [(x_{ik} - x_{jk})^2 + (x_{ki} - x_{kj})^2]}$$

where x_{ik} is the value of the tie from actor i to actor k on a single relation. In-creasing values of d_{ij} indicate increasingly equivalent patterns. Various group-ing techniques, such as hierarchical clustering or smallest space analysis, can use d_{ij} to graphically group equivalent actors.

Equivalence analysis exposes the similarities and differences in relational patterns among members of the Erls. Given the primary group nature of the traveling group, one might expect that members within the same group would have similar patterns of relations—that is, they would be structurally equiv-alent. Or one might expect the different leaders, hangers-on, and so forth to have similar patterns of relations vis-à-vis the rest of the group. Using the last equation, figure 7.2 shows the eigenvalue decomposition of the Euclidean dis-tances among actors, where the x-axis is defined by the eigenvector for the first

eigenvalue, and y-axis is defined by the second eigenvalue.[14] The clo members are clustered, the more alike are their patterns of relations.

Figure 7.2 shows a close clustering of the boys in Tatter's traveling indicating that compared to other members their patterns of relations are turally similar. In contrast, K-Man's group lacks such equivalence and i is split into two somewhat different clusters. This might suggest a hier within the subgroup or at the very least some important role differenti Figure 7.2 also shows that the patterns of relations among the "hanger and periphery members are distinct from members of the traveling gr Namely, their patterns of relations—or their positions in the structure distinct from those in the traveling groups.

This analysis of cohesive and equivalent subgroupings suggests that, the traveling group distinctions are significant, particularly for Tatters's gr other structural distinctions can be made. Smaller cliques within the Erls have some functional importance in such matters as dispute resolution, tergang activities, or other types of behavior. Furthermore, although the do not have a formal organizational structure, equivalence analysis imp clear role differentiation among the members *and* the traveling groups. Th contrary to Fleisher's (chapter 6 in this volume) findings among female ga members, sociocentric analysis reveals network attributes within the Erls th create a rather tangible "structure"—a claim supported by Suttles's ethn graphic observations and by other network research on gangs elsewhere (se e.g., McGloin 2005).

Social Capital and Structural Holes

The phrase *social capital* is theoretically chic and, unfortunately, method-ologically ambiguous. The concept refers to a spectrum, from the number of bowling leagues or volunteer associations one belongs to, to the number of neighbors one can count on in a tough situation. The network version of the concept rests on Coleman's (1988) assertion that "social capital" is a form of social organization in which the structure of ties and relations between indi-viduals makes possible certain actions. It is not simply the sum of individual, neighborhood, or group characteristics but rather the structure of an individ-ual's or group's social ties and how such ties are used with reference to action. Unlike human capital, which is a property of individuals, social capital is a property created *between* individuals. While human capital refers to individual attributes, social capital refers to opportunity (Burt 1997). It is, in this sense, a function of the structure of a given network and a social unit's position in it.

Burt's (1992) theory of structural holes gives concrete meaning to social capital in this network sense. A structural hole refers to a gap in a social network,

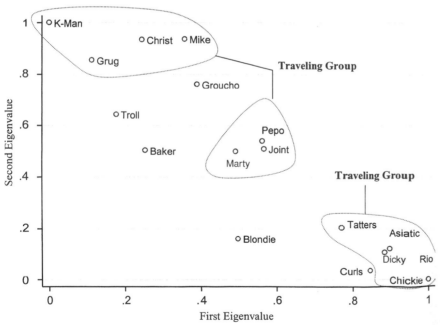

FIGURE 7.2
Structural Equivalence among Members of Erls

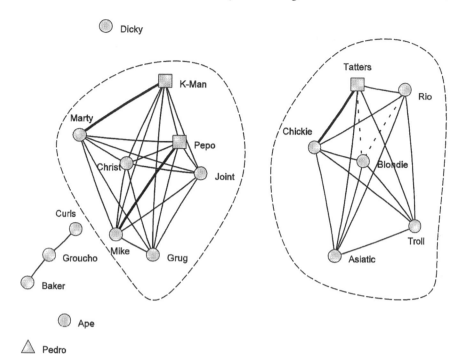

FIGURE 7.3
Relationships among Erls without Ties between Groups

group. Very little gang research has focused on what types of members hold such groups together.[15]

Discussion and Conclusion

Applying advances in network analysis to the Erls illustrates several important aspects of gang structures and processes. Patterns of relations among the members are far more complex than a simple core-periphery distinction, although such a distinction appears to exist to some degree. Density measures and analyses of subgroupings suggest that while the gang as a whole is not remarkably cohesive, there exist strong pockets of cohesion inside the traveling groups identified by Suttles. Several smaller subgroupings, such as cliques, and several nonprominent members serve important functions in maintaining cohesion of the larger group. Leadership itself does not appear to be solely determined by prominence and must consider a range of nonstructural attributes. Pursuing and empirically analyzing such factors in a systematic fashion can push the boundaries of gang research *and* increase its relevance within the social

Chapter 7

APPENDIX
Relationships among Members of the Erls

	K-Man	Marty	Christ	Pepo	Mike	Joint	Grug	Dicky	Groucho
K-Man	0	2	1	1	1	1	1	1	0
Marty	2	0	1	1	1	1	1	0	1
Christ	1	1	0	1	1	1	1	0	0
Pepo	1	1	1	0	2	1	1	0	0
Mike	1	1	1	2	0	1	1	0	0
Joint	1	1	1	1	1	0	1	0	0
Grug	1	1	1	1	1	1	0	0	1
Dicky	1	0	0	0	0	0	0	0	0
Groucho	0	1	0	0	0	0	1	0	0
Curtis	0	−1	0	0	0	0	0	0	1
Baker	0	0	0	0	0	0	0	0	1
Ape	0	0	0	0	0	0	0	0	0
Pedro	0	0	0	0	0	0	0	0	0
Asiatic	0	0	0	0	0	0	1	0	0
Troll	0	0	0	0	0	1	0	0	0
Chickie	0	0	0	0	0	0	0	0	0
Tatters	−1	0	0	1	0	0	0	0	0
Rio	0	0	0	0	0	0	0	0	0
Blondie	0	0	0	0	0	0	0	0	0

	Curtis	Baker	Ape	Pedro	Asiatic	Troll	Chickie	Tatters	Rio	Blondie
K-Man	0	0	0	0	0	0	0	−1	0	0
Marty	−1	0	0	0	0	0	0	0	0	0
Christ	0	0	0	0	0	0	0	0	0	0
Pepo	0	0	0	0	0	0	0	1	0	0
Mike	0	0	0	0	0	0	0	0	0	0
Joint	0	0	0	0	0	1	0	0	0	0
Grug	0	0	0	0	1	0	0	0	0	0
Dicky	0	0	0	0	0	0	0	0	0	0
Groucho	1	1	0	0	0	0	0	0	0	0
Curtis	0	0	0	0	0	0	0	0	0	0
Baker	0	0	0	0	0	0	0	0	0	0
Ape	0	0	0	0	0	0	0	0	0	0
Pedro	0	0	0	0	0	0	0	0	0	0
Asiatic	0	0	0	0	0	1	1	1	1	1
Troll	0	0	0	0	1	0	1	1	1	1
Chickie	0	0	0	0	1	1	0	2	1	1
Tatters	0	0	0	0	1	1	2	0	1	−1
Rio	0	0	0	0	1	1	1	1	0	−1
Blondie	0	0	0	0	1	1	1	−1	−1	0

0 = no relation between members; 1 = "cool with" each other or in same "traveling group"; −1 = animosity or conflict between members; 2 = family/kin relation between members.
Source: Suttles 1968.

sciences more generally. This chapter has only briefly discussed some extensions of social network analysis to the study of gangs, the application of which can open exciting new avenues of inquiry.

Notes

I would like to thank the editors and Mark Fleisher for their comments on earlier versions of this work.

1. Recent work by Fleisher (2002a, 2002b, 2005); Kennedy, Braga, and Piehl (1997); McGloin (2005); Papachristos (2004a; 2004b); and Tita and colleagues (2005) all explore the utility network approach in the study of gangs. Early studies by Whyte (1943), Suttles (1968), and Klein (Klein and Crawford 1967) also used early versions of sociometry and social network analysis.

2. This is commonly referred to as "one-mode" data, as rows and corresponding columns refer to the same social unit. For a discussion on nonsquare data, see Wasserman and Faust (1994).

3. Generally, a sociomatrix is coded where 1 equals the presence of a tie and 0 equals its absence. If the strength of ties is of interest, the additional weight can be given to that particular tie. Or, if a sociomatrix contains negative relations, such as disliking or animosity, ties can be given a negative sign.

4. Most definitions of gangs include some element of interaction. Thrasher (1927), for example, explicitly distinguishes a gang from other groups by the extent to which it partakes in collective action in space and over time; his definition also mentions specific types of interactions common to the gang (e.g., milling, conflict, moving through space, etc.). One of the most widely cited definitions by Klein (1971) defines a group as a gang when its interactions, especially deviant ones, elicit some collective response to the group and self-group identification. In particular, group process definitions such as those suggested by Short (e.g., 1997), posit that the focus of gang research should be on the internal and external dynamics of the gang as a group, which are specifically generated by the type, degree, and intensity of inter- and intragang interactions.

5. Fleisher bases his conclusions on a rather literal interpretation of Homans's ideal type rendering of a "social group," which rarely fits with any empirical group, let alone a street gang. Homans, in fact, spends two chapters analyzing the sociograms found in *Street Corner Society* (Whyte 1943) and concludes that the corner group epitomizes his notion of a human social group even given the intergang "friendship" between Doc and Chic. While I agree with some of Fleisher's conclusions, the techniques discussed here, such as equivalence analysis, might provide more direct tests of his claims about cohesion and the "group" nature of gangs more generally. For example, using sociocentric network techniques McGloin (2005) finds that while gangs in Newark are not monolithic organizations, pockets of cohesive subgroupings hold the larger "group" together (see also Klein and Crawford 1967). Whyte (1943), like Homans, finds a similar distinction among the Nortons, with cohesive subgroups surrounding Angelo's and Nuty's friends.

6. The review of network techniques is in no way exhaustive but is designed to discuss the selected measures and their interpretation. For a more detailed discussion of the mathematics behind these measures as well as alternative and additional measures, see Wasserman and Faust (1994).

7. Network measures are calculated using STRUCTURE 4.2 (Burt 1991), Pajek (Batagelj and Mrvar 2004), and UCINET 6.0 (Borgatti, Everett, and Freeman 2002) with all equations, unless otherwise noted, following those listed as the defaults in these programs. Directed graphs and network diagrams were created using Pajek. For a discussion of available network software and its applications, see Huisman and Van Duijn (2005).

8. Suttles (1968) bases his analysis on a variety of ethnographic, observation, and interview data. I translate his ethnographic and observation data into the sociomatrix of the members of the Erls found in the appendix. The data is taken directly from Suttles's figure 1, entitled "Pattern of Relationships among the Erls: 1963," as well as from the associated text (189).

9. However, there exist rather fine distinctions of when centrality equates with prominence, influence, status, and so on. In directional networks, for instance, *indegree* centrality is generally associated with prominence (i.e., the number of times an actor is chosen by others), whereas *outdegree* is associated with influence (i.e., the number of connections an individual can utilize). For a discussion and review, see Wasserman and Faust (1994).

10. In fact, members of the Boston Gun Project used such centrality measures to target the most volatile and "active" gangs and gang members responsible for a disproportionate amount of violence (see Kennedy, Braga, and Piehl 1997).

11. This underscores Fleisher's (chapter 6 in this volume) suggestion that leadership traits within a gang need not be associated with purely structure properties; ethnographic and description data, such as Suttles gives, thus become essential in decoding such structural characteristics.

12. Additional measures of subgroups, such as *k-clans, k-cores, k-clubs, neighborhoods,* and *components,* exist that are based on more complex restrictions and definitions of cohesion (see Wasserman and Faust 1994).

13. In contrast to structural equivalence, which focuses on ties to the *exact* same actors, *role equivalence* refers the similarity in the overall patterns of relations with any other actors in the network (see Wasserman and Faust 1994).

14. The first eigenvalue is 6.22 found in nine iterations. The second is 2.46 found in fifteen iterations. Both axes are scaled from zero to one.

15. Recent work by McGloin (2005) provides an excellent example of how using network techniques can locate such individuals *and* positions within the network. Her research in Newark locates key structural positions within gangs called "cut points" occupied by such members who hold together the larger group.

8

A Public Health Model for Studying Youth Gangs

Bill Sanders and Stephen E. Lankenau

THE DISCIPLINES OF PUBLIC HEALTH and sociology have a considerable history of collaborating.[1] Sociology's influence and image within the field of public health is especially apparent within epidemiology, which provides information pertaining to the promotion of health and prevention of disease. Working traditionally, either in health departments or clinical settings, epidemiologists have examined the distribution of infectious diseases within populations, endeavoring to ascertain what helps explain such distributions (Syme 2000). More recently, certain health behaviors, such as drug use, sexual behavior, and violence, have been framed epidemiologically (see, e.g., Adimora and Schoenbach 2005; Farrington and Loeber 2000; Yacoubian 2003).[2] In the study of health behaviors, examining the "environment" is crucial (e.g., Adimora and Schoenbach). Yet, within epidemiology, the focus has traditionally remained on the "host" (infected) and "agent" (pathology), with "environment" (context, setting) receiving relatively limited attention (Agar 1996; Syme). Sociological research, with its emphasis on context and meaning, compliments epidemiological data by placing the environment in the forefront of the host/agent/environment equation, thus more appropriately identifying and situating risk factors associated with risk behaviors (Syme).

The health of youth gang members is a topical concern, as evidenced by the National Institutes of Health's recent prioritization of research on youth gang members.[3] This seems logical, as young men and women involved in gangs are exposed to multiple health risks, such as those stemming from violence, substance abuse, and sexual behavior. Involvement in youth gangs is a high-risk behavior that accelerates and exacerbates additional high-risk behaviors. Negative health outcomes that may result from these behaviors include sexually transmitted infections (STIs), such as HIV, as well as cognitive impairment, injury, disability, and death.

Although the research interests of those studying gangs from a public health perspective differ in significant ways from traditional criminological and criminal justice approaches, these fields have employed similar qualitative methods to answer their questions. Many criminological studies on youth gangs have utilized interviews and observations to collect data (see Hughes 2005a). Public health researchers have also made use of these methods in the form of ethnoepidemiology, combining the epidemiological focus of host and agent with an ethnographic focus on environment, meaning, and context (e.g., Agar 1996; Clatts, Welle, and Goldsamt 2001; Lankenau and Clatts 2002, 2004; Lankenau et al. 2004; Lankenau et al. 2005).

Whatever definition of *youth gang* is chosen, it is clear that gangs are a type of group within which young people socialize. This finding has special implications for public health researchers in terms of their social networks. Social network research collects data concerning an individual's position and relationships within the group, and relationships between group members and others outside the group (Fleisher 2002a; chapter 6 in this volume). The usefulness of this approach has been demonstrated in studying risk behaviors among groups of young people, such as runaway and homeless youths (Ennett, Bailey, and Federman 1999; Kipke et al. 1995) and injection drug users (IDU) (Friedman et al. 1997), and the transmission of STIs among sexual partners (Adimora and Schoenbach 2005). Social network data about youth gang members are helpful in identifying such risky behaviors as sexual and/or IDU partners within a youth gang and the extent to which behavioral norms regarding violence are shaped by gang members and others.

Youth Gangs and Risk Behaviors

Youth gangs are typically associated with inner-city areas, where poverty, social deprivation, and welfare dependency are endemic (Curry 2001; Esbensen 2000). Surveys suggest that the majority of youth gang members in large U.S. metropolitan cities are juveniles (under 18), most are either African American or Hispanic/Latino, and perhaps 90 percent are male (Esbensen; Howell, Egley, and Gleason 2002). Precursors to juvenile gang involvement include poor school performance; difficulties within conventional employment; familial alcohol, substance, physical, and sexual abuse; and familial involvement in street gangs and crime more generally (Brotherton and Barrios 2004; Esbensen and

Lynskey 2001). Although other such behaviors common among gang members have been identified, such as offending in general and involvement in informal "street" economies, this first section focuses on three risk behaviors of particular interest to public health researchers: sexual behavior, drug use, and violence.

Sexual Behavior

The initiation of sexual behavior within adolescence and young adulthood is a critical period for the transmission of HIV and other STIs, such as chlamydia, gonorrhea, and human papillomavirus (HPV)—the most prevalent STIs among youth (Cates 1999; Centers for Disease Control and Prevention 2000). Of an estimated 12 million cases of STIs diagnosed annually in the United States, two-thirds are among those under the age of twenty-five (Centers for Disease Control and Prevention 2001). Young people are also at risk for HIV infection through sexual transmission, particularly since those infected with an STI are more likely to contract HIV if exposed sexually. Estimates indicate that over half of all *new* HIV infections occur among those under twenty-five (Rosenberg, Biggar, and Goedert 1994). Moreover, studies demonstrate that alcohol and/or illicit substance use impairs decisions regarding sexual behavior, increasing the risks of transmitting or becoming infected with STIs (Adimora and Schoenbach 2005).

Gang youth, compared to nongang youth, are more at risk for a range of negative health outcomes associated with sexual activity. Compared to the national average, gang-involved youth, particularly those within minority communities, generally experience sex at earlier ages (Cepeda and Valdez 2003). Gang youth have more sexual partners and have been found to be at higher risk of becoming infected with STIs, such as gonorrhea and trichomonas vaginalis (Wingood et al. 2002). Gangs are also more likely to be intoxicated on drugs or alcohol when having sex, which further increases their chances of becoming infected with an STI, including HIV (Adimora and Schoenbach 2005; Voisin et al. 2004).

Sexual behavior among heterosexual teenage partners is a significant public health concern in the United States due to the country's higher rates of teenage pregnancies and birthrates compared to other developed countries (Cepeda and Valdez 2003). In addition to becoming infected with an STI through sexual activity, youth gang members are also at a significantly high risk of becoming teenage parents, compared to nongang youth (Browning, Thornberry, and Porter 1999; Voisin et al. 2004). Young women who are gang members are at a high risk of becoming pregnant in their teenage years, many by male gang members (Harris 1988; Moore and Hagedorn 2001). Teen pregnancy among gang members poses significant health risks, not just for youth gang members, but also for their children. Many gang members have children who are raised primarily by their mothers, either due to their father's abandonment or imprisonment (Moore and Hagedorn). These processes, in turn, generate new waves of at-risk young people and exacerbate difficult conditions for young women living in socially and economically marginal communities and engaging in risk behaviors.

Other topics concerning sexual health among male gang members include undisclosed men-having-sex-with-men (MSM) relations, particularly during episodes of incarceration. Very few researchers have discussed MSM behavior among male youth gang members. Within the United States, the percentage of known cases of HIV within the prison population is roughly 10 percent higher than known cases of HIV within the general population, and the overall rate of confirmed AIDS cases in state and federal prisons is about five times the general population rate (Centers for Disease Control and Prevention 2003; U.S. Department of Justice 2001). MSM behavior among young men while incarcerated apparently places them at greater risk of HIV infection. Moreover, rape in male prisons is not uncommon. While these figures are surely underreported, research suggests that roughly one in every five male prisoners in the United States (22 percent) is a victim of rape; that young people in particular are victims of male prison rape; and that incidents of prison rape among males often involve one victim and multiple offenders (Mariner 2001). Because youth gang members are at a greater risk of becoming incarcerated than nongang youth, rape victimization is also a significant risk.

Alcohol and Drug Use

Compared to nongang youth, gang youth have higher rates of alcohol and drug use, including cocaine, crack cocaine, marijuana, heroin, and crystal methamphetamine, often in combination (Hill, Lui, and Hawkins 2001; Hunt and Joe-Laidler 2001; Wingood et al. 2002). Hill, Lui, and Hawkins found that, over a six-year period, twice as many gang members as nongang youth used drugs. Alcohol and drug use are important public health issues because they have been linked to significant adverse health outcomes, such as overdose (Coffin et al. 2003), increased risk of exposure to blood-borne pathogens, such as human immunodeficiency virus type 1 (HIV-1) and hepatitis C (HCV) (Peters, Davies, and Richardson 1998); dependence (Leri, Bruneau, and Stewart 2003); decreased cognitive functioning (Dillon, Copeland, and Jansen 2003); and increased sexual risks (Adimora and Schoenbach 2005; Wingood et al.).

Little is understood about the sequencing or timing of alcohol and drug use, drug forms consumed, and modes of drug administration, all of which influence health risks. Drug form, for example, is often indicative of its purity and potency because form influences the mode of administration, which, in turn, shapes the risk of transmission of blood-borne pathogens, such as HIV-1 and HCV. Intravenous administration presents the highest risk for transmitting blood-borne pathogens (Rich et al. 1998). The most crucial risk related to injecting drugs in general is the risk of transmitting infectious viruses, including HIV, HCV, and hepatitis B (HBV) (Des Jarlais et al. 2003; Hagan et al. 1991). IDUs account for more than one-third (36 percent) of AIDS cases in the United States and are among the leading risk cohorts associated with new infections (Centers for Disease Control and Prevention 2003; Holmberg 1996). HCV is a common chronic blood-borne infection in the United States (Alter et al. 1998), and both HCV and HBV are associated with IDUs via indirect sharing of injection equipment (Hagan et al.). The risk of becoming infected with these viruses is not uniform among social groups, however. Important age differences exist regarding safe injection practices, with younger and recently initiated injectors experiencing disproportionate risks associated with syringe and paraphernalia sharing (Clatts et al. 1998). Qualitative studies (Lankenau et al. 2004; Lankenau et al. 2005) suggest that an individual's propensity to and frequency of injecting drugs is shaped by social and economic factors, such as family background, peer group, and involvement in the street economy. Qualitative studies of youth gangs that focus on all these aspects of drug use permit the exploration of drug-using trajectories, the impact of drug use on other aspects of members' lives, and identification of high-risk behaviors associated with general drug use.

Interpersonal Violence

For a variety of reasons, compared to nongang youth, gang members are at substantially higher risk of both violent victimization and engaging in violence (Howell and Decker 1999): intergang rivalry; territorial disputes; conflict over drug sales (Esbensen and Lynskey 2001; Sanders 1994); redress of insults and pursuit of masculine ideals such as toughness, courage, and respect; avoidance of humiliation; and adherence to gang and community norms (Anderson 1999; Katz 1988; Messerschmidt 2000; Miller 1958). These same masculine ideals are also championed by many female gang members (Campbell 1991; J. Miller 2001) and related to their fighting.

In large U.S. cities such as Los Angeles and Chicago, approximately half the total number of homicides in recent years have been considered gang-related (Egley and Major 2003). Youth gang firearm use in assault crimes (aggravated assault, robbery) and in gang-related homicides is higher in cities with long histories of youth gangs, compared to smaller cities where gangs are a more recent phenomenon (Howell, Egley, and Gleason 2002). Accessibility to and possession of firearms clearly facilitates lethal violence (see Sanders 1994), and there is a strong association between gang membership and possession of firearms (Browning, Thornberry, and Porter 1999; Howell and Decker 1999). Interpretive accounts of interpersonal violence are necessary in order to permit examination of the contexts, extent, and frequency of violence among individual gang members, gang members' conceptualizations of risks associated with various violent episodes, and such practical issues as how young people negotiate these risks (see Hughes and Short 2005). Pathways (if any) that youth gang members have to medical recourse also need to be understood.

Ethnoepidemiology and Youth Gangs

Ethnoepidemiology (sometimes called epnography or ethnodemiology) combines conventional epidemiological concerns for agent, host, and environment with an ethnographic focus on significance and overall context (Agar 1996; Lankenau and Clatts 2002, 2004; Lankenau et al. 2004). Ethnography facilitates documentation of subjective worlds and "missing epidemiological data," while epidemiology permits the generalization of "ethnographic results" (Agar, 392). Regarding drug use, for example, epidemiology frames the agent as the drug, the host as the person using the drug, and the environment as the physical and social space in which drugs are used (e.g., shooting gallery, friend's house, park). The primary concern with epidemiology, however, lies with the agent (the drug) and the reason or cause (etiology) that an individual becomes infected (using the drug) (Agar). Ethnography fills in missing data by bringing the concept of host and environment to the foreground, recognizing that the host is not passive, and identifying how environments reveal much about individual and group drug use (e.g., Agar; Parker, Williams, and Aldridge 2002).

Ethnoepidemiology utilizes quantitative data for describing trends and patterns and an interviewing modality that captures narrative detail for context. This approach also applies observations from natural settings to contrast and validate data generated during interviews. An epidemiologic profile of risk behaviors, such as sexual activity, violence, or drug use, may be constructed through the use of ethnographic methods. This approach appears to be a logical methodology from which to generate data concerning public health issues related to youth gang members. Juarez (1992, 44) argues that violence-related injury, like infectious diseases, "can be conceptualized as an interaction between agent, host, and environment." Here, agent refers to the cause of the injury, host to the victim, and environment to the socioeconomic setting in which the violent act occurred. By examining violence among youth gangs in this fashion, researchers will be better able to identify the root causes of such behaviors among different populations, thereby facilitating violence intervention and prevention efforts and quashing common myths and stereotypes of gangs and violence. Some researchers have questioned the validity of the claim that youth gangs are responsible for a disproportionate share of an area's violent incidents (Katz 2000; Katz and Jackson-Jacobs 2004). The public health model offers a new perspective from which to test the extent and nature of violence involving youth gang members.

Consistent with previous research on risk behaviors amongst IDUs (e.g., Lankenau and Clatts 2004), data collection on risk behaviors among youth gang members through an ethnoepidemiological approach is expected to unfold in two phases. The purpose of the first stage is to gather "local knowledge" of youth gangs by interviewing people within the community who are locally "wise" (Becker 1970; Goffman 1963) about such groups, such as high school administrators, youth and community program managers, directors of local health departments and STD clinics, directors of needle exchange programs, directors of youth outreach programs, police officers, gang researchers, youth and community workers, outreach workers, health services staff, and intake personnel at drug treatment programs. Outreach or "street" workers are especially important because they work primarily on the street, away from an office, shelter, or community center. While not all of those interviewed will have intimate or direct knowledge about youth gangs, the information gathered is important for understanding youth gangs and their risk behaviors.

Such local knowledge informs the next phase of research: interviews with and observations of youth gang members. Youth gang members comprise "hidden populations" in that "the size and boundaries of the population are unknown" (Heckathorn 1997, 174). Moreover, there are likely to be strong privacy concerns among them because membership may involve stigmatized or illegal behavior. Because a lone researcher approaching gang members is likely to be suspected as representing the police (see, e.g., Douglas 1972; Sanders 2005), an efficient way to negotiate access into the worlds of gang members is through the aid of those who work directly with them.

Outreach or street workers often serve as gatekeepers into the lives of youth gang members, providing a crucial link between them and the researcher (see Klein 1971; Sanders 2005; Short and Strodtbeck 1965/1974). Such individuals may themselves be former gang members, or have lived in the same or similar environments to those of the gang members. Sanders's research in inner-city London found that detached youth workers, the English equivalent to the outreach worker, were raised within the communities they now assisted and were highly revered by other youth and community workers for working with serious young offenders. Sanders notes that the detached workers discussed knowing the families of many young people and others who were involved in serious levels of offending. Compared to the other adults, including "professionals" who work with youth, the detached workers were in close contact with young people who were involved in serious levels of offending and violence, highlighting an important point concerning the differential levels of offending within gangs. Because young people within any one gang are likely to engage in various levels of offending (cf. Brotherton and Barrios 2004; Klein 1995a), special efforts need to be made to establish contacts with gang youth through other youth and community members, such as those working at health clinics, youth and community centers, and schools. Outreach and other youth and community workers have established trust with the gang members, and a researcher who gains the trust of the worker is more likely to be allowed research access to gang members, especially if they can be convinced that the research will be beneficial. Securing the trust of the outreach worker ultimately lies in the social skills of the researcher.

During fieldwork for a current research project, researchers approached various individuals from health clinics, youth and community centers, community organizations, and drop-in centers.[4] The researchers also inquired about health issues among youth gang members with whom these individuals worked, and discovered that those closest and most directly involved with gang-identified youth were individuals at youth and community centers, including outreach workers. These individuals discussed being raised in the communities within which they now work, and they appeared genuinely concerned (and somewhat guarded) about the gang youth they assisted (cf. Sanders 2005). After much discussion, they agreed to facilitate contact with gang youth for another study. Importantly, these workers noted that they worked with a *range* of gang youth; some were involved in relatively less risky behaviors (marijuana use, infrequent fights, marginal involvement in offending), others were involved in more risky behaviors (cocaine/heroin use, fights involving weapons, heavy involvement in offending), and still others were somewhere in between these extremes. Interviewing the gang youth that these individuals work with should allow for assessment of a broad spectrum of trajectories into risk behaviors.

Thus far, the ethnoepidemiological method unfolds in a similar fashion to previous qualitative studies of youth gangs. Differences lie in the types of questions asked and the behaviors observed. Criminologists and criminal justice researchers interested in drug use may want to know which drugs a gang member uses, the frequency of use and attitudes toward use of particular drugs, how drugs are obtained, and the contexts of drug use. Public health researchers would be interested in these questions as well, plus a few others. In particular, identifying the form of the drug and how it is administered are important in determining levels of risk. For example, sniffing, smoking, swallowing, and injecting a particular drug present different levels of risk for negative health outcomes. Individuals who share needles during episodes of injecting drugs or share paraphernalia during episodes of sniffing drugs (bills, straws, etc.) may be at risk of becoming infected with HBV, HCV, and/or HIV (Des Jarlais et al. 2003).

Other questions of interest to a public health researcher concern how gang members conceive of their risk behaviors and the extent to which they negotiate these risks and anticipate and handle the consequences. Questions such as the following might be asked: What do you find pleasurable about using drug x? Can you tell me how people become infected with STIs? How likely do you think it is that you will get in a fight on a normal day? If you were injured seriously, and needed stitches or a bone to be placed in a cast, what would you do?

Through the interview process, and with additional assistance from others who work directly with gang youth, researchers may be able to observe youth gang members in areas where they work, live, and recreate. Informal observations are an additional aspect of the ethnoepidemiological approach, as they allow the researcher to validate information gained via interviews and help to contextualize risk behaviors. Not all the risk behaviors lend themselves to informal observation, for example, sexual activity and violence. Nonetheless, observing the overall socioeconomic conditions and immediate environments of such behaviors builds on interview data. It is often possible to observe incidents of drug use, including observing injecting-drug episodes, in which the researcher can record details of interest (see Clatts et al. 1999). Again, the objective of such observations is to better contextualize risk behavior and validate or refine interview information.

Youth Gangs, Social Networks, and Risk Behaviors

A social network is a "web of social relations within which individuals . . . are embedded" (Fleisher 2002a, 200). Social network data provide information on the structure and dynamics of the group, mapping out social relationships between individuals within the group and with persons outside it, and an individual's overall position within the group. Network analysis assumes that "the structure and content of social relationships have important behavioral consequences for individuals. The power of networks resides in the ties among members—ties that structure the flow of information, social norms, and social support" (Ennett, Bailey, and Federman 1999, 64).

Social network data have the ability to identify how individuals within cliques interact and influence one another, others in the gang, and persons outside the gang. This, in turn, reveals much about the extent and nature of risk behaviors, the transmission of norms and values regarding such behaviors, and the degree to which certain actors within and outside the group shape the extent, nature, and transmission of these norms and values (Adimora and Schoenbach 2005; Friedman and Aral 2001). By understanding the gang as a social network, public health researchers are able to better design intervention and prevention efforts aimed at minimizing or removing negative health outcomes of risky behaviors. Specific questions asked during the interview generate network data regarding risk behaviors, for example, With whom do you spend most of your time on an average day? With whom do you use drugs x, y, and, z? With whom have you fought against or alongside? Whose opinion within the gang do you most value?

We know that the frequency, nature, and extent of risk behaviors in which gang-involved youth engage are far from uniform (e.g., Brotherton and Barrios 2004; Short and Strodtbeck 1965/1974; Spergel 1995). The social network approach has the ability to inform which gang members are most at risk for negative health outcomes and which individuals hold influence over others regarding such behaviors. Risk behaviors within any one group (youth gangs, homeless youth, IDUs) tend to overlap and influence one another; offending and use of illicit drugs are likely to shape one another (e.g., people using drugs and then committing offenses; people committing offenses in order to obtain drugs); and drug use has been shown to manipulate sexual risks and episodes of violence (Adimora and Schoenbach 2005; Nurco, Kinlock, and Hanlon 2004; Wingood et al. 2002). A study of sexual behavior, substance use, and general offending among young Mexican American females "associated" with male gangs found that these young women were socially categorized by how they related sexually to the gang members (Cepeda and Valdez 2003). This categorization, in turn, indicates the extent to which the women were at risk of intoxication (from alcohol or illicit drugs), of becoming pregnant, and of general offending. Overall, the research suggests that, for gang-associated females, those who engaged in casual sexual relations with several male gang members were more likely to engage in other risk behaviors at much higher levels, compared to gang-associated females in long-term, sexually monogamous relationships with a male partner. Examining the youth gang as a social network has the potential to reveal the extent to which risk behaviors overlap and influence one another.

Members of youth gangs vary in the extent to which they associate with one another. Most gangs are loosely structured, consisting of smaller "cliques" who "hang out" with each other (e.g., Spergel 1995). Network data on youth gangs regarding risk behaviors thus may be examined at different levels: risk-potential networks, egocentric networks, and total sociometric networks (see Fleisher 2002a; Friedman and Aral 2001). A *risk-potential network* is a series of ties between two people within a group. Two people in a youth gang who inject drugs and/or have sex together would be considered a risk-potential network. An *egocentric network* might consider the direct ties one person (ego) has with other members of the group. A broader *sociometric network* would explore linkages among an entire group and others.

Network analysis can be conceived of as a mathematical model employed to assess an individual's or group's probability of behaving a certain way or becoming victimized by particular behaviors. Network analyses have been applied to study the spread or containment of viral infections, such as HIV-1, HBV, and HCV (Friedman et al. 2000), and such risky behaviors as violence, delinquency, and drug use among populations of homeless youths (Ennett, Bailey, and Federman 1999). Social network analyses have the potential to highlight patterns of linkages between sex partners and IDUs, leading, in turn, to a greater comprehension of high-risk behaviors associated with sex and intravenous drug administrations (Adimora and Schoenbach 2005; Friedman and Aral 2001) as well as norm transmission regarding high-risk behaviors (Ennett, Bailey, and Federman; Friedman et al.; Kipke et al. 1995).

Summary and Discussion

The aim of this chapter was to outline a public health model for the study of risk behaviors among youth gang members. Large research literatures exist concerning youth gangs, risk behaviors, the application of ethnoepidemiological methods, and the collection of social network data. This chapter links these concerns and methods into one focus.

Why do this and why now? Over the last hundred years, youth gang members have held a special place within society's rogues' gallery. Youth gangs may be clearly defined or amorphous, prosocial or antisocial, responsible for a disproportionate amount of an area's crime and violence or very little of it (Brotherton and Barrios 2004; Egley and Major 2004; Katz 2000; Katz and Jackson-Jacobs 2004; Klein 1995a; J. Miller 2001; Sanders 1994; Spergel 1995). Youth gang members have even been considered terrorists and officially charged under antiterror laws, perhaps reflecting the country's current moral panic concerning terrorism.[5] The questions asked by public health researchers complement those asked by criminologists. A public health agenda regarding the study of risk behaviors typical of youth gang members may help to generate policies that heretofore have been underutilized or undiscovered. Incarcerating youth gang members entails a tremendous cost to society, further marginalizing and stigmatizing young people who are already marginalized and stigmatized. It seems clear that efforts aimed at developing intervention and prevention measures for reducing these risk behaviors among youth gang members should include a public health perspective.

Notes

1. See, for instance, academic journals, such as *Sociology of Health and Illness*, the *Journal of Health and Social Issues*, and the *Journal of Health and Social Policy*, and monographs, such as *Social Epidemiology* (Berkman and Kawachi 2000), *Drugs, Alcohol, and Social Problems* (Orcutt and Rudy 2003), and *Health and Health Care as Social Problems* (Conrad and Leiter 2003).

2. See Bhopal (2002) for more on paradigm shifts within epidemiology.

3. See, for example, Request for Application (RFA) number RFA-DA-04-012. http//grants.nih.gov/grants/guide/rfa-files/RFA-DA-04-012 (accessed January 20, 2004).

4. A NIDA funded study (RO1 DA-15631) examining health risks among young IDUs.

5. In 2004, individuals from the St. James Boys, a gang from the Bronx, New York, were charged with terrorism, under an antiterror law that went into effect on September 17, 2001 (see New York City Police Department 2004).

9

The Value of Comparisons in Street Gang Research

Malcolm W. Klein

T HIS CHAPTER IS BASED ON A SINGLE ASSUMPTION: Street gang research is nowhere near as cumulative as it could be (or could have been). After many decades of studies of many kinds, largely uncoordinated, we have reached the point where we "know" much about the nature of street gangs and their contexts. In proof, I offer the knowledge syntheses available in Covey, Menard, and Franzese (1997), Spergel (1995), Curry and Decker (1998), and Klein (1995a, 2004). But it took us six decades to reach this point of cumulative knowledge. How might the process have been accelerated? How might it yet be accelerated?

My answer comes in many variations of a single theme: Gang research would be far more productive if it were based on *comparisons*. The variations have to do with *types* of comparison—gang members, gangs as units, gang locations, gangs over time, and gangs studied by coordinated rather than disparate methods. In the several sections of this chapter, I cite studies involving such comparisons, but the studies chosen are selected to be illustrative. This is not the place to be exhaustive.

It is the place, however, to be definitive about what I mean by the term *street gang*. For this chapter and for my future writing, I have adopted the "consensus Eurogang definition" developed over five years and agreed upon by over one hundred gang research scholars in the United States and Europe. It is a minimalist definition specifically designed to enhance comparative street gang research. It reads as follows: *A street gang is any durable, street-oriented youth group whose own identity includes involvement in illegal activity.*

Point 1: *Durable* is a bit ambiguous, but a period of at least several months can be used as a guideline. Many ganglike groups come together and dissipate within a few months. The durability refers to the *group*, which continues despite turnover of members.

Point 2: *Street-oriented* implies spending a lot of group time outside home, work, and school—often on streets, in malls, in parks, in cars, and so on.

Point 3: *Youth* can be ambiguous. Most street gangs are more adolescent than adult, but some include members in their twenties and even thirties. Most have average ages in adolescence or early twenties.

Point 4: *Illegal* generally means delinquent or criminal, not just bothersome.

Point 5: *Identity* refers to the group, the collective identity, not the individual self-image.

These are four definers of street gangs, here the necessary and sufficient components: durability, street orientation, youthfulness, and identity via illegal activity. All other gang characteristics we are accustomed to citing are not definers, but descriptors (e.g., ethnicity, age, gender, special clothing and argot, location, group names, crime patterns, and so on). This consensus definition has now been employed with considerable success, and its history and applications can be reviewed in Klein and colleagues (2001), Klein (2002), and Decker and Weerman (2005). It allows us to distinguish street gangs from prison gangs, terrorist groups, motorcycle gangs, and adult criminal organizations. Such distinctions are often blurred in media reports and law enforcement pronouncements. The definition also allows us to distinguish street gangs from the far more numerous informal and formal youth groups whose members may occasionally engage in illegal activities but for whom such activities or orientation is not a definer of their gang's identity. There are far more youth groups than there are street gangs.

In the sections that follow, I spell out and illustrate a number of comparative areas of study in gang research, a larger number than we normally think about in generalizing about gang knowledge. The instigation for my discussion occurred many years ago, when I first became acquainted with gang research and read a few fascinating gang ethnographies. Both then and now, my question in each case has been, Is this study part of a pattern, or is it an anomaly? Was the researcher attempting to build generalizeable knowledge, or merely taking advantage of a fortuitous situation where a street gang was available and interesting?

Illustrative Case Studies

Let us consider several oft-cited case studies. Leon Jansyn (1966) studied a Chicago gang over a period of a year. He demonstrates that a major turning point in the group's life came when its solidarity or cohesiveness ebbed to a particularly low point. When that point was reached, remaining active members deliberately increased their criminal activity, with a view to reenergizing the gang, reestablishing its solidarity. The process described by Jansyn makes sense conceptually; maintaining group cohesion is critical to gang maintenance. But whether Jansyn observed an exemplar of a larger pattern or a unique episode cannot be known. One technical problem is that his observations over a one-year period might have been merely an expectable seasonal pattern, as gangs tend to show activity patterns related to summer and winter periods.

More importantly, however, Jansyn was not able to place his case study in a wider array of cases, even though many Chicago gangs were under study at the time, with extensive recorded observations (Carney, Mattick, and Calloway 1969; Short and Strodtbeck 1965/1974). What needs demonstration is not that gang cohesiveness or gang activity ebbs and flows but that this is deliberately fostered by gang members' activities (increasing at low points—again, deliberately). Such intentionality would be an antidote to the many descriptions of gang crime as merely the outcome of group processes (Klein 1971; Thornberry et al. 2003).

A second example arises from Chicago data of the same era. In 1995 Laura Fishman reported a delayed analysis of the activity of a black female gang, the Vice Queens. The group consisted of about thirty girls in a gang having auxiliary status to the famous Vice Kings. The ages ranged from thirteen to nineteen, with about nineteen of the girls described as "hard core." The group had functional rather than structural leadership and a moderate level of cohesiveness. Members were largely out of school, unemployed, sexually active with the Vice Kings, and otherwise exhibiting versatile or "cafeteria-style" delinquency patterns.

Fishman declares that, to judge from these 1960s data, not much has changed about the nature of girl gangs, but she offers no modern comparisons. More to the point, we can in this case know that the Vice Queens were very similar to many other female auxiliary gangs in the 1960s and 1970s, as described by Klein (1971), and Moore (1978) in Los Angeles. Thus the Fishman depiction "makes sense," and we have the potential for a two-city, same-era pattern of findings. But how delicious it would have been way back then if the Chicago and Los Angeles projects could have joined forces to plan coordinated data collection on similarly defined and measured variables. What a quantum leap might have resulted in the then relatively barren area of female gang research.

A third example is provided by Sudhir Venkatesh's 1999 report on a traditional Chicago "supergang" heavily engaged in the drug trade. The gang numbered in the several hundreds and was highly structured around the sale of crack cocaine. Venkatesh scored a research coup in gaining access to the gang's financial records of drug proceeds and expenditures (including amounts dedicated to wages, weapons, and funeral expenses).

This was obviously a unique opportunity, and the author deserves credit for taking advantage of it. But is it a unique instance, part of a small, identifiable pattern among drug gangs, or something yet broader? Venkatesh claims that there was a "dramatic transformation known as corporatization" in the 1970s, yet in support he cites only Taylor's troublesome work in Detroit on a project that started in 1980 (see Klein 1995a for a critique). Venkatesh clearly implies that he is describing a general pattern, and of course he may be correct. Nonetheless most research on the organizational capacities of street gangs argues the opposite (Decker 2001a; Klein 1995a; Weisel 2002). How useful it would be to have a comparable set of drug gang studies that included data on how sales proceeds were spent.

In fact, a contrary case, also from Chicago, is offered by Felix Padilla (1992). He describes a Puerto Rican drug-dealing gang that is an offshoot of a larger traditional gang. About twenty-four members aged mostly between fifteen and eighteen work for distributors in their twenties. They seem less unstable than most street gangs in their criminal pursuits, but more cohesive and more hierarchically organized. Conceptually this makes sense for a gang "in business." Empirically it fits the pattern for "specialty" gangs described first by Maxson and Klein (1995), and soon thereafter by Klein (2002) and Weitekamp (2001). But how much more solid would the pattern be if Padilla had been able to compare the same variables across several drug gangs; he reports that there were a dozen others around at the same time in the Chicago area he frequented. He also provides no description of the "parent" gang from which his evolved; was it similar to the one described by Venkatesh? Again, my purpose is not to fault ethnographies for undertaking single-case studies; they often have no other choice. Rather, the point is to suggest that a set of coordinated studies by several researchers would add *generic* knowledge to the rich *case* knowledge that single studies provide.

Finally, let me escape the confines of Chicago and move marginally southwest, to Kansas City. Mark Fleisher's (1998) ethnography of the Fremont Hustlers in that city is quite a departure from most gang studies, in part because it is truly an ethnography, not just an observational or field study. Fleisher got an inside look at the gang, its members, and the neighborhood and family setting in which they were embedded. He came to understand the gang culture from the inside out, as few of us do.

Fleisher's description of a mixed-gender, drug-oriented, amorphous street gang is unique to date among ethnographies, because it illustrates the "collective" gang type described by Maxson and Klein (1995). But as rich and illuminating as the description is, it stands alone as an exemplar of the type (which was derived from police reports and structured inquiries). Maxson and Klein found collective gangs to be the least common of their five structural types, so it is not surprising that other depictions like Fleisher's are absent. To judge the type from the Hustlers alone may be appropriate, but we cannot know this. Is Kansas City different? Was the time period unique? Does ethnography reveal an image that cannot be captured by field observations or gang member surveys? A field that cannot adequately answer such questions has not yet achieved its potential, has not grounded itself in generic knowledge.

These five good research studies illustrate the inherent limitations of unique attributes in time, location, and method. But what if such limitations could be reduced? Let us consider comparisons that could move us forward and faster.

Available Comparisons

Of all the comparative studies gang researchers have undertaken over the years, it is surprising to find that most types of comparison have been given relatively scant attention. Most surprising is the paucity of cross-gang comparisons, despite the obvious fact that gangs are *groups*, that groups are potential units of analysis, and that gangs proliferated at their peak to over four thousand jurisdictions (National Youth Gang Center [NYGC] 2000). Instead, we have concentrated our efforts on gang *member* comparisons, so let us review these first.

Gang Member Comparisons

Examples of research cataloguing the different characteristics of gang members abound (Chin 1996; Decker and Van Winkle 1996; Klein 1971; J. Miller 2001; Short and Strodtbeck 1965/1974). Researchers have been able to document the wide ranges and central tendencies of members' ages, ethnicities, behavior patterns, familial and socioeconomic backgrounds, gang joining, participation levels, and leaving patterns. Two patterns among these seem to be so universal and yet surprising to the lay public that they deserve special attention, namely the versatility rather than the specialization of gang member crime (Klein; Robin 1967; Short and Strodtbeck) and the dramatically changing level of criminal involvement associated with joining and leaving gangs (e.g., Thornberry et al. 2003 and replicated in studies in Denver, Pittsburgh, Seattle, Montreal, and Edinburgh).

Attention should also be drawn to gender differences, which have drawn increasing attention over time (Fagan 1990; Klein 1971; Maxson and Whitlock 2002; J. Miller 2001; J. Moore 1991). Several descriptive facts stand out: Gang girls are younger and leave earlier than boys, gang girls are not merely the sex objects and weapon carriers described in early research, and gang girls exhibit the same general illegal behavior patterns as the boys but at lower levels. A comparison between police reports of female gang participation on the one hand and ethnographies and survey reports on the other makes it clear that the police greatly underestimate levels of female gang membership, which often reaches between 20 and 40 percent at younger ages (below sixteen). However, these statements are more cumulative than directly comparative. Studies looking at male and female members of the same group are uncommon (but see Fleisher 1998; Klein 1971; J. Moore 1978, 1991).

Gang versus Nongang Members

Another important approach to understanding gang members is to compare them with nongang youth. Preferably, such comparisons would encompass the same communities, in order to control for broad contextual differences. Recent work by Maxson, Whitlock, and myself in San Diego and Long Beach, yet to be published, drew members and nonmembers from the same neighborhood where gangs were known to be present. The differences we are finding are fewer than those taken from less-stringent comparisons (same schools, same communities) but nonetheless are striking with respect to a subset of variables distinguishing members from nonmembers (see preliminary analysis in Maxson, Whitlock, and Klein 1998). A few other gang/nongang comparisons illustrate the sorts of findings that seem particularly instructive about the nature of gang members.

- A series of papers by Short and his colleagues explore comparisons between gang and nongang youth on structural dimensions. One of these (Short, Rivera, and Tennyson 1965) reports predictable differences in exposures to legitimate and illegitimate opportunities. A second (Short, Rivera, and Marshall 1964) reports surprisingly *few* differences in the ways gang and nongang youth rate nine adult roles (politician, minister, policeman, etc.), suggesting a minor place for adult protest in explaining gang membership. Yet a third paper (Rivera and Short 1967) reports large differences between gang members and nonmembers in how the adults they know respond to them. Gang-nominated adults are far less responsive and more likely to "pin the blame" on the boys rather than on the conventional structure of opportunity.
- Huff (1996) reports that differences in social activities between members and nonmembers are far smaller than differences in illegal activities; gang members, contrary to popular conception, often engage in the same social and recreational activities as their nongang peers. However, Huff's data show illegal activity differences to be significant in two-thirds of all

categories of crime, with ratios ranging from 3 to 1 up to 20 to 1, member to nonmember. It is the rare acts (e.g., forgery, kidnapping, sexual assault) that show nonsignificant differences.

- Fagan (1990) found ratios over twelve categories of crime to favor gang members from between 2 to 1 and 4 to 1 among males. Female comparisons were almost equally large. As in the Huff analysis above, the more serious offenses showed the larger ratios.

- Esbensen, Huizinga, and Weiher (1993) advanced the issue with gang members and two categories of nonmembers: "nongang street offenders," and "nonoffenders" (relatively, that is). They, too, found no differences in levels of conventional activities but expectable major differences in crime rates. Unexpectedly, however, while there were significant differences in attitudes and perceptual variables between gang members and nonoffenders, this was not true when comparing gang members and nongang street offenders. Only one of eighteen variables distinguished these two groups. Different but reasonable comparison groups provide different conclusions, depending on the category of variables employed, in this case behavioral versus cognitive variables. More of this kind of work will inform our conceptualizations of what makes gang members different.

- Thornberry and colleagues (2003) added another comparative variation by comparing gang members with quartiles of nongang groups who nonetheless had delinquent peers—another reasonable comparison. They found the highest quartile to be similar to the gang members in mean peer delinquency, but *not* in general delinquency rates. The gang processes were adding something beyond the effects of delinquent peers. These differences remained among eight waves of data collection in all quartiles, with violence differences being the greatest. Similar results were obtained for females across the first four waves, but then the female gang membership disappeared.

- Finally in this listing is the work of Jody Miller (2001) with gang and nongang girls. She found major differences in self-reported delinquency on twenty of twenty-six items. Additionally, she reports differences in exposure to or awareness of gang issues in the neighborhood, along with differences in family problems and gang membership within the families. The stability of the comparisons is established by drawing the gang respondents from two contrasting urban settings, Columbus and St. Louis.

In sum, there have been enough studies using comparison groups and analyses that a rather stable depiction of gang members has emerged, a depiction that allows us to speculate on factors that make gangs and gang members qualitatively different from nongang youth. It is our historical emphasis on studying individuals that has permitted this to occur. This is less true of the other comparisons to which I turn next.

Cross-Gang Comparisons

When I started my career in gang research, I was fortunate to be presented with four large clusters of black street gangs, which I later augmented with intensive exposure to a large Hispanic gang. I had five gangs to compare, but did not appreciate until later how valuable this opportunity was. When, during this same period, I traveled to Chicago and Boston to compare notes with Jim Short and Walter Miller, I learned that they were studying gangs of much the same type, what we now call traditional gangs. Traditional gangs are large, self-regenerating clusters of subgroups with cafeteria-style crime patterns and territorial orientations. Joan Moore's gangs are of the same type (Moore 1978), as are many described in New York, San Francisco, Philadelphia, and El Paso. This research took place largely before 1980, and while it provided wonderful data on traditional gangs, we did not appreciate that such gangs were special. We could study them *because* they were stable over time, providing easy and continuing access. They were available; they were not necessarily typical.

Various attempts at typologizing gangs were undertaken, but they yielded different typologies, based on different methods (see Klein and Maxson 2005 for a full exposition of the typological approach). Short and Strodtbeck (1965/1974) had the luxury of gathering data from sixteen Chicago groups, and the comparisons allowed them, among other things, to extract gang behavior patterns that failed to support popular typologies.[1]

The structural typology first described by Maxson and Klein (1995) was based on gang descriptions from fifty-nine cities—one gang in each—and then was validated in hundreds of others both in the United States and abroad (Klein 2002). Traditional, neotraditional, compressed, collective, and specialty gangs account for between 74 and 95 percent of gangs studied, representing variations on durability, size, age structure, subgrouping, territoriality, and crime pattern. The strength of the typology rests on its stability when even statewide and national comparisons are made. And while it is based on male gangs for the most part, J. Miller (2001) has found it applicable to female gangs in Columbus and St. Louis as well.

Recent deliberately comparative studies have also helped lay to rest the stereotype of street gangs based on media reports of the mythical character of the Crips and Bloods of Los Angeles and the "supergangs" of Chicago. Reports by Decker (2001a) and Weisel (2002) compare the most serious gangs in San

Diego, St. Louis, and Chicago (two gangs in each city) to search for the quasi-corporate structure that feeds both the public image and the claims of many enforcement agencies. Only one of the six gangs, the Black Gangster Disciples in Chicago, fits the bill. The others do not, based on organizational variables such as differentiated levels of membership, strong leaders, regular meetings, written rules, specialization of functions, organization of drug sales, profits used for gang purposes, owning legitimate businesses, engaging in local political activities, relationships with local businesses, and collaborative relationships with other groups. This important research dispels popular notions, just as the typological results clarify both the variety and patterns of gang structures.

One vital comparison is still missing: We know little about gangs, as defined in this chapter, as different from other youth groups. I am referring here specifically to using groups as units of analysis. If street gangs (by definition) are different from other youth groups—beyond the several defining characteristics—and different from such groups as prison gangs, motorcycle gangs, and drug cartels, what are the important differences and what do they tell us about street gang structure and street gang life? I cannot, offhand, think of a single comparative study that looks at these different group units.

Comparisons across Locations

Locations can refer to different neighborhoods in a given community, to different communities within a given city, to different cities, or even to different countries. While there are a number of examples of the first three, it is often the case that data are aggregated *across* locations without specific comparisons *between* locations. My first four gang clusters in the early 1960s (Klein 1971) were compared on gang structures in each of the four locations as well as on the cohesiveness of the four clusters, but the analysis of the offense patterns was aggregated across all four. Short and Strodtbeck (1965/1974), with sixteen gangs in several locations, aggregated most of their data analyses. So did Miller with his Boston gangs.

An exception to the aggregation pattern is provided by Dennis Mares's (2001) study of the gangs in three contrasting neighborhoods in Manchester, England. One of these was a downtrodden housing development area, the second a working-class area, and the third a changing suburban area. Dear to my heart is Mares's attempt to relate the different areas to differences in gang structure: neotraditional gangs in the first two areas and compressed gangs in the third. This was an ethnographic study, with no serious attempt to aggregate data across contrasting settings.

Across cities, Fagan (1989) drew gang members from Chicago, Los Angeles, and San Diego to illuminate a typology of social, party, conflict, and delinquent gangs, but otherwise aggregated his data across the three locations. Similarly, Huff's (1996) gang/nongang comparisons were aggregated across several cities without intercity comparisons. Cross-city comparisons are difficult for two very practical reasons. First, it is a logistic nightmare to launch a sustained, multicity research project. It is expensive in finances, time, and effort. Second, a decent cross-city comparison is of limited value unless those cities (and neighborhoods) are described and studied to understand why one would expect differences and similarities between the gangs drawn from them. For example, Decker's (2001a) commendable comparison of the most serious gangs in San Diego, St. Louis, and Chicago concentrated on the organizational capacities of the gangs, but not on what we might have expected given their very different urban and historical contexts.

I can think offhand of only one cross-city study that deliberately selected contrasting cities, described their social, economic, and historical contexts, and then collected gang data to investigate in part what differences might emerge that made sense given those contrasting contexts. This was Jody Miller's study of female gang members in Columbus and St. Louis, cities with very different economic states of health and different histories of gang development. Miller provides a model that could easily be followed by others.[2]

One report stands out for its examination of cross-city data on a number of dimensions. As part of a program evaluation, Esbensen and Lynskey (2001) compared school survey reports from young gang members in eleven cities. Included were responses about four topics: demographics, gang characteristics, self-report delinquency, and reasons for joining gangs. While some notable differences emerge, the more striking pattern is that of similarities across most cities with respect to twenty-eight items in the fourth category. This is all the more striking as the eleven sites range from rural to urban and from small cities (under 100,000 population) to major urban centers such as Philadelphia and Phoenix.

There is a way in which this situation could be further improved without great effort. The National Youth Gang Center (see NYGC 2000 and other yearly reports) has collected gang data from law enforcement agencies over about a decade, with literally thousands of communities included in the database. While the material is necessarily somewhat superficial, it covers a number of areas of interest: percentage of reporting gangs; numbers of gangs and gang members; distribution of age, gender, and ethnicity; use of member, motive, or other definitions of gang crime; various crime rates; approaches to gang control; and so on. Changes in levels of gang crime per city are available over the ten-year period. What is required first is the melding of these data with census and other city databases to get at the patterns of gang prevalence. Then the stage would be set for adventuresome researchers to engage in both quantitative and on-site qualitative comparative studies.

Another stage-setting exercise has already taken place to add cross-national comparisons (with instrumentation equally applicable to neighborhood and city comparisons). The Eurogang Program (Klein 2002) has since 1997 brought together over a hundred American and European gang scholars and policy officials in a series of seven international workshops. To date, two volumes of research reports have been produced (Decker and Weerman 2005; Klein et al. 2001).[3] These include studies in the United States, Holland, England, Scotland, Norway, Denmark, Germany, France, Russia, Belgium, and Italy. Included are several comparative studies, employing the same instruments, by European and American gang researchers. The gang definition employed in this chapter and described in its first pages derives from the Eurogang effort. The Decker and Weerman collection illustrates clearly how comparisons across countries are facilitated by the use of this definition in each contribution. Common terms cannot help but improve comparative efforts.

Historical Comparisons

Here we are on even thinner ground. One of the reasons for needing historical comparisons is, of course, the enormous changes in gang prevalence, structure, and crime patterns that have taken place over the last several decades (Covey, Menard, and Franzese 1997; Klein 1995a; Spergel 1995). In addition, gang activity has been shown to go through cycles, ranging from seasons to many years. These changes and cycles led me to comment some years ago:

> With respect to changes in gang characteristics, it might be thought that the cyclical nature of gang activity would yield a picture of little linear change over time—that is, the back and forth swings of the pendulum would cancel each other out. But this is not the case. Through all the periodic cycles, gangs and gang problems have grown. The cycles end at higher plateaus, on average, as if the pendulum seldom reverts to its original lower level, while often reaching a higher level on the upswing. Thus, over several decades, the upper age limit has increased; the variety of ethnic minority gangs has increased; the variety of gang structures has increased; associated gang violence has increased. (Klein 1995b, 233)

In the face of these sorts of changes, some continuity in the research process would be valuable, but this requires researchers who are willing and able to stay at the table over long periods of time or, at the very least, who are interested in recapturing the past and comparing it with the present. Only a few examples present themselves. Taylor (1990a) reports an evolution in gang structures from what he calls scavenger to territorial to corporate gangs in Detroit. This analysis is low on data but at least yields testable hypotheses. Joan Moore (1978, 1991) returned to East Los Angeles to assess changes in two traditional gangs. She found them to have become more institutionalized, with the groups coming to have more influence over members, with greater drug involvement, violence cyclical rather than changing linearly, deviance generally but not dramatically increased, more isolation from other peer groups, and less tolerance by community adults. These gangs, she notes, are "... no longer just at the rowdy end of the continuum of local adolescent groups—they are now really outside the continuum" (J. Moore 1991, 132).

Obviously we can compare research findings from one period to another and assess aggregate changes. But such comparisons do not control for location or gang, and thus they give little sense for the dynamics of gang evolution within gangs or within locations. Models such as Taylor's or Moore's are far more promising in understanding such dynamics, but they are rare.

Methodological Comparisons

In the mid-1960s, I found myself in an odd argument with Walter Miller. We had both been collecting extensive data on gang delinquency from similar sets of traditional black street gangs, he in Boston and I in Los Angeles. In a very long phone conversation, Miller reported a heavier (albeit not extensive) level of violence among his gangs than I did among mine. Were Boston and Los Angeles gangs so similar in type, yet so dissimilar in behavior? After considerable discussion, we discovered that the dissimilarities lay not in the gangs, but in the researchers.

Miller's data were based on informal interviews and detached worker reports of gang member conversations. Miller was listening to violence. My data were based on street observations and detached worker reports of gang member behaviors. I was observing. Gang members, it seemed, talked a more violent game than they played. A listening researcher will "find" different levels of violence than an observing researcher. If Miller had taken his ears to Los Angeles and I had taken my eyes to Boston, the pictures likely would have been reversed.

The anecdote reminds us of the obvious fact of methodology; different methods may, or even must, yield variations on what we trust as independent reality. Further, entry into the gang world via different doors will probably yield different perspectives. There are important implications from starting out with gang member contacts, or street worker contacts, or school contacts, or police and correctional contacts. Different "truths" may emerge (see, for example, the data reported for Chicago by Curry 2000). Only the application of different methods to the same phenomenon, in the same time and location, can lead us to a more comprehensive and interpretable "reality."

A planned comparative methods approach can expose the limitations of the separate methods. It can give a rounder picture of gang realities. It forces a better appreciation of the "ecology" of gangs versus the "nature" of gangs that single methods cannot provide. Too often, and for very understandable reasons of practicality and training, gang researchers have depended on a single method. This has been especially true of survey researchers, whose data are most often taken from youth samples in school or household surveys, or occasionally from surveys of police respondents. It is also often true of archival researchers, who dig into police, correctional, or court files and databases.

It has been somewhat less true of field observers and ethnographers, where one finds an admixture of experiential, observational, and interview data (see, for example, Fleisher's 1998 depiction of the Fremont Hustlers in Kansas City). Yet even in these instances, the combination of methods is not usually planned as a comparative methodological design. Perhaps the most comprehensive pattern of methods has been associated with researchers undertaking evaluations of gang intervention programs (Carney, Mattick, and Calloway 1969; Klein 1971; Miller 1962; Spergel 1995). Still, this is not enough. A definitive statement of the street gang picture as seen from differently selected methods is not yet available. However, it might soon be possible.

After six years of interactions between U.S. and European scholars, a series of research instruments designed for comparative cross-national, multimethod research has emerged. To varying degrees, these instruments have been translated and back-translated into several languages, pretested and revised in a number of countries, and are now being employed by a variety of gang researchers here and abroad. They are publicly available and can now be used to assess the comparative gang pictures they produce. All of them are based on the consensus Eurogang definition introduced in the beginning of this chapter, and the three principal instruments incorporate operational measures of this definition. The instruments are as follows:

The Youth Survey

The survey protocol contains three levels of items as judged by the Eurogang researcher consortium. Core items are those necessary to establish a youth's group affiliations as gang or nongang, according to the program's definitional stance. Secondary items are those judged very important for basic comparisons of street gangs across different sites. Tertiary items are those of general interest to most gang researchers but not critical to establishing the nature of the gangs and gang members. Users of this interview protocol are required to use the core items, strongly urged to use at least the secondary set as well, and encouraged to use the tertiary set. They can, of course, add any items they deem useful for their research purposes.

The Ethnographic Guidelines

These are an explicit listing of information to be gathered in the course of an ethnographic street gang study. They correspond in content, though not of course in format, to the three levels of information gathered in the youth interview. They allow for systematic collection of the same information across gangs and across ethnographic study sites, as well as comparisons to data drawn from youth surveys in those sites. Nothing in the guidelines prevents an ethnographer from gathering additional data of interest in any form deemed feasible.

The Experts' Survey

This is an interview or questionnaire protocol designed for respondents who are knowledgeable about the street gang situations in their area or jurisdiction. It is appropriate for police, social service practitioners, teachers and school officials, local businessmen, crime reporters, neighborhood leaders, and even selected veteran or ex-gang members. It uses the same definitional items as the youth survey, and then seeks structured information on known street gangs in the respondent's purview. Cross-site ecologies of street gangs are easily derived from the experts' survey.

Two other standardized instruments are also available. The first is a set of guidelines for city descriptions. Tested out for general availability of such information, it lists historical, cultural, geographic, and demographic data that can normally be collected about a research site to provide the broad social context within which to locate street gang problems. The fifth instrument is a survey of gang prevention and control programs, with special emphasis on those that have been subjected to some evaluation effort.

It is my first fantasy that within a few years we will see planned, comparative method studies of street gangs using these standardized instruments. It is my second fantasy that we will see such studies in multiple sites—comparing gangs, gang neighborhoods, and gangs in different cities and countries. The technological means are now available through the Eurogang Program, and the opportunity, as called for by Maxson (2001) in the first Eurogang collection of papers, now exists. More comparisons mean better knowledge and, for those so inclined, better practices in improving the worlds inhabited by street gangs.

Caveats and Conclusions

Fantasies such as these are easily come by. The realities of conducting comparative research teach hard lessons: It is difficult work and requires a good deal of tolerance, especially for the different perspectives of one's collaborators. Beyond this, good comparative research brings several requirements of particular note:

- It means using the same or similar definitions of the central concepts, such as *street gang* (thus my use of the consensus Eurogang definition in this chapter).
- It means using the same or very similar forms of data collection procedures, be they ethnographic protocols, survey instruments, or archival coding schemes.
- But common definitions and common instruments do not necessarily yield common sample procedures. Comparative research should also mean careful attention to sample selection (members, gangs, locations) that yield either similar units, or units deliberately selected to compare the impact of their contrasts, for example, similar types of gangs or very different types; gang members from the same community or drawn from very different communities; and gangs all in "emergent" or "chronic" gang areas or gangs deliberately chosen to represent those two different contexts. In other words, we must know beforehand what the relevant parameters of comparison are.
- All of this, obviously, implies careful planning prior to launching comparative studies, and a commitment to resolving differences among collaborators' perspectives. Additionally, it means that comparisons across types of data collection must also be carefully considered. The "depth" of ethnography, the "breadth" of surveys, and the selectivity of archives (police reports, court transcripts, news articles) must be appreciated and assessed for their differences. As a colleague remarked to me, "Quantitative factors have qualitative consequences."
- Finally, research on different gangs or in different locations, with several types of data collection methods, means that we are dealing with different contexts of knowledge development. To be thorough, we must not only understand the elements of our methodological outputs but the contexts of those data sources as well.

My fear is that all the foregoing will discourage most readers from undertaking comparative gang research. I hope not; I hope it will instead be read as a challenge. I hope the challenge will appeal to researchers who thrive on complexity and on the satisfaction of bringing order out of chaos. I write with them in mind.

Notes

The author has benefited from the early draft comments of Scott Decker, Finn Esbensen, Inger-Lise Lien, Cheryl Maxson, and Frank Weerman.

1. They also employed another comparison of great merit, using their data to assess the validity of competing gang theories (Cohen 1955; Cloward and Ohlin 1960; Miller 1958; and Yablonsky 1962, inferentially).

2. It should be noted that Miller's design was derived from the distinction between "emergent" and "chronic" gang cities. Vigil's (2002) cross-ethnic comparison is not a cross-city comparison, but the model he uses is worth consideration because he searched for the connections between different *ethnicities* and gang characteristics for explanatory purposes, much as Miller did for different cities.

3. One should note as well the recent compendium of gang studies put together by Herbert Covey (2003). In this volume, Covey attempts secondhand comparisons of various sorts, including the structures described in Maxson and Klein (1995).

10

Hate Groups or Street Gangs? The Emergence of Racist Skinheads

Pete Simi

ALTHOUGH THE EMERGENCE of racist skinheads during the 1980s provided gang researchers with a rich opportunity to examine one type of white gang, skinheads typically have been excluded from gang studies on the grounds that they are better understood as "hate groups" and/or "terrorists," sharing little in common with traditional street gangs (Curry and Decker 2003; Hamm 1993; Hicks 2004; Klein 1995a; Moore 1993; Schneider 1999).[1] In contrast to street gangs, racist skinheads have been portrayed as closely organized around an ideological system of "Aryan supremacy" (Hamm; Hicks; Klein)[2] and as lacking traditional gang territorial claims. Moreover, it is commonly believed that skinheads differ from traditional gangs in that they do not spend significant amounts of time "hanging out" on the streets; instead, they are said to be "inside...working on their materials; or if outside, they're looking for a target, not just lounging around.... Skinheads and bikers are focused, always planning... Skins prefer narrower ranges of trouble" (Klein, 22).

A careful review of the literature suggests the inadequacy of conceptualizations of racist skinheads as distinct from traditional youth street gangs. Baron's (1997) study of Canadian racist skinheads and Anderson's (1987) study of San Francisco skinheads, for example, found these youth to be neither highly organized nor politicized. Skinhead youth lived on the streets or in other transient circumstances (e.g., crash pads) and often used violent and other criminal means for survival and the settlement of disputes with other urban and suburban youth cliques.[3]

This chapter examines the early development of Southern California skinheads (1981–1985) in relation to the larger sociohistorical context of gang formation.[4] Racist skinheads are shown to parallel conventional gangs along three dimensions: (1) organizational structure, (2) territoriality and group conflict, and (3) participation in nonspecialized criminal activity.[5]

Defining Skinheads as Gangs

A gang is defined here as an age-graded peer group that exhibits some permanence and establishes a sense of boundaries through gang-identified territory, style, and such oppositional practices as fighting and criminal activity (Decker and Van Winkle 1996; Klein 1995a; Short and Strodtbeck 1965/1974). Although I share reservations about the inclusion of criminal activity in the definition of gangs, I argue that regardless of whether the street, youth, or criminal dimension is emphasized, skinhead groups meet the criteria commonly used to define gangs and thus fall within the same conceptual rubric. Some observers (Anderson, Mangels, and Dyson 2001) argue further that all "hate groups" should be viewed as gangs. This overly broad position, however, ignores the overtly political nature of hate groups such as the Ku Klux Klan.[6] While the Klan has consistently used racial intimidation and violence throughout its long history, it is more accurately conceptualized as a social movement organization (McAdam and Snow 1997) rather than a street or youth gang. Most members are adults, their territorial claims have always been broader than the local neighborhood, and throughout most of its history the Klan has sought political power in order to enact a broad platform of ideals that include conservative traditional patriarchal family forms, prohibitions against "race mixing," extreme anti-Semitism, and militant Aryan nationalism (Ferber 1998). In contrast, most skinheads become involved between the ages of twelve and nineteen (Anti-Defamation League 1995; Moore 1993; Wooden and Blazak 2001),[7] and they tend to coalesce around a unique music, style, argot, and set of practices that are autonomous and distinct from adult hate groups such as the Klan (Bjorgo 1998; Wooden and Blazak).

History of U.S. Skinheads

British scholars analyzed the original skinheads in England during the late 1960s using a neo-Marxist-inspired conception of youth subculture (Brake 1974; Clarke 1976; Hebdige 1979; Knight 1982). These studies tend to focus exclusively upon style, which they explain as an attempt to resolve a marginal working-class status in a class-based society.[8] Following the emergence of skinheads in the United States during the late 1970s, most American observers—like their British predecessors—also portrayed skinheads as qualitatively distinct from traditional gangs (Curry and Decker 2003; Hamm 1993; Hicks 2004; Klein 1995a; Moore 1993; Schneider 1999).

The relatively small literature examining U.S. skinheads describes their emergence, development, and organizational characteristics at the broadest possible level, offering little specificity regarding the ground level of social action (for example, see Etter 1999; Hamm 1993; Hicks 2004; Kaplan 1995; Knox 2000; McCurrie 1998; Moore 1993; Wood 1999; Wooden and Blazak 2001; for an exception, see Anderson 1987). These broad depictions of skinheads have not been well suited to examining issues related to the local dimensions of skinhead emergence and development. Additionally, conceptualization of American skinheads has been divorced from the historical precedence of racial antagonism typical of many conventional gangs (see Curry and Decker 2003; Hagedorn 1988; Schneider 1999; Short and Strodtbeck 1965/1974).

The development of skinhead gangs was directly related to conflict with other youth groups (jocks, cowboys, rockers, minority gangs, etc.). This is not to say, as claimed by some observers, that early skinheads were "nonracist" (Sarabia and Shriver 2004; Wood 1999). My data clearly indicate that racism has been a component of skinhead identity from the beginning (see also Moore 1993); however, it was not initially attached to a broader political agenda and did not include participation in racist political activism.

Methods and Data

Between 1999 and 2004, I conducted participant observation and in-depth interviews in a variety of settings in order to examine the emergence and development of Southern California skinheads. I used a snowball sampling technique to locate skinheads in the Los Angles area, where the largest number have been thought to exist (Anti-Defamation League 1989). In all, I obtained data regarding seventeen Southern California skinhead gangs and their members.

My analysis is based primarily on 127 interviews conducted with forty-three current and former racist skinheads. These interviews were supplemented with data from interviews that I conducted with fourteen law enforcement officers and several "nonskinhead" white-power movement leaders (e.g., Tom Metzger and Richard Butler), who were among the first to promote the importance of recruiting skinheads to the white supremacist movement.[9] Skinhead interviewees were selected by means of purposive snowball sampling strategies, which enabled me to access a wide range of skinheads from various different groups (e.g., Orange County Skins, Norwalk Skins, American Firm, etc.). Most of the skinhead interviewees were male, reflecting the predominance of males in the skinhead subculture (Blee 2002). No clear social class pattern was found among interviewees, which is not surprising in view of the cross-section of social classes represented among skinheads in general (Anderson 1987; Hamm 1993). Interviews focused primarily on group history, how individuals became skinheads, group activities and practices, organizational characteristics, and recruitment strategies.

The range of events I observed with skinheads in Southern California included house parties and other social gatherings, white-power music concerts, and twenty-three home visits, ranging in length from one day to three weeks. Participant observation provided data regarding group practices and allowed me to build rapport with key informants who served as gatekeepers, introducing me to other skinheads and providing much-needed references for further interviews. Participant observation and interviewing allowed for close examination of a wide range of information that is impossible to obtain solely through secondary sources (Blee 2002).

Secondary data sources included antiracist watchdog organizations' (e.g., Anti-Defamation League) official reports, newspaper accounts, court documents, and various types of documentary evidence that law enforcement officials provided (e.g., videotaped interviews of skinheads conducted by law enforcement personnel, written correspondence among skinheads, etc.). These documents, as well as skinhead texts, such as newsletters, websites, and Internet discussion groups, were content analyzed and studied for corroboration or contradiction of insights gleaned from primary interview data.[10] This multimethod approach allowed for triangulation across an array of data (Denzin 1978).

There are methodological difficulties with studying skinheads. Because I am not a member of these groups, entree was difficult. Skinheads are often antagonistic toward outsiders and tend to prefer secrecy. Moreover, skinhead networks are diverse and loosely structured. After meeting a skinhead in his midthirties who was originally from Long Beach, California, at an Aryan Nations gathering in northern Idaho, I obtained e-mail access to several other relatively older skinheads from Southern California. I made contact with these skinheads (via e-mail) requesting, as a sociologist, opportunities to observe various skinhead events and to conduct life history interviews. Eventually these requests were granted, the only condition being that I was white. The first meeting occurred at a bar in Orange County, at which time contacts were made for further observations and interviews. The initial contacts led to further communication with other skinheads from various groups. These contacts snowballed into the sample described above. Reliance on nonprobability sampling was necessary, due to the hidden character of the population (see Heckathorn 1997, 2002 for an alternate respondent-driven sampling approach for hidden populations). At times my status was challenged, and I was accused of working in concert with law enforcement agencies or as an agent provocateur. Some of these challenges resulted in threats of bodily harm, although none occurred. Clearly these obstacles prevented me from gathering certain types of data (e.g., gang rosters), as did the refusal by certain skinheads to participate in the study.[11] My generalizations about racist skinhead gangs must, therefore, remain modest and tentative.

Subcultural Schism and the Transition from Punk to Skin

Although the skinhead style spread to America through a process of international cultural diffusion, Southern California skinheads formed in response to microlevel changes in the local punk rock scene and macrolevel changes in the wider social structure. In the late 1970s, Southern California punk started getting "hardcore" (Blush 2001; Spitz and Mullen 2001), signaling a more violent and suburban trend in punk rock. *Hardcore* referred to a faster style of music and a hostile attitude, which was expressed through random violence directed at other punks during music shows. For young suburban kids, hardcore aggressiveness provided an important security device against those antagonistic toward punk style:

> Around that time [late 1970s] there were a lot of kids [punks] who were getting seriously fucked up by these long-haired redneck hicks in their 4x4 vehicles, real Lynyrd Skynyrd kind of guys. They were going to punk shows and hiding out in the parking lot and ambushing us, and I think a couple of people died.... Nobody was doing anything about it. No disrespect against the Hollywood party punks ... but they just weren't prepared to defend us out in the 'burbs where kids were getting beaten on all the time.... (quoted in Spitz and Mullen 2001, 192)

By the late 1970s, individuals were experimenting with the skinhead style (Moore 1993); however, these youths were submerged within the punk rock scene, and a "skinhead collective identity" had not yet developed. As hardcore continued to radicalize the punk scene, some punks merged hardcore with a "cholo" style to form punk gangs (e.g., the Suicidals, some sets of the Los Angeles Death Squad, etc.), while others formed skinhead gangs by building on the hardcore style, emphasizing a hypermasculine, clean-cut, working-class identity:

> Hardcore and skinheads were definitely connected. Hardcore took punk to a different level, to a more extreme level. You could see it with the music, the dress.... That's where there was a lot of overlap between skinhead and punk, and there was an overlap in members ... (Order Skinhead interview, 11/20/02)

One historian of punk also notes the stylistic connection between hardcore and skinhead:

> The rise of Hardcore coincided with the rise of Skinhead culture. In some ways the scenes overlapped. Edgier HC [Hardcore] types adopted Skinhead style. A shaved head provided the perfect fuck you to Hippies. . . . Very few embraced the style and remained unfazed by the politics. Some racists' hatred was heartfelt; for others it was just a confrontational tool . . . (quoted in Blush 2001, 31)

As these quotes suggest, there were stylistic and ideological overlaps between hardcore and skinheads, as well as important organizational linkages (Wood 1999).

Skinhead Organizational Characteristics, Social Gangs, and Street Socialization

The first skinhead gangs formed around 1981, after hardcore began splintering the punk scene. Skinhead gangs like the Northside Firm, the South Bay Skins, and the Order Skins formed across Los Angeles, Orange, San Bernardino, and Riverside counties. The early skinhead gangs were, as one member put it, "identity groups"; skinhead gangs bonded around identity markers and shared interests (e.g., shaved heads, clothing styles, musical preferences, slang, tattoos, etc.). Skinheads were building an identity with organizational names, initiation rites, semihierarchical social roles, and participation in the same type of nonspecialized, garden-variety delinquency that characterizes traditional street gangs (e.g., vandalism, underage drinking, petty theft, and, perhaps most importantly, fighting). Skinhead identity was loose, unstructured, and tied to social gatherings that were relatively unregulated, allowing for the innovation needed to create oppositional identities.

Early skinhead gangs were organized primarily around fraternal relations among members and conflict with other gangs, resembling what various observers describe as social gangs (see Fagan 1989; Maxson and Klein 1995; Schneider 1999; Short and Strodtbeck 1965/1974; Yablonsky 1962). They did not adhere to an explicit political ideology and did not engage in the conventional political activities (marches, leafleting, rallies, etc.) that eventually came to characterize some of the later skinhead gangs. Unlike Pinderhughes's (1997) Brooklyn white ethnic youth groups, which he differentiates from gangs on the basis of their lack of official names and clearly established leadership positions, the skinheads that I studied used initiation rites to mark group membership and, in some cases, established relatively formal leadership positions and other organizational roles. The level of involvement among skinheads ranged from core to peripheral, mirroring what others have found among traditional gangs (Decker and Van Winkle 1996; Klein 1995a).

Skinhead gangs were part of a larger youth scene (Bennett and Petersen 2004; Cavan 1972; Gaines 1994; Irwin 1977; Polsky 1967) organized around a particular style, music, specialized language, and a range of oppositional practices that included violence (e.g., fighting) and garden-variety crime (e.g., vandalism, petty theft, drugs). The early skinhead scene was an umbrella without clearly demarcated boundaries, allowing fluid forms of participation; yet there emerged within the scene subgroups with clearer boundaries of membership (skinheads often refer to these as "crews").

> Yeah there were all the different crews and that's who you ran with. . . . Some of us got along pretty well and others didn't and we would fight with each other all the time. Back then it didn't matter if you were skinheads or not; if there was a problem between different crews we brawled. . . . They [crews] were usually about 20 or 30 skins; some were bigger and some got a lot bigger after they started recruiting heavy in the late 1980s. . . . (American Firm interview, 6/14/04)

While resembling Los Angeles Latino gang *klikas*, early skinhead crews had less age-graded organization than the much older Latino gangs (see J. Moore 1978, 1991; Vigil 1988, 2002); they were also less hierarchical. Such differences, however, may disappear if recent trends continue. The older traditional gang structures with age-graded subgroups and relatively well-defined territorial boundaries seem to be giving way "to relatively autonomous, smaller, independent groups, poorly organized and less territorial than used to be the case" (Klein 1995a, 36). "Gangs are more mobile now and their territories may include a shopping mall rather than (or in addition to) a street or neighborhood or an area drug market" (Short 1996, 238). To some extent, the emergence of skinhead gangs reflects these changes. Although skinheads attempted to establish turf claims similar to traditional gangs, the development of high levels of mobility was necessary for attendance at hardcore music concerts and other functions of special significance to these youth. Thus early skinhead gangs included a combination of new trends (increasingly found among gangs in general) and traditional patterns of gang organization.

Street socialization is a street-based process involving peer guidance and the adoption of an alternate set of values and norms by youth who lack parental supervision and positive school experiences (Vigil 2002). Most skinheads describe their early participation as street socialization within urban and suburban locales, such as malls, parks, and music shows. Most reported spending evenings and nights walking the streets with other young skinheads and congregating at music shows and neighborhood schools and parks. In many cases this process began prior to formal affiliation with any one particular skinhead group. Subjects reported that these experiences were vital to forming bonds with other skinheads and loosening attachments to family and school, hence lessening these institutions' ability to regulate their behavior.

> We would meet up pretty much every night at the park or the school over by our house. A lot of us lived out here in Anaheim Hills or nearby so it wasn't hard for us to get together and hang out. We'd raise all kinds a hell once we were together, you know spray painting shit about skinheads ruling the streets, all kinds of shit. We'd go over and beer raid the 7–11 and go down and start fucking with other kids hanging around the park. . . . It was a blast. I wouldn't come home 'til the middle of the night and my parents would yell at me and shit, but I didn't care. . . . I stopped listening after a while. After that I started missing school and when I did go I was usually in trouble. . . . (White Aryan Resistance Skinhead interview, 6/21/04)

> I remember going out and hanging out on the street all night with "Popeye" and "Snake" you know before they started PENI [Public Enemy Number One] and before I got hooked up with WAR [White Aryan Resistance] Skins. . . . I was probably fifteen or so and we all lived pretty close. We just ran the streets getting into fights with punk gangs like the LADS [Los Angeles Death Squad] and doing all that stupid gang shit. (White Aryan Resistance Skinhead interview, 2/3/00)

Social Change, Skinhead Discontent, and Violent Territoriality

In addition to schisms in the local punk scene, skinhead formation was related to macrolevel changes involving the larger sociopolitical environment. Since the mid-1960s, increasing "nonwhite" immigration has been significantly altering California's demographics (Waldinger and Bozorgmehr 1996).[12] The initial skinhead response to these rapid social changes resembled the kind of conflict that ethnic/racial migration spurred in New York and other large urban centers a few decades earlier (see Adamson 2000; Meyer 2000; Schneider 1999; Suttles 1968). As Schneider explains regarding New York gangs:

> After World War II, the massive expansion of African-American and Puerto Rican communities redefined these conflicts, created unity among Euro-American groups around their "whiteness" and focused resentment on the newcomers . . . while efforts by African-Americans to integrate New York's schools in the 1950s led to boycotts and threats of violence by Euro-American parents. (9)

A Huntington Beach Skinhead describes in similar fashion more recent conflict between skinheads and "nonwhites":

> The blacks, we don't like the blacks. . . . We get along with some Chicanos, we don't like the Iranians, the Pakistanis, Afghanistanis, we don't like people. . . . These immigrants coming to our country that's who we're against. We didn't want them

here ... get them out if they moved into our neighborhood. We encouraged them to leave and they usually did ... We would burn crosses uh Molotov cocktails, whatever it took (Huntington Beach Skinhead interview, 3/12/89 [referring to the early and mid-1980s])

Other skinheads echo the effect of immigration on skinhead formation:

You had all these beaners and other muds coming in here and we didn't have a chance. Jobs that should have been filled by white Americans were getting taken away and given to illegals under the table. . . . (American Front Skinhead interview, 7/19/99)

[Orange County] was still predominantly white when I was a kid but my parents moved out here in '73 from Chicago and it was pretty white, you know. It was right about the time they started shipping boatloads of Vietnamese refugees over here and then the Hispanics, illegal aliens, started coming up in droves and you saw the neighborhoods ... crime-free white areas go to nonwhite cesspools. (White Aryan Resistance Skinhead interview, 3/17/02)

These statements express the social and economic anxiety and frustration that is often associated with waves of immigration (see Green, Strolovich, and Wong 1998). Skinhead perceptions of this "social problem" were not mono-lithic, however. The Huntington Beach Skin expresses a degree of "tolerance" for "some Chicanos," while the American Front Skin views Hispanics as a sig-nificant threat. Thus, even among racist skinheads, ideology has important variations rather than being homogenous. In a city where they are greatly out-numbered by Hispanic gangs, white gangs that "tolerate" Hispanics are far more likely to develop ties and even alliances with Hispanic gangs. This occasionally results in "crossover" membership. What is most curious about these types of relationships is that they do not necessarily spell an end to racist beliefs. For ex-ample, in the city and surrounding areas of La Mirada (located in southern Los Angeles County), the racist skinhead gang La Mirada Punk (LMP) began in the mid-1980s as a multiethnic gang (white and Latino). As racism became a stable feature of the gang, some Latino members were purged. Today, LMP remains an active racist skinhead gang with links to various other skinhead gangs (some of whom maintain a strict "whites-only" policy of membership); yet LMP re-tains a membership that both a law enforcement interviewee (5/11/02) and an LMP interviewee (6/14/04) estimate is 40 percent Latino (including at least one Latino member who is in a leadership position).

Some skinhead gangs were formed to provide refuge from the perceived threat posed by minorities. This perception was related to larger structural changes, such as shifting neighborhood composition, increasing numbers of minority street gangs, and the anxiety-provoking policies surrounding busing (see also DeSena 1990; Hagedorn 1988; Meyer 2000; Rieder 1985; Schneider 1999). Each of these changes heightened interracial hostility and fear of minority-generated aggression being directed toward white youths:

> In my opinion nonwhite street gangs led to the rise of skinheads. Many whites growing up in gang-afflicted areas become victims. After being victimized or *feeling as if you are* [my italics], it's not a huge step to begin to hate that tormentor and to soon begin to hate his whole race. (White Aryan Resistance Skinhead interview, 9/10/02)

> I grew up in a pretty dark neighborhood and most of my homeboys did too . . . We were surrounded by mostly spic gangs and all we had was each other and if we didn't want to get punked all the time then we needed to have some reinforcements to fight back . . . so yeah that [racial conflict] played a big role in how we got started and I think that was true for other skinhead gangs as well you know maybe not so much for some of the ones down in OC [Orange County] but even they were starting to get invaded by all these nonwhite gangs trying to take over neighborhoods and all that bullshit. (Norwalk Skinhead interview, 3/16/01)

These comments articulate sentiments widely shared among skinheads. Even those who did not directly experience racial antagonism were informed by the fear and resentment such conflicts engendered. From this vantage point, skinheads were not only necessary, but were a rational response to an environment that violated white youths on the basis of skin color.[13] The "victim status" (Berbrier 2000; Holstein and Miller 1990) evident in skinheads' self-definition as "working-class, white kids" who were the "new minority" tapped into the cultural heritage of working and minority populations' claims for social justice. These identities did not always correspond with objective conditions, however, as revealed by examples of kids from relatively affluent areas (e.g., Anaheim Hills) appropriating a working-class identity.[14] In this respect, skinhead gangs illustrate the elasticity of identities built around feelings of disaffection from the status quo (De Certeau 1984).

Schneider (1999) argues that protecting turf and engaging in a pattern of conflict distinguish other youth formations from gangs. Defending turf, honor, and racial/ethnic pride helps gang members construct a framework for understanding their world by identifying "enemies" and crystallizing core values. The skinhead gangs I examined were not devoid of local neighborhood-based forms of territoriality, as some observers contend (Hamm 1993; Klein 1995a; Moore 1993). Reflecting the tradition of street gang culture, skinheads attempted to claim territory, which could be seen in their choice of gang names (e.g., Huntington Beach Skins, Chino Hills Skins, South Bay Skins, Norwalk

Skins, etc.) and their claims of specific locations (such as parks or music clubs) through the use of graffiti "tags" and other more physically aggressive means. Of the seventeen skinhead gangs I studied, thirteen attempted to claim territory by such methods as graffiti, hanging out, and/or accosting individuals who entered their turf.

Skinhead identity was formed in part around notions of protecting and defending local symbolic or turf boundaries. Situational conflict was directed toward two types of targets: First, racist skinheads attacked members of minority groups when they transgressed perceived boundaries (e.g., an African American family moving into a predominantly white neighborhood); second, racist skinheads developed rivalries with other gangs (both white and "nonwhite") primarily as a result of interpersonal disputes. A member of the American Front Skins and a member of the Huntington Beach Skins explain each type of territorial conflict:

> Well if a nigger moved in, we'd start fucking with 'em right away you know, like we'd drive by and shout, "Niggers, go back to Africa" or we'd spray paint their garage or somewhere else nearby their house to just let 'em know that we wanted them to get the fuck out. . . . (American Front Skin, 7/12/00)

> *Interviewer:* In regards to territory, if someone from a rival gang comes into that territory, do skinheads protect that territory? And how would you do that?
> *Skinhead:* They tell 'em to leave, only they wouldn't do it that kindly. . . . They'd usually beat that person up you know. If it was someone from a gang, we didn't . . . like say if a LAD [predominantly white punk gang] member came into the territory in Huntington Beach that LAD would get jumped. . . . (Huntington Beach Skinhead interview, 3/12/89)

Although early skinhead violence was sometimes racially motivated, there is little evidence to suggest that these early skinhead gangs went beyond the long-standing pattern of white gangs' defense of racial neighborhood boundaries (see Adamson 2000; Meyer 2000; Rieder 1985; Short and Strodtbeck 1965/1974; Thrasher 1927). Skinhead racial identity was oppositional in localized terms, but there was no clear political program for broad social change along racial lines that is typically associated with adult hate groups like the Klan or Aryan Nations. As indicated above, much skinhead violence was directed toward other subcultural groups (e.g., other skin gangs, punks, surfers, etc.) that were also willing participants in the action. Skinheads defined their violence as a means of protecting themselves from aggressive nonskinhead groups.

> We went to all the different punk shows and mainly just fought with anyone who tried us, 'cause you had a lot of punk gangs thinking they were all cholo, like the

Suis [the Suicidals gang] who were always looking to start shit. So we just went at it at pretty much every show back then. Back then we were pretty loosely organized. You know, we were a tight crew, you know, when it came to fighting, but we weren't politically organized like we were later. (Boot Boy Skinhead interview, 9/12/01)

Despite some efforts to build a neighborhood base in communities, skinheads have not developed into "quasi institutions" or even fundamental components of local neighborhoods. In this respect, early skinhead gangs resembled what Cloward and Ohlin (1960) refer to as "conflict subcultures" that lack strong neighborhood ties and engage in high levels of violence in order to gain status. Although skinheads clearly did not have the same kind of neighborhood ties as some Latino gangs that have existed in their barrios for several generations (J. Moore 1978, 1991; Vigil 1988, 2002), this difference may be due largely to historical circumstance. As these change—and if skinheads continue to maintain a presence in neighborhoods—it is possible that such ties between skinheads and their communities may develop.[15]

Conclusion

In this chapter I discuss the early development of Southern California racist skinheads and their parallels to conventional gangs. The focus on persistent and pervasive poverty has led to the view of gangs as "quasi institutions" (Hagedorn 1988; J. Moore 1991; Vigil 2002) within traditionally marginalized communities. The "underclass" emphasis, however, has neglected gang formations that are not associated with impoverished economic conditions (Horowitz 1987) and has inadvertently reproduced a narrower conception of gang membership than can be sustained in view of the economic, ethnic, and racial diversity of gangs.

At the same time, while the shaven-headed, swastika-tattooed, jackbooted youths who spew racist venom have become a powerful image associated with contemporary hate groups, few ground-level case studies explain the development and organizational characteristics of skinheads. Viewing racist skinheads primarily as terrorists and hate groups obscures their similarities to traditional minority street gangs. Overemphasis on the politicized character of racist skinheads ignores three important findings: (1) Most of the early skinhead groups meet criteria widely used for defining youth and/or street gangs; (2) although some skinhead gangs gravitated toward a political orientation, this transition did not include all racist skinheads, and even among politicized gangs not all members shared the same level of commitment to this orientation;

and (3) currently the two largest racist skinhead gangs in Southern California are entrepreneurially organized primarily around the increasingly lucrative methamphetamine trade rather than a political agenda (Simi and Smith 2004).

Observers speculate that the total number of skinheads nationwide remains relatively small; however, recent developments among skinhead gangs in Southern California demonstrate how quickly these gangs can change. Between 1996 and 2000, the Nazi Low Riders (NLR) grew from twenty-eight confirmed members to over 1,500 members in California alone (Anti-Defamation League 2004). Another Southern California–based skinhead gang, Public Enemy Number One (PENI), has grown from a few dozen members in the mid-1990s to more than five hundred current members. Despite these gangs' white supremacist orientation, their predominant focus is on profit-motivated criminal activity (e.g., methamphetamine production and distribution, identity theft, home invasions, and counterfeiting) designed for personal gain. There is no evidence that either gang uses the profits derived from these enterprises for funding larger political endeavors related to the white supremacist movement. Like early racist skinhead gangs, the NLR and PENI do not participate in racist political activism, and while their violence is sometimes racially motivated, they are more likely to engage in instrumentally motivated violence related to criminal operations or spontaneous violence related to interpersonal disputes (Simi and Smith 2004). Some skinhead gangs have become branches of the contemporary white supremacist movement, yet many other skinhead gangs remain oppositional in localized terms without a clear political program for broad social change along racial lines.

Notes

1. Adamson's (2000) analysis points to both similarities and differences between black and white gangs but does not address skinheads. A national estimate of skinheads is extremely difficult to ascertain, but most estimates suggest that skinheads are a relatively small portion of the overall gang picture (Etter 1999; Kaplan 1995). Despite small numbers, skinheads have maintained a continuous presence in the United States for the past twenty-five years and can be found in every region of the country.

2. Although antiracist and nonracist skinheads exist, this article focuses on racist skinheads (see Sarabia and Shriver 2004; Wood 1999). The distinction between racist and antiracist skinheads is relatively clear-cut; however, this was not the case initially, as factions along lines of racial ideology were originally much blurrier. Some ambiguity continues to persist as skinheads change allegiances between racist and antiracist (Blazak 2001; Finnegan 1999). Stereotyping and sound-bite terms like *racist* and *antiracist* actually obscure the process of becoming racist and encourage overly simplified explanations for this process.

3. There are far more empirical studies of European skinheads, and European scholars often distinguish between street-level skinhead youth cliques (gangs) and right-wing youth who possess an organized ideology and are actively involved in extremist political movements (Bjorgo 1998; Fangen 1998; Kersten 2001).

4. In this chapter, I focus on skinheads in Southern California. During the course of fieldwork, I conducted interviews with early skinheads in Chicago, Dallas, Denver, Detroit, Las Vegas, New York City, Philadelphia, Phoenix, Portland, Salt Lake City, and Seattle (n = 18). The data obtained from these interviews suggest important similarities between the emergence of skinheads in Southern California and in other locales; however, these impressions must be confirmed with in-depth case studies of skinheads in locales outside of Southern California. One interesting comparison would be skinheads' self-identification. In Southern California it is common for skinheads to describe their group as a "gang," while in other areas there is a strong stigma attached to using the term.

5. I am not arguing that no differences exist between racist skinheads and minority gangs, merely that empirical evidence suggests that conceptualizing skinheads as gangs is warranted.

6. The Klan has existed since 1865. By the 1920s, Klan membership reached a high of between 1.5 and 5 million followers, including high-ranking political figures (MacLean 1994; L. Moore 1991).

7. Because skinheads have maintained a presence in the United States since the late 1970s, there are now skinheads in their forties. However, we know very little about these "O.G." (Original Gangster) skinheads or more generally about how aging affects a skinhead's identity or life course trajectory.

8. This focus upon subcultural style has been criticized by several observers for lacking a solid ethnographic foundation (Cohen 1980; Leong 1992; Moore 1994).

9. This approach departs from previous studies of skinheads, in that I combine law enforcement data with primary interviews of skinheads. Hamm (1993) did not conduct law enforcement interviews, and his interviews of skinheads were more akin to survey questionnaires, which are not well suited to obtaining historical data. Other researchers have claimed that, because of the difficulty accessing skinheads, it is necessary to rely primarily on secondary sources in order to compile a history of skinheads (see Blee 2002; Wood 1999).

10. While some might claim that skinheads' presence on the Internet differentiates them from conventional gangs, this would be a mistake, as various gangs have developed a presence in cyberspace (e.g., 18th Street, Crips, etc.). Newspaper articles on the skinheads were drawn primarily from the *Los Angeles Times*, the *Orange County Register*, the *Los Angeles Weekly*, and the *San Bernardino Tribune*. I selected these articles through a structured, exhaustive search of the Lexis-Nexis database and microfilm indexes of the *Los Angeles Times* to 1980 using the following search terms: *skinhead, neo-Nazi, white supremacy, white power, hate** (including *hate crime, hate group*, etc.).

11. For example, one former skinhead, who was a founding member of one of the first skinhead gangs in Southern California and who is now a corporate attorney, refused to talk with me when I phoned him at his home.

12. This analysis does not posit that the predominantly suburban white neighborhoods where skinheads emerged were objectively under attack; rather, white youth who formed and joined skinhead gangs perceived that such conditions existed and were a threat—a perception with significant precedent among the larger white population (Meyer 2000).

13. Skinheads' "folk devil" status has obscured some of the motivating factors that led to their increasing racialization and has prevented a fuller understanding of the effects of external forces on skinheads' racial sentiments. While some research tends to portray skinheads as dominated by violent and irrational tendencies (see Hamm 1993; Moore 1993), skinhead grievances and violence resemble a long tradition of "normative" racial conflict in the United States (Meyer 2000).

14. Interestingly, appropriating a working-class identity can become a self-fulfilling prophecy (Merton 1968). After adopting the skinhead identity, some youth from middle- and upper-middle-class families experience downward mobility resulting from the loss of educational and economic opportunities that often accompany the skinhead emphasis on "toughness," "getting into trouble," and "anti-intellectualism" (Blee 2002; for an explanation of "how working-class kids get working-class jobs," see Willis 1981).

15. This question will be especially interesting to monitor as national demographic changes continue and "whites" become a numerical minority in the United States.

11

Youth Gang Research in Australia

Rob White

THE ISSUE OF YOUTH GANGS has received considerable media, political, and police attention in Australia in recent years. Periodic media reports about the perceived proliferation and criminal or antisocial activities of youth gangs have long been featured in press stories about young people in many parts of the country—from Melbourne to Adelaide, Perth to Sydney (see, e.g., Bessant and Hil 1997; Collins et al. 2000; Healey 1996; Pudney and Hooper 1999). Until recently, however, there has been little concerted research into the nature and dynamics of youth gangs in the Australian context.

Much of the knowledge of youth groups, including gangs, has typically been based on anecdotal information and popular media imagery. Disputes regarding the existence and magnitude of the alleged gang problem in the Australian context hinge on how particular youth group formations are defined (see Perrone and White 2000; White 2002). Media and political representations of youth gangs, and in particular ethnic youth gangs—many of which are sensationalistic and highly inaccurate—have, however, spurred greater academic interest in researching the life worlds of street-present young people. This has been the case especially since the early 1990s, when in cities such as Sydney and Melbourne there were numerous moral panics over the alleged gang problem, a phenomenon that researchers wished to test empirically and that activists wished to challenge politically.

A group of like-minded researchers decided to form the OzGang Research Network in 2001. Members of the group include experienced youth researchers in Sydney, Melbourne, and Hobart (that is, people who had already begun to study gang-related behaviors and group formations in the 1990s), community organizations such as the Australian Multicultural Foundation, and liaison agencies such as the National Police Ethnic Advisory Bureau. The impetus for the formation of the OzGang Research Network was partly technical, in the sense of providing a forum for the learning and transfer of expertise, insofar as it is only recently that social research on youth gangs in Australia has been undertaken in any sort of systematic fashion. The formation of the group was also partly driven by political concerns. The network is composed of individuals who broadly adhere to a human rights and social development approach to youth issues. This is in counterpoint to the prevalent right-wing "law and order" discourses that emphasize punitive perspectives and coercive intervention.

The purpose of this chapter is to provide an overview of youth gang research undertaken in Australia over the past ten years or so. Such research is relatively new to this country. This chapter sketches out some of the conceptual problems and methodological issues faced by Australian researchers so far in their varied studies. It then provides a snapshot of relevant gang research from various cities around the country. The chapter concludes with a brief summary of key trends and concepts associated with gang research in Australia.

Perceptions of Youth as a Social Problem

The first issue confronting Australian social researchers was how best to define what a youth gang is. Not surprisingly, much of the discussion and analysis of the mid-1990s centered on these questions. The first major research effort on youth gangs, undertaken in Melbourne, was entitled *Ethnic Youth Gangs in Australia: Do They Exist?* (White et al. 1999). As the authors of these reports emphasized, the term *gang* is highly emotive and rarely has a fixed definition in terms of social use or legal meaning. It can mean very different things to different people. The ambivalence of perception, definition, and representation is acknowledged as an important concern in most Australian writings on the topic.

The specific features of any particular youth group formation will vary greatly, and this, too, has been recognized in the Australian research. In particular, effort has been made to distinguish different types of group formation, and to locate "gangs" as such within a wider sociological context. That is, it is important that distinctions be made between different sorts of groups—that may include gangs, youth subcultures, friendship networks, school cohorts, sports teams, and so on. Similarly, the reasons for group formation and the typical focus of activities can provide insight into differences between groups— as with distinguishing between social-centered and criminal-centered activity (Perrone and White 2000; White 2002). Nevertheless, the presence of large groups of young people on the street, or young people dressed in particular ways or with particular group affiliations, appears to have fostered, at least within the media, the idea that Australia has a gang problem.

What is known about street gangs in Australia seems to confirm that their actual, rather than presumed, existence is much less than popularly believed, and that their activities are highly circumscribed in terms of violence or criminal activity directed at members of the general public. To a certain extent, much of the concern about gangs is really a misunderstanding of the nature of youth subcultures, of how young people naturally associate with each other in groups, and of the material opportunities open to them to circulate and do things in particular places (White 1999). The idea of gangs has been associated over time with various kinds of youth group formations. For example, from the mid-nineteenth century to the end of the 1800s, much public concern was directed at the "push larrikins" of Melbourne and Sydney (Murray 1973). These were groups of young men (the groups were called pushes) who, through their appearance (e.g., wearing of pointed-toed boots) and behavior (e.g., getting drunk, getting into fights), became easily identified as threats by the media, the police, and the general public. The streets were the meeting places of the pushes, and they had their origins in poverty and want. The push larrikins were born out of a very unsettled state of society, and reflected the lack of amusements, recreational outlets, jobs, and overall means of livelihood for these young people.

By contrast, public consternation about young people in the mid-twentieth century revolved around the "bodgies and widgies," young working-class men and women who were identifiable by their particular visual styles and leisure concerns (Stratton 1992). The bodgies and widgies represented a new teenage culture, with an emphasis on fashion (long hair styles for the boys, gabardine skirts for the girls), street presence, dancing, and rock and roll music. From 1950 to 1959, the phenomenon of the bodgies and widgies captured the imagination of the media. These were working-class young people with jobs, and they were engaging in the first stirring of a distinctive teenage consumer-oriented culture. In doing so, they represented a threat to middle-class values and culture, and much of the media condemnation (and distortion) centered on alcohol use, sexual behavior, and family breakdown associated with the bodgies and widgies.

In Australia, today, "ethnic youth gangs" generally constitute the focus of media fear and loathing. The term *ethnic minority* refers to non-Anglo-Australians who are nonindigenous. In recent years, the hype and sensationalized treatment of youth gangs have tended to have an increasingly racialized character. That is, the media have emphasized the "racial" background of alleged gang members, and thereby have fostered the perception that, for instance, "young Lebanese" or "young Vietnamese" equals "gang member." The extra visibility of ethnic minority youth (relative to the Anglo "norm") feeds the media moral panic over youth gangs, and bolsters a racist stereotyping based upon physical appearance (and including such things as language, clothes, and skin color). Whole communities of young people can be affected, regardless of the fact that most young people are not systematic lawbreakers or violent individuals. The result is an inordinate level of public and police suspicion and hostility being directed toward people from certain ethnic minority backgrounds (see, e.g., Lyons 1995; Maher et al. 1997; White 1996).

Most of the studies cited below were generated, at least in part, by the high level of public anxiety about particular youth behaviors in particular places at particular times. For instance, the specific impetus for the 1999 Melbourne study was the extensive media and political concern about ethnic youth gangs that surfaced in the early 1990s. An informal meeting of youth and community workers, academics, and government representatives was held in 1994 to discuss the rise in public attention on the issue, and to consider whether or not there was in fact such a problem in this city. Certainly the moral panic was real, if we take as the measure the extent of the media storm surrounding alleged youth group misbehavior (see Cohen 1980 for discussion of the concept of moral panic). Contrary to perceptions, however, there was at the time no empirical evidence of a crime wave involving youth in groups, nor any indication that groups of young people constituted a threat to the general public. In such circumstances, social research is essential.

Doing Gang Research

The preferred method of youth gang research in Australia has tended to be qualitative, and most studies have been mainly based around interviews with young people themselves. Importantly, getting funding for gang research has, until very recently, been notoriously difficult. This has put severe limitations on the design and implementation of research strategies, and on the ability of researchers to gain extensive and good-quality data. Often the research has relied upon goodwill and doing things on the "smell of an oily rag," rather than having access to long-term funding and professional staff. Governments have been generally reluctant to fund gang research due to other fiscal and political priorities. Perhaps too the lack of baseline data and lack of a singular and uniformly acceptable definition of a youth gang has contributed to the paucity of funded research (see Lozusic 2002; Perrone and White 2000). As more commentaries, discussion papers, and research reports have become available (particularly since the late 1990s), governments seem to have taken a greater interest in supporting research in this area.

In addition to intrinsic problems associated with research that relies upon outsider-insider connections, there have been major difficulties in undertaking gang research in a volatile social and media context, and under financially restrictive conditions. A Melbourne-based gang study commenced in 1996, for example, took three years to complete because it had to rely on the volunteered services of the researchers—the community interviewers were paid, but the research design, data collection, processing, analysis, and report writing were provided gratis by the four main contributors (White et al. 1999). It was decided to interview young people from diverse ethnic backgrounds: Vietnamese, Turkish, Pacific Islander, Somalian, Latin American, and Anglo-Australian young people. While specific local areas were the initial focus for the research, on the assumption that certain ethnic minority groups tended to reside or hang around in these locales (e.g., Vietnamese youth in Footscray), it was discovered early on that a more sophisticated and complex pattern of movement often took place. There were certain corridors within the metropolitan area within which the young people moved, and while these were not suburb specific, they ranged in specific territorial directions (e.g., fanning out from the city center toward the western suburbs for one group, mainly concentrated along the coastal beaches for another group). In addition, many of the young people did not in fact live in the place within which they spent the most time. All these factors had time and cost implications for the research.

There was considerable variation in how the young people were selected, and in the nature of the interviewer–young person relationship. As much as anything, this had to do with the contingencies of social research of this kind: The diverse communities and the sensitivity of the subject matter were bound to complicate sample selection and the interview process in varying ways. In recruiting interviewers, care was taken to ensure that, where possible, the person spoke the first language of the target group and/or had prior contact with or was a member of the particular ethnic minority community. The specific sample groups for each defined ethnic youth population were selected and interviewed according to the social connections and research opportunities of each community-based interviewer.

The Vietnamese sample, for instance, was based upon prior contacts established by the interviewer, who had had extensive experience working with and within the community. This person was Anglo-Australian but was fluent in Vietnamese and traveled to Vietnam several times a year. The young people who were interviewed preferred to speak with him, rather than with another member of the Vietnamese community. They felt that they could be more open in what they had to say, without exposing themselves to possible leaks to other members of their families or community. The interviewer was a teacher and a community worker in the neighborhood, and over a long period of time he had built up strong trust relations with the local young people.

The composition of the sample, and the dynamics of the interview process, were thus bound to be quite different depending upon the group in question. For instance, the Turkish sample involved two interviewers, reflecting the cultural mores of having a male interview young men and a female interview young women. This was not the case in regards to other communities. Methodologically, it is therefore important to acknowledge that the prior research background and ethnic background of each interviewer inevitably plays a role in facilitating or hindering the sample selection and information-gathering processes. The presence or absence of guardians, the closeness to or distance from the young person's family on the part of the interviewer, and the basic level of familiarity or trust between interviewer and interviewee will all affect the research process.

So too will the social experiences and social position of the particular group in question. For example, in cases where the interviewer was not known to a particular migrant family, the young people (and their parents) tended to be suspicious about what was going on, suspecting that perhaps the interviewer was a government employee sent by child protection services to determine the fitness of the family to raise children. There were also other instances in which young people may have been reluctant to speak about certain matters. This was most apparent in the case of some refugees who were deeply suspicious regarding questions about authority figures such as the police. In a similar vein, the notion of "gangs" was also culturally bounded for many refugees from war-torn countries. In their experience, gangs are men brandishing weapons, who roam the streets robbing people, pilfering, raping, and engaging in all manner of serious offenses, including murder. Such gangs do not exist in Australia.

Close observation, continuous interaction over a period of years, and culturally sensitive investigation have been the hallmarks of the best kind of gang research so far undertaken in Australia. This is certainly evident in the work of Collins and colleagues (2000), undertaken in western Sydney in the late 1990s and beyond. What makes this study so significant is that it is really a *community study*, rather than gang research as such. This provides for a complex and sophisticated analysis that captures the ebbs and flows of communal life, including conflicts within the community and those involving authority figures such as the police. Undertaking this kind of research, however, demands extraordinary commitment, resources, contacts, and funding sources.

One of the hallmarks of Australian research has been the recognition that youth behavior does not exist in a social vacuum. Researchers have been acutely aware that, given the media focus on ethnic youth gangs, it is essential to study the contours of immigration policy, the various waves of migration, and the diverse histories of distinctive migrant groups. Sensitivity to such background issues is highlighted, for example, in the 1999 Melbourne study (White et al. 1999). This study found huge differences in the resettlement process within communities, such as within the Vietnamese community (based largely around issues of class, time of movement, and mode of entry into Australia). There were also major differences between specific ethnic minority communities, such as the Somalian community (where great emphasis was placed on incorporation into the educational, work, and cultural mainstream) and other communities, such as the Turkish community (where in the early period of mass settlement the emphasis was more insular and premised upon social separation, reflecting the communal experience of being "guest workers" in Europe). Which group or who, specifically, is the object of "moral panic" can, to some extent, be linked to particular moments in Australian immigration history—in the 1970s it was the Greeks and Italians who dominated the headlines, the 1980s saw Asians as the folk devils of the mass media, and by the 1990s the problem began to feature those with "Middle Eastern appearance."

Media preoccupation with ethnic minority groups is often reflected in so-cial research, with changing emphasis on who in particular is to be included. The 1999 Melbourne study and the 2000 Sydney study, for example, involved selective samples of young people, but not on the basis of gang membership. That is, while certain ethnic minority young people were selected, the sample did not initially distinguish between gang and nongang members (since such categorization was itself subject to contestation). However, more targeted sampling has begun to feature in later gang research, as in a national study involving interviews with street-present young people in each capital city (Sydney, Canberra, Brisbane, Hobart, Melbourne, Adelaide, Perth, Darwin). This research is funded by an Australian Research Council grant, under the direction of the present author, and commenced in 2002. After extensive discussions within the OzGang Research Network, and consultations with community agencies and youth workers, it was decided that this project should attempt to explicitly target gang members. Accordingly, the sample was to include members of actual gangs (as self-defined and/or as perceived by authority figures in that local area), and to focus on hot spots where perceived gang activity occurs.

Generally speaking, the experience in Australia has been that youth and community workers can provide an effective entry point for obtaining access to young people whose personal trajectories suggest they could usefully participate in these kinds of projects. The quality of data collection does vary considerably, however, depending upon the experience of the interviewer and research team, their connection with the young person, their understanding of the study, the length of time over which the research takes place, and the local political environment.

Australian Research Findings

This section presents in schematic form findings and opinions on the nature and presence of youth gangs in various cities around Australia. No systematic literature review of gang research exists, partly due to the paucity of quantitative data and the fact that most research has been based upon interviews with relatively small numbers of young people in specific locales. This review is intended to be indicative rather than definitive vis-à-vis the nature and dynamics of youth gangs in Australia.

Sydney

Sydney is the largest city in Australia, with some 4 million people, followed by Melbourne, with about 3 million people. Cities such as Brisbane, Perth, and Adelaide each have over 1 million residents. Australian cities are very diverse culturally, although the specific ethnic composition of each city varies considerably. This is important insofar as, in a national climate in which "ethnic youth" are seen as problematic, which ethnic youth are meant depends upon specific locale. In Sydney the key target for government intervention and media concern since the mid-1990s has been Lebanese youth. Prior to this, and with some overlap chronologically, it was Vietnamese young people who were seen as especially problematic, particularly around drug-related issues. There have been several attempts to deal with gang issues in the state of New South Wales, with particular reference to Sydney.

The 1995 Sydney Inquiry

A 1995 inquiry in New South Wales turned up little or no evidence that the overseas style of gangs (i.e., the stereotypical gangs of the United States) exist in that state. The inquiry report stated that usage of the term *gang*, which implies violence and an organized structure, has little relevance to youth activities in Australian communities (Standing Committee on Social Issues 1995). Furthermore, while the police service reported the existence of some fifty-four street gangs in 1993, there was no other evidence to support either this or related allegations of extensive memberships.

Nevertheless, there was evidence that certain types of youth gangs do exist, albeit not to the extent suggested in media accounts (Standing Committee on Social Issues 1995). Even here, it was noted that most gangs limit their criminal behavior to petty theft, graffiti, and vandalism. Few gangs have a violent nature. Moreover, when violence such as homicide does involve a gang member, it is usually not gang-related. By and large, it was concluded that most bands of young people in Australia are not *gangs*, but *groups*.

The 2000 Sydney Study

Another study, looking more specifically at ethnic minority youth, particularly in relation to the issue of crime, was undertaken in Sydney's western suburbs (Collins et al. 2000). The research involved interviews with Lebanese young people and other community members. Over a period of several years, the researchers interviewed some twenty young people and undertook observational fieldwork. The researchers also interviewed Lebanese immigrant parents, Lebanese community leaders, community workers, police officers, and others in the local area. The study included systematic media and policy analysis. The research found that a major problem was the "racialized" reporting of crime when the media dealt specifically with Lebanese youth. Ethnic identifiers were used in relation to some groups but not others (such as Anglo-Celtic Australians). Moreover, the explanations for such "ethnic crime" tended to pathologize the group, as if there was something intrinsically bad about being Lebanese or Middle Eastern.

Social exclusion was central to the explanation of youth offenses involving particularly disadvantaged groups. The concentration of specific communities in particular local areas, and the reputation of some places as being "ethnic" enclaves, also contributed to and reflected complex exclusion-inclusion processes. Marginalization was central to explaining the perception of widespread involvement in "youth gangs" among Lebanese youth. Even so, the main forms of association among Lebanese young people were first and foremost friendship groups. These groups also functioned as a defense against experiences of racism and exclusion from the cultural mainstream.

This Sydney study found an intersection of masculinity, ethnicity, and class—in such a way as to affirm social presence, to ensure mutual protection, and to compensate for a generally marginalized economic and social position.

> This performance of the "gang" functions in several ways: it provides a venue for cultural maintenance, community and identity; and at the same time provides the protection of strength in numbers in the face of physical threats by other youth, and harassment by police and other adults. . . . Central to their partial negotiation of their experience of racialization, they affirm a masculine and "ethnic" identity of toughness, danger and respect. (Collins et al. 2000, 150)

Assertion of gang membership can thus be interpreted as an attempt by the young men to valorize their lives and empower themselves in the face of outside hostility, disrespect, and social marginalization.

Some of the young men who were interviewed thus presented themselves as a "gang" in order to gain a measure of respect (Collins et al. 2000). Representation of themselves as members of a gang was more symbolic (i.e., presenting an image of being tough and dangerous) than reflective of criminal activity. The point of claiming gang status was to affirm social presence, to ensure mutual protection, and to compensate for a generally marginalized economic and social position.

In follow-up work, these researchers have explored in greater depth the social processes underpinning the emergence of the "Arab Other" as the preeminent folk devil of our time (Poynting et al. 2004). They discuss how public presentations of asylum seekers fleeing repressive regimes in the Middle East are represented as dangerous, criminal, and dishonest. They examine the effects of the attacks of September 11, 2001, and the Bali bombings on the stereotyping of Arabs and Muslims as not having respect for Western laws and values and being complicit with terrorism. The net result is that whole communities are being stigmatized and vilified. One consequence of this is that many Arab and Muslim people report experiences of various forms of prejudice because of their ethnic background or religion. Arab and Muslim youth feel that they are particularly at risk of harassment. This has led to feelings of frustration, alienation, and loss of confidence in themselves and trust in authority (Human Rights and Equal Opportunity Commission 2004). In light of the Sydney gangs research involving members of the Lebanese community, this bodes ill for future youth and community relations.

While the Sydney study did not involve a large number of young people directly as interviewees, it provides an important and insightful picture of the local area and of the key players involved in the lives of Lebanese young people. Methodologically, the research is robust, in that the researchers have strong connections with relevant local people, built up over a period of years and involving the development of trust relationships and familiarity. The Sydney research is also notable for its critical and extensive treatment of the media portrayal of people and issues, a concern that has carried over into present research.

Melbourne

The city of Melbourne boasts some of the largest Greek and Italian populations in the world, as well as many other nationalities, religions, and languages. The weight of numbers of some ethnic minority groups, and the interpenetration of people and cultures (from coffee shops to soccer stars), provide for a cosmopolitan feel to the city. However, the link between drugs and Asian youth reinforces negative images of Vietnamese young people in particular. Group conflicts, involving fights among Vietnamese youth and including several deaths, have also heightened the notion that these particular ethnic minority youth are linked to gangs and are more likely to engage in gang-related behavior. The first small study of gangs in Melbourne, however, did not consider ethnicity as such. This was carried out in the early 1990s and involved students from the University of Melbourne interviewing street-present young people on a random basis.

The 1994 Melbourne Study

This analysis of youth gangs found that, while some characteristics of the groups mirrored media images (e.g., the masculine nature of youth gangs, their preferred hangouts, and shared identity markers such as shoes or clothes), the overall rationale for the group was simply one of social connection, not crime. Aumair and Warren (1994) cited five key characteristics of youth gangs:

- overwhelming male involvement, which in turn reinforced certain "masculine" traits (such as fighting prowess, sexual conquest, substance use, minor criminal acts) in the group setting
- high public visibility, given the lack of money and therefore a reliance on free public spaces for recreational purposes
- an outward display of collective identity, in the form of the wearing of similar styles of clothing, adopting a common name for the group, and so on
- organization principally for social reasons, and consequently low rates of criminal activity, as indicated in the absence of formalized gang rules and a social rationale for gathering together, rather than a criminal objective
- differences between public perceptions of the "gang problem" and the real nature of the problem, as illustrated by the fact that most criminal activity seemed to be inwardly focused, involving one-on-one fights and substance abuse

Much of the criminality exhibited by youth gangs, thus, is inward looking and linked to self-destructive behavior such as substance abuse, binge drinking, and the like. The popular perception is that gangs seek to violate the personal integrity and private property of the public in general; however, closer investigation reveals the insular nature of much of their activity, a conclusion both challenged and reaffirmed in a later Melbourne study, which found that, while most activity occurs within the group, there is also evidence of conflict and ongoing violence between different groups.

The 1999 Melbourne Study

This study examined the issue of youth gangs by talking directly with young people about the nature of group formations and group activities in their communities and neighborhoods (White et al. 1999). The study was based on in-depth interviews with 120 young people from six different ethnic and cultural backgrounds across metropolitan Melbourne. A major focus of the research was to investigate the specific problems, challenges, and opportunities faced by ethnic minority young people: Vietnamese, Somalian, Turkish, Pacific Islander, and Latin American, as well as Anglo-Australian.

A major finding of this research was that very often the notion of "youth gang" was ill-defined or contentious on the part of the young people who were interviewed. It could refer to types of activities, group associations, and/or use of violence. It could refer to youth group formations involved in legal and/or illegal sorts of activities and behaviors. The ambiguities surrounding the term were apparent in the young people's perceptions on the types of gangs in their own areas. "Gang" membership was easily conflated or mixed up with membership of particular friendship or ethnic groups. The idea of a "criminal" gang had less relevance than concepts pertaining to group identification and social identity.

Membership of a defined group tended to revolve around similar interests (such as choice of music, sport, style of dress), similar appearance or ethnic identity (such as language, religion, and culture), and the need for social belonging (friendship, support, and protection). Group affiliation was perceived as the greatest reason why certain young people were singled out as gang members, an identification process that was in turn associated with hassles by authority figures such as the police and private security guards, and conflicts between different groups of young people on the street or at school.

Two main types of group conflict were mentioned: Street fights were seen as violent, occasionally involving weapons, often linked to racism, and between different ethnic groups as well as within particular communities; school fights consisted of verbal and physical assaults, also often associated with racism. In both cases, the young people tended to make assumptions and generalizations about other groups of young people from different ethnic backgrounds, including Anglo-Australian young people.

The specific reasons for fighting between different groups were identified as due to perceptions regarding what are acceptable and unacceptable ways to relate to particular groups and individuals. Racism and treating people with disrespect are crucial elements in the explanation. So too is the sense of ownership and belonging associated with particular local areas and membership in particular youth groups. Social status is thus something that is both contested and defended, and this in turn is generally tied to one's identification with certain people and places.

Although the Melbourne study was one of the largest city-based interview samples of young people, it basically is a snapshot survey. The study relied upon the goodwill and expertise of youth and community workers, both of which varied greatly. Nevertheless, the study was invaluable, in that it brings together the social histories of each group studied and demonstrates the diverse and dynamic nature of the migrant experience in areas such as the resettlement process, work, welfare, education, and policing. Racism is also highlighted as a matter requiring urgent and ongoing attention and sustained analysis.

Adelaide

As with other Australian cities, Adelaide is composed of a diverse range of ethnic groups, with the northern suburbs being particularly well known as a haven for British migrants, due to targeted recruitment in the 1950s for workers in the white goods and car industries. Moral panic has been associated with groups of indigenous young people, especially around the nightspot areas of Hindley Street, but rarely are groups of indigenous young people portrayed as "gangs" as such (see White 1990). The term *gang* has tended to be reserved for ethnic minority youth from, in particular, Italian and Greek backgrounds. This is the substance of an investigation undertaken in the late 1980s.

Media concerns about street kids and loutish behavior on the part of some young people in the inner city led to a study to investigate the potential and actual needs of young Italo-Australians who frequent Adelaide city streets (Foote 1993). Participants were recruited through advertisements in the local newspaper and at a local high school. A total of twenty-one young people (seven male and fourteen female) ranging in age from thirteen to twenty-one were interviewed. The study was intended to shed light on how Italo-Australian young people themselves perceive gang issues.

The study found that groups of young men, united around their common Italian heritage, met regularly, both in the suburbs and in specific "Italian" areas of the inner city. The groups essentially formed on a social basis, with "hanging around" being an important activity. Periodically fights between Italo-Australian young men and other groups occurred, based upon ethnic identification: Italians, Greeks, and "Australians." Sometimes the Italians and Greeks would find solidarity with each other in their common differences with the Anglo-Australians. It was the "wogs" versus the "Aussies."

Fights tended to occur due to taunts and jeers between groups of young people. For the Italo-Australian young men, this often took the form of racist discourse that attacked their legitimacy as Australian citizens and residents ("They call us wogs and they say go back to Italy"). Group behavior and protection reinforced group cohesion and identity. The 1980s brought the active assertion of identity and legitimacy among certain ethnic minority groups.

Thus graffiti in Adelaide bus shelters started to feature spray-painted slogans such as "Wogs Rule, OK"—an indication that the minorities are here to stay and are proud of who they are.

The Adelaide study was basically a once-off study, again restricted to a small group of young people. The impetus for the study was the heightened media and public concern about the behavior of an identifiable group of young people frequenting Adelaide inner-city streets. The researcher was a youth worker who was employed at the time by the Coordinating Italian Committee, a welfare agency for the Italian community in Adelaide. The research was thus directly related to and inspired by social welfare concerns, rather than a criminal justice perspective. The importance of community context for understanding and dealing with young people is reflected in the author's final comment: "It is what the young people do that needs to be tackled, not who they are" (Foote 1993, 128).

Perth

The city of Perth, on the west coast of the country, is noted for its beaches and outdoor lifestyle. Youth who cause the greatest media consternation in this city include indigenous young people and Vietnamese and Chinese young people. However, the moral panic varies depending upon the group. In the case of indigenous young people, issues surround the welfare of sometimes quite young children being on the streets at night, particularly in the restaurant area of Northbridge. Regarding Vietnamese and Chinese young people, the concern is much more clearly about crime. Recent fights in local nightclubs and the death of alleged gang members have heightened concern about criminal youth gangs in Perth.

The aim of a recent Perth project was to provide information about the nature and prevalence of youth gangs in the Perth metropolitan area and to identify appropriate strategies to deal with gangs (White and Mason 2004). The key concern was the nature of school-based or school-related gang formation and gang-related behavior in a western Australian setting. A survey questionnaire targeting high school students was administered to a selection of students from grades 10 through 12 at six schools throughout the Perth metropolitan area and one country school. A total of 743 students responded to the questionnaire. Information was solicited about a wide range of issues, such as how safe young people feel in their local neighborhood, what recreational and social activities young people engage in, whether racism is a problem at their school, drug and alcohol use among students, what kind of youth groups exist within local areas, whether students had experienced or witnessed violence, the reasons young people join particular groups, and so on.

The survey was based upon a synthesis of questions and ideas used in research instruments employed in Europe (by the Eurogang Research Network) and in the United States and Australia. For the purposes of the research, students were asked two related questions in order to identify gang status:

Do you consider your special group of friends to be a gang?
Are you a member of a gang?

These questions are related to what Klein refers to as the "funneling technique," a means to operationalize the distinction between gangs and other kinds of nongang youth group formations (see Klein 2002).

The Perth study found that gang culture is largely a culture of violence. To understand this fully, it examined both the nature of gang membership and the nature of gang-related violence. The study demonstrates that there are significant differences between those young people who identify as being gang members and those who do not. Key differences are that gang members engage in criminal and antisocial activities (versus social and recreational for nongang members), intensive and extensive violence (versus sporadic experiences), poly drug use (versus experimental and soft drug use), and social isolation (versus social connection).

The study also indicates that, while many young people in school experience and/or witness conflict of some type, the nature of the violence differs greatly depending upon whether or not one is a gang member. Gang members tend to have different motivations, experiences, injuries, and occasions of violence compared with nongang members. The conclusion is that everybody fights (young men, that is), but they do so very differently and for different reasons.

In contrast to most other gang studies previously undertaken in Australia, the Perth study was based upon a survey questionnaire rather than face-to-face interviews. The questionnaire was carefully prepared, drawing upon international expertise and instruments, and it was piloted before being distributed in the schools. The data from the survey basically confirm much of the street-based interview findings, and so act as a useful means of triangulation in relation to gang research generally. The survey results provide an informative picture of what is happening in the lives of school-age young people, and they indicate that gangs and gang-related behaviors are of concern to young people in school as well as on the street.

The National Study

The sample for the national study varied, depending upon local variations in "hot spots" and which groups of young people are deemed to be problematic on the basis of their gang membership and activities. Data from more than three hundred interviews conducted over a three-year period (2002 to 2005) are being analyzed to discern a number of important aspects of youth group participation, including the impact that ethnic background has upon a person's recreational opportunities, preferences, and type of group membership, and the differences and similarities in the activities engaged in by gang and nongang members. Preliminary results are summarized below.

- There is acknowledgement in each city that "gangs" do indeed exist, although the specific character and composition varies, depending upon social characteristics and behavior of specific groups of young people. The majority of respondents describe gangs in terms of violence and illegal acts. Membership of group formations tends to be based on ethnicity (e.g., cultural or family links), territory (e.g., a particular location or venue), or activity (e.g., graffiti). The main members are boys and young men, rather than girls and young women. Females are rarely mentioned in relation to questions concerning gangs and gang-related behavior. Gang activity is still very much tied up with masculinity and "boys in groups." Girls may engage in gang-related behavior (e.g., illegal drugs, occasional street aggression), but gang membership is another matter.
- Gang-associated violence tends to be group-based and involves trouble with other groups. All the self-identified gang members report fighting with other groups. In some cases, a gang will engage in "mobbing"— that is, surrounding an individual member of another recognized gang or group and violently assaulting him. The groups know each other and where they hang out. An element of ritualized brawling exists in many parts of the country, suggesting that such activity is considered by many young people to be exciting, dangerous, and, ultimately, a thrill—something to look forward to.
- It is difficult to gauge what proportion of serious and violent crime to associate with youth gang members; for that we would need a fine-grained analysis of particular kinds of criminal activity. For instance, several recent youth homicides in Perth and Melbourne were related to gang behavior, but others were linked to groups of young people gate-crashing parties and getting into fights with strangers. Both gang members and nongang members commit crime, although gang members tend to commit a greater variety of criminal acts and with greater frequency than nongang members. But gang members also need to be distinguished from smaller groups of teenagers who might commit crimes (such as breaking and entering) but who have no gang association.

- As to whether or not gang-related behavior and membership are related to ethnicity, the answer is both yes and no. Much of the serious gang violence (especially that involving homicide) in Australia is in fact intracommunal violence, involving different groups of young people within the same ethnic community (e.g., Vietnamese gangs in Perth). On the other hand, in other places (such as western Sydney), the marginalization of certain young people, and often their experiences of racism, mean that some (but definitely not all) are seeking to identify themselves and friends as members of a gang in order to protect themselves and to project a strong image that affirms their communal identity. Issues of identity and inequality are often central to how and why particular ethnic minority groups become linked with gang processes and discourses. The number one reason for both carrying a weapon and joining a group is protection.
- It is difficult on the surface to distinguish between gang and nongang members. It is important to acknowledge, for instance, that many nongang members also frequently engage in fights with others. However, this violence tends to be more spontaneous, less ritualized, and sporadic. If a fight breaks out between two individuals, then in many cases a group fight will result. This may take the appearance of a gang fight but may not be related to gang membership or identification or motivation. This is one of the gray areas of gang research and the development of antigang strategies.

The data suggest that subtleties of perception, association, and activity need to be teased out in any analysis of gang formation and gang-related behavior. This is a task that remains to be done. The national study will assist the process of gathering comparative data that will allow better evaluation of the similarities and differences among cities and among diverse youth group formations.

Conclusion

In Australia, youth gangs are increasingly perceived to be a problem. More empirical study is needed to ascertain (1) whether or not gang-related activity is on the rise; (2) whether youth gang prevalence is increasing and/or whether conflicts between diverse groups of young people generally are increasing; and (3) to whom youth gangs are a problem (i.e., to other gangs, to members of the general public, to nongang young people). The last decade has seen a cumulative picture of gangs in Australia emerge, a picture that is gaining more clarity as research techniques and questions are refined and greater networking among researchers takes place. We are now in a position to make broad statements about gangs and gang-related behavior, while conceding that we cannot extend these generalizations across whole groups and whole communities. Gang issues (including media portrayals) are very much contingent upon time, place, and specific individuals and groups. If the nature of youth group formation is to be understood, it thus is essential to undertake localized studies that incorporate analyses of diverse social histories and specific group dynamics.

Given the dearth of baseline studies, it is difficult to answer whether or not the gang problem is larger than before. To the extent that this is the case, a combination of racism and marginalization appears to be creating the ground for an expansion of antisocial behavior and gang-related activities, but this too depends on the setting and the group in question. For example, unpublished material from gang research in Hobart indicates that the most prominent publicly and self-identified gang is the Glenorchy Mafia. This group is mainly composed of Anglo-Australian working-class youth who are invariably portrayed in class rather than ethnic terms (i.e., as "bogans," who wear distinctive flannel shirts and tight jeans). In relation to problems associated with gang activities, there is some indication that the rules of engagement have changed between diverse groups on the street and in the school. The gang problem is intensifying with respect to apparently heightened levels of physical violence, use of weapons, and frequency of the violence. This is particularly so in relation to those young people who self-identify as gang members.

One of the key findings of recent research is that ethnic background and identity are often equated with gang membership. In the end, perhaps the issue is less one of gangs per se than one of social identity and the frictions associated with group interaction. Thus, as the Adelaide study found:

> Rivalry and physical conflicts with other racially based groups reinforce their identity both as Italians and as "macho men". In this context, especially as victors in the fight, they can turn their status as "wogs" from a point of derision to something of which they can be proud. (Foote 1993, 127)

It is clear from recent studies (Collins et al. 2000; White et al. 1999) that group protection from perceived and actual threats is integral to both group identity and to the use of violent means to protect oneself. Ironically, being in a group also increases the chances of getting into a fight. Standing back from gang research, we find similar themes in the literature dealing with issues of immigration, resettlement, and the relationship of ethnic minorities to the dominant Anglo-Australian mainstream (see, e.g., Guerra and White 1995; Hage 1998; Jamrozik, Boland, and Urquhart 1995). Hence, different kinds of social studies are basically coming to very similar conclusions.

Of major concern to researchers (and, increasingly, to policymakers) are the immediate harms stemming from gang membership and gang-related behaviors, and the potential for gang members to negatively affect their future prospects. Intervention strategies have to be conscious of these considerations, as well as of the importance of local community factors in fostering gang formation. Social inequality and criminalization based on social difference are never far from the surface in any consideration of youth gangs in Australia.

12

The Global Impact of Gangs

John M. Hagedorn

WHY STUDY GANGS? The short answer is that gangs are a significant world-wide phenomenon with millions of members and a voice of those marginalized by processes of globalization. Understanding these social actors is crucial to fashioning public policies and building social movements that can both reduce violence and erode the deep-seated inequalities that all too often are reinforced by present economic, social, and military policies.

The American study of gangs can no longer start and stop with local conditions but must also be rooted in a global context. How else do we come to grips with Jamaican posses in Kansas (Gunst 1995), San Diego's Calle Trente and their past relationship to Mexico's Arellano brothers cartel (Rotella 1998), the Russian "mafiya" in Chicago (Finckenauer and Waring 1998), female Muslim gangs in Oslo (Lien 2002), LA's MS-13 and 18th Street as the largest gangs in Honduras and El Salvador (Decesare 2003), Nigerian drug smugglers coming through Ronald Reagan International Airport (Greman et al. 2000), Crips in the Netherlands (van Gemert 2001), the ties of U.S. tongs to Chinese Triads (Booth 1999), and other examples of a global web of gangs?

Gang research is important today for six related reasons:

1. Unprecedented worldwide urbanization has created fertile conditions for the growth of gangs, particularly in Latin America, Asia, and Africa.
2. Unlike the expansion of the state in the earlier industrial era, in the global era the state has retreated in the face of instantaneous financial flows and neoliberal monetary policy, while emphasizing punitive policies toward marginalized communities. Gangs and other groups of armed young men

occupy the vacuum created by the retreat of the social welfare policies of
the state.

3. The strengthening of cultural identities by men and women is a central
method of resistance to marginalization. While fundamentalist religion
and nationalism have been adopted by many gang members, hip-hop
culture and its "gangsta rap" variant also provide powerful resistance
identities and influence millions.

4. Globalization's valorization of some areas and marginalization of others
has meant the flourishing of an underground economy for survival and
as profitable, internationally connected enterprises run by gangs, cartels,
and similar groups.

5. The wealth of the global economy has led to the redivision of space in
cities all across the globe. "Economic development," "making the city safe,"
and "ethnic cleansing" are among the reasons given for the clearing out
of "the other" from urban spaces desired by dominant ethnic or religious
majorities. These spatial changes have influenced the nature and activity
of gangs.

6. Some gangs *institutionalize* and become permanent social actors in communities, cities, and nations, rather than fading away after a generation.
These gangs often replace or rival demoralized political groups and play
important, albeit often destructive, social, economic, and political roles
in cities around the world.

The Explosion of Urbanization

A UN-Habitat (2003) report finds that nearly 1 billion people live in "slums"
in the world today. In developing nations, slum dwellers make up 43 percent
of the total population, compared to 6 percent in developed countries. Eighty
percent of the population of Latin America is now urban. In sub-Saharan
Africa, nearly three-quarters of those who live in cities are slum dwellers. India
has 25 cities of 1 million or more, and China, as of this writing, has 166 (French
2004).

The present urban population is greater than the entire population of the
world in 1960 (Davis 2004). Urbanization has accelerated worldwide in processes that were so well described by Robert Park, Frederic Thrasher, and the
Chicago School as prime conditions for the growth of gangs. Malcolm Klein's
(1995a, 3) argument that "the common varieties of street gang still are an essentially American product" leads in the wrong research direction. The vast
majority of gangs and gang members are from Latin America, Africa, and
Asia—recent products of urbanization.

Gangs did not originate in the United States. Dickens and others described London gangs long before their American cousins existed (Pearson 1983). Even female gang members—"scuttlers"—may have roamed Manchester in the nineteenth century (Davies 1998). Gangs have formed all over the world whenever and wherever industrialization and related processes drive people into cities.

For example, industrializing Third World countries like South Africa had gangs, or "skollies," for most of the twentieth century (Pinnock 1984). "Number gangs" have been known in South African prisons for nearly a century (Shurink 1986). In the wake of post–World War II urbanization, gangs like the *rarry* boys in Sierra Leone (Abdullah 2002) were formed by the children of urban migrants. In New Zealand, Maori gangs have built a national network since the mid-twentieth century (Hazlehurst forthcoming). And one familiar figure, Yasser Arafat, learned guerrilla tactics as a street gang leader in Cairo in the 1940s (Aburish 1998).

Other forms of the gang have been around even longer. In China, Triads began in the eighteenth century and morphed into gangster activity in Hong Kong, Shanghai, and other large Chinese cities (e.g., Booth 1999). The mafia, originally a rural nineteenth-century Sicilian rebel force, took root in U.S. cities and transformed local gangs, like Chicago's Taylor Street crew, into powerful illicit organizations (Hobsbawm 1969; Nelli 1969).

Much of the current world literature on gangs, unlike the "at-risk youth" literature in the United States, does not use the label *gangs*. The World Bank, for example, documents millions of "street children" around the world, a term that includes various semiorganized forms (World Bank Institute 2000). The "child soldiers" literature, newly supplemented by the category of "children in organized armed violence," is another source of reporting on gangs (Dowdney 2003; Human Rights Watch 2004). By perusing the global organized-crime literature and the human rights studies (e.g., Amnesty International 2004; United Nations 2000), other snapshots of youth gangs can be garnered. The Social Science Research Council has begun an international working group on "children and armed conflict," looking at armed groups as diverse as gangs, vigilantes, death squads, drug cartels, and paramilitaries (Social Science Research Council 2004).

But what is a *gang*? Group process definitions, from Thrasher (1927) to Short and Strodtbeck (1965/1974) to Moore (1978), describe unsupervised youth developing organizations through conflict with other groups and authorities. They pointedly exclude criminalization as a necessary characteristic of the definition of gangs, as claimed by Klein (1971) and Miller (1982/1992).

In today's cities, particularly in less-developed countries, such unsupervised groups of youth are often "supervised" by a variety of criminal groups and recruited by nationalist and religious militias. Prisons both receive and create gangs that spread back to their communities, as in South Africa (Shurink 1986), California (Moore 1978), and Rio de Janeiro (Dowdney 2003). The present era has witnessed the proliferation of gangs and other groups who are outside the control of formal state authority. Thrasher's diagram (1927, 70) of the various paths a "casual crowd" can take was prescient.

The central issue is that gangs today are organizations of the socially excluded, most of whom come and go as their wild, teenage peer group ages. But a substantial number institutionalize on the streets, either through self-generated processes or with the assistance of already institutionalized armed groups.[1] The similarity of these institutionalized gangs to other groups of armed young men requires that the global study of "gangs" broaden its focus (see Hagedorn forthcoming-a). While I am a theoretical soul mate of Short and Moore, it is clear that one central mechanism for the persistence of "institutionalized" gangs is participation in the underground economy.

There are no comprehensive, comparative studies of gangs across the world (but see Hagedorn forthcoming-b; Hazlehurst and Hazlehurst 1998; Klein et al. 2001; Kontos, Brotherton, and Barrios 2003). It is possible, however, to estimate that, depending on the definition, there are *at least* tens of millions of gang members in the world today.

Globalization and the Retreat of the State

The study of gangs began in an era of optimism about the role of the state in solving problems of poverty and diverting youth from delinquency (Thrasher 1927; Wirth 1928/1956). The social disorganization that accompanied immigration, the theory propounded, could be overcome by social programs, settlement houses, and the juvenile court "in loco parentis" (Addams 1920/1960). The key to combating delinquency, Shaw and McKay (1942) argue, is the organization of communities to control delinquent behavior.

Gang studies in the 1960s argued for new social programs that stressed "opportunity" as part of a societal war on poverty (Cloward and Ohlin 1960; Yablonksy 1962). Much current gang literature continues to urge increased state intervention (e.g., Klein 1995a; Spergel 1995), while others follow Shaw and McKay and stress community empowerment, in part through leveraging state resources (Bursik and Grasmick 1993; Sampson and Groves 1989).

Social disorganization theory is theoretically grounded in the Enlightenment notion of the progressive nature of history and the belief that the secular state would continue to grow as religion and tradition were weakened by modern society (Elias 1939/1994; Nisbet 1980; see especially Touraine 2000). The only way to overcome the loss of the bonds of old-world culture, Kornhauser (1978) argued, is to strengthen community institutions, an approach that continues to guide social theory today (Sampson, Raudenbush, and Earls 1997; Wilson and Sampson 1995). The role of the state has changed, however, and the gang literature has all but ignored the decline of the state and the rise of global cities that are at the cutting edge of urban political economy (see Castells 1997; Sassen 2002).

The vast transformation of the U.S. economy has resulted in economic restructuring that prioritizes information and services over heavy industry, contingent labor over unionized labor, and consumption over production (see, e.g., Bell 1960; Castells 1998/2000). These developments have been accompanied by public policies that stress security and the needs of the new wealthy and fray the safety net for the poor and a weakened working class (Bourdieu 1999; Touraine 2001). In the wake of reduced opportunity for unskilled labor, many gang members have remained in their gangs as adults, and gangs have become important ghetto employers (Hagedorn 2001).

These policies have been accelerated by the war on terror (Calhoun, Price, and Timmer 2002). In Europe and other advanced countries, the Reagan-Thatcher agenda has been more controversial and contested (Hagedorn 2001; Pitts 2000; Wacquant 1999). In the Third World, International Monetary Fund strictures to reduce social spending, pay on foreign debt, allow foreign capital penetration, and continue a strong military have resulted in the erosion of the social welfare policies of already weak states (Bauman 1998; Castells 1998/2000), while increasing what Wacquant (2004) calls "neoliberal penalty."

Latin American and African academics have long been skeptical about the progressive nature of development (e.g., De Soto 1990; Frank 1970). The retreat of the state in the Third World has created anew what might at first blush be considered conditions of "social disorganization," with weakened and delegitimized social institutions unable to contain a rapidly urbanizing population. As a result, various sorts of "armed young men" (Hagedorn forthcoming-a; Kaldor 1999), including gangs, paramilitaries, death squads, and drug cartels have proliferated that parallel, replace, or complement public authority. The Social Science Research Council working group focused on the role of the state in perpetuating and repressing armed groups. Some armed groups aim to replace or overthrow the state, others are employed as repressive agents of the state, and still others seek to perform their activities with minimal state involvement (Social Science Research Council 2004).

The state in many countries can no longer be said to have a monopoly on violence, Weber's (1921/1968) standard definition of the modern state. For example, in Rio de Janeiro, drug factions control and patrol the *favelas*, and police enter only with massive armed force and then quickly withdraw

(Dowdney 2003). In Haiti, the state lost all capacity to control the populace and various types of groups of armed youth, leading to the deposing of Aristide and an uncertain status for the new state (Farmer 1994; Kovats-Bernat 2000). Recent press reports from Haiti tell of pro- and anti-Aristide youth gangs, who now refuse to put down their arms and have turned full-time to crime (Children in Organised Armed Violence 2004).

The proliferation of death squads in this sense is another indication that the state no longer can enforce its rule without resorting to extralegal violence. Like gated communities with their private security guards for the wealthy, armed groups or vigilantes, like the Bakassi Boys in Nigeria (Human Rights Watch 2002), are filling a vacuum within poor communities, where the state is unable to maintain order. In many cases, the state, in order to preserve "plausible deniability," subcontracts tasks of violence to informal death squads (Campbell and Brenner 2000). In Colombia, militias, cartels, revolutionaries, and the military all draw teenage warriors from the large pool of youth gangs in urban areas (Children in Organised Armed Violence 2003). Castells (1998/2000, 210) sums up this point:

> In a world of exclusion, and in the midst of a crisis of political legitimacy, the boundary between protest, patterns of immediate gratification, adventure, and crime becomes increasingly blurred.

This does not mean that gangs are the same thing as death squads or terrorists. *It does mean, however, that "social disorganization" and "juvenile delinquency" are too narrow definitions for the study of gangs.* The structuralist emphasis of most U.S. gang studies is also undermined by "the power of identity."

The Power of Identity

Globalization and the retreat of the state have meant more than a loss of social control. The failure of modern institutions and the lack of faith in the certainty of a better future have strengthened *resistance identities*, that is, identities formed in opposition to the dominant culture and the uncertainties of an unstable modernity (Castells 1997). Touraine (1995) argues that the modern era can be understood best as the clash between the unfettered power of the market and the resistance of national, ethnic, and religious identities.

Within poor communities, resistance identities are held by a wide assortment of people, including gangs and other groups of armed youth. Nationalist, religious, and ethnic cultures have grown strong by resisting the homogenizing influences of westernization. Islamic fundamentalism today is but one example of the strength of cultural resistance identities.

Often overlooked is the resistance of women who share ethnic or religious identities but also challenge the male dominance of traditional culture. As Moore (forthcoming) notes, there is scant literature on female gangs around the world, though such gangs may be increasing. Although most female gangs still appear to be adolescent groups, adult forms may differ markedly from adult male gangs, and both are woefully understudied (Chesney-Lind and Hagedorn 1999). In the United States, the conflicted voices of women can be seen in "gangsta rap" music, where misogyny and violence reign but female rappers strongly protest, while defending black males against racist attacks on their music (hooks 1994; Rose 1994).

The power of rap music is not often discussed in gang studies, though its strong influence contradicts the premise that culture is everywhere in decline, and even more so in subcultures (Kornhauser 1978; Park 1940; but see Finestone 1957, 1967). The present era is marked by the strength of culture, driven by the international dominance of the U.S. media, the resurgence and reinvention of traditional cultures, and the dominance of youth street cultures, even in Islamic countries. In Nigeria, gangs of Muslim youth enforce sharia for the state, while wearing gold chains, using and selling drugs, and listening to rap music (Casey 2002). Throughout Africa, Latin America, and Asia, homegrown styles of rap music have captured the imagination of youth.

Although media corporations promote "gangsta rap" to run up profits, and the lure of sex and violence celebrates values of the dog-eat-dog "cowboy capitalism" of globalization, the broader cultural power of hip-hop helps forge a more complex resistance identity for youth modeled after African American rebellion to white authority (see Short 1996). Among the founders of hip-hop were former gang members, like Afrika Bambaataa in the South Bronx, who consciously saw hip-hop as a way to pull youth away from gangs (Kitwana 1994, 2002). The fact that rap now contains conflicting ideals of violence and antiviolence, consumerism and anticonsumerism, religion and antagonism to religion, misogyny and feminism, only attests to its overall power in identifying the locus of the struggle.

To say that gangs can be understood through the lens of hip-hop culture is different than saying gangs are subcultures (Cloward and Ohlin 1960; Cohen 1955; Miller 1958). Miller and Cohen both saw subculture as an ethnically neutral and temporary outlook of working- or lower-class youth and adults. Cloward and Ohlin saw the source of gang subculture in the particular characteristics of opportunity structures within kinds of neighborhoods and downplayed its ethnic dimensions.

Hip-hop culture, and its gangsta rap variant, is avowedly African American, with African and Jamaican roots. Originating in communal, life-affirming values (Rose 1994), like all cultural goods today, it is also shamelessly exploited by media companies "merchandizing the rhymes of violence" (Ro 1996). Gangster rap is also nihilistic, worshiping destruction and violence in a way more extreme than Cohen's reaction formation, a paean to black survival and a violent response to the no-way-out life of the ghetto.

However, the gangster identity exists within a broader, worldwide hip-hop culture and represents an outlook of millions of the "socially excluded." This contested "resistance identity" is no longer a transient "subculture" of alienated youth but a permanent oppositional and racialized culture arising in the wake of the retreat of the state and the parallel strengthening of cultural identities. The power of gangtsa rap within hip-hop culture attests to the importance of the global criminal economy to socially excluded youth.

The Underground Economy

The criminal economy has been estimated by the United Nations as grossing more than $400 billion annually, which would make it the largest market in the world, including oil. Peter Reuter's (1996) more conservative estimates (his low-ball figure of $150 billion in annual drug sales) are nevertheless breathtaking. The U.S. gang literature has often described drug dealing as unorganized, and low-paying, but the sale of drugs in the United States is tied to an international network of drug suppliers, cartels, and mafias that exercise enormous influence in communities and nations on a global scale (Castells 1998/2000).

The literature on gangs and the underground economy in the United States is extensive (J. Moore 1991; Taylor 1990a; Venkatesh and Levitt 2000). But these are local studies, and their emphasis, as in my own prior work, is on the insular world of drug dealing in a single city. These studies describe the importance of the drug market to both young gang members and to the community (see especially Pattillo 1998; Venkatesh 2000). They also describe drug-dealing gangs as the main street-level employer of youth in the poorest areas of cities, forsaken by industrial jobs (Hagedorn 2001).

The underground economy, however, has changed over the decades. Portes, Castells, and Benton (1989) explain how globalization has transformed illegal markets into an integral part of the world system. The underground economy has survival functions in urban areas when the formal economy disappears, providing goods and services in unregulated ways that are in demand by more affluent customers. On the U.S. border, a crusading prosecutor who was later killed admitted, "It is sad to say, but while the drug lords are here the economy is strong. This money activates the economy, injects new money" (Rotella 1998, 254). In many areas, profitable illegal markets in drugs are but one business among many which include arms sales and trafficking in women and children. When the formal economy falters, the informal one steps in.

An important feature of the global era is the coexistence/convergence of different kinds of nonstate actors, including groups of armed young men (see also Goldstone 2002). Political movements often rely on the underground economy, and many state security forces have been corrupted by massive profits derived from selling drugs and guns. As left-wing political movements wane, demoralization sets in, and militants, many of whom have few skills outside of armed struggle, are faced with the dubious moral choice of unemployment or working for drug gangs. Thus the inability of the new government in South Africa to assimilate all Spear of the Nation guerrillas into the police or military has led some former guerrillas into the world of crime. Protestant militias in Belfast, faced with the "greening" of Northern Ireland and what appears more and more certainly a future reunification with the south, have turned their guns on one another in a war over drug turf. Mexico is the poster child for the integration of military and police forces with the local drug cartels. In Central America, journalist Silla Boccanero sadly reported, "Until recently, a rebellious youth from Central America would go into the mountains and join the guerrillas. Today, he leaves the countryside for the city and joins one of the street gangs engaged in common crime without political objectives" (Children in Organised Armed Violence 2002).

The informal underground economy is now a structural part of the world order, assured by the uneven development of globalization. Violence is not a necessary condition for illicit enterprises, but when regulation by peaceful means fails, gangs and other groups of armed youth rise in prominence.

Urban Redivision of Space

Peter Marcuse (1997) argues that the vast expansion of wealth in the global economy has produced global cities that are separated into the "citadel" and the "ghetto." Space in globalizing cities is redivided, as the wealthy and well-paid "knowledge workers" hew out spaces for themselves near the banks and central business districts (see Sassen 2002). This "yuppie" landgrab is accompanied by renewed emphasis on safety, crime, and ethnic antagonisms. The spatial concentration of ethnic minorities—often people of African descent—in the poorest areas of old cities has meant that lands coveted by the wealthy must be "cleansed" of the criminal, the violent, and the "other." Thus Chicago has displaced one hundred thousand African Americans by demolishing the high-rise housing projects that were built to contain them less than half a century ago (Hagedorn and Rauch 2004). Sao Paolo is compared to Los Angeles in

Caldiera's (2000) brilliant study of the two cities erecting walls of segregation to keep the dark poor away from the white elite (see also Massey 1996).

This worldwide trend has meant the politicization of policies on crime and violence, even though in most cities of the industrialized world violence declined in the 1990s. In the United States, this law-and-order trend has targeted alienated and jobless African American youth, resulting in an unprecedented expansion of prison building. America's prisons, at least 50 percent black in a country where African Americans make up about 12 percent of the population, can be seen as but another device for control of the "social dynamite" of the ghetto. Wacquant (2000) argues that the prison and the ghetto are but two nodes on a continuum of social control dating back to slavery. While prisons are often built far from urban areas, they have become virtually contiguous to ghettoes and barrios, as gang leaders continue to run their organizations from their cells. Most gangs in both Rio de Janeiro and Chicago are run from the prison (Dowdney 2003; Hagedorn forthcoming-a). Some gangs have their origins in prison, like La Eme, and later dominate the streets (Hayden 2004).

The Institutionalization of Gangs

Violence in cities of the world varies widely, from very low rates of homicide in Europe, China, Japan, Oceania, and the Middle East, to very high rates in cities of many countries in Africa, Latin America, and the Caribbean. Within the United States, as in South America, Asia, Eastern Europe, and Africa, some cities have very high rates, some low.

Gangs are to be found in cities all over the world, in those with low rates of violence as well as those with high rates. However, in some cities, gangs have become *institutionalized* and have been present for decades. To say that a gang has institutionalized is to say that it persists despite changes in leadership (e.g., killed, incarcerated, or "matured out"), that it has an organization complex enough to sustain multiple roles of its members (including roles for women and children), that it can adapt to changing environments without dissolving (e.g., as a result of police repression), that it fulfills some needs of its community (economic, security, services), and that it organizes a distinct outlook of its members (a gang "subculture").

That some cities are home to institutionalized gangs and others not reinforces the importance of local conditions. My research suggests that in every city in the world that has had persisting high rates of violence, there are institutionalized groups of armed youth—Chicago, Los Angeles, Rio de Janeiro, Medellin, Caracas, Kingston, Cape Flats, Lagos, Mogadishu, and Belfast—though causality is likely to be recursive. The divided cities literature (Hagedorn and Perry

2002; Marcuse 1997) suggests that gangs or other groups of armed youth institutionalize in contested cities with high levels of racial, ethnic, or religious (rather than solely class) oppression, where demoralization and the defeat of political struggle have occurred, and in defensible spaces that provide natural protection opportunities for illegal economic activity.

Institutionalized gangs are more than a crime problem. Many are deeply involved with politics, real estate, religion, and community organizations and cannot be easily destroyed by suppression or repression of the drug economy. Drug sales also provide opportunities for large-scale corruption and the purchase of heavy weapons. Gangs thus are *social actors*, in Touraine's and Park's sense. As social actors within poor communities with weak mechanisms of formal social control, gangs, militias, factions, and cartels have the capacity to not only wage war but also to rein it in (see Brotherton and Barrios 2003; Bursik and Grasmick 1993; Hayden 2004 for different elaborations of this thesis). Differences among cities—for example, why Chicago and Los Angeles are home to institutionalized gangs and New York City is not—have not been satisfactorily explained. Understanding the factors underlying the institutionalization of gangs and the persistence of violence are among the most pressing reasons for studying gangs.

Conclusion: Gangs as Social Actors

The U.S. Justice Department war on terror has redirected funds for research (Savelsberg, Cleveland, and King 2004), with the result that fewer social scientists will be doing gang research, and perspectives are likely to be polarized. Federally funded studies are likely to stress gang links to terrorism, while nonfederally funded studies may continue to "puncture stereotypes" and stress local conditions. A more realistic and productive future for gang research lies in neither of these directions. Instead, we should combine our sociological and anthropological orientations with urban political economy and the analysis of gangs and other organizations of the socially excluded in the globalizing city. Gangs cannot be understood outside their global context, nor can they be reduced to epiphenomena of globalization or cogs in an international terrorist conspiracy. To a far greater degree than in the past, we need to study the racialized identities of male and female gang members and the salience of culture.

Gangs are being reproduced throughout this largely urban world by a combination of economic and political marginalization and cultural resistance. We ignore organizations of the socially excluded at great risk. Although the collapse of socialism and the demoralization of left-wing forces have been followed by new social movements that show promise for social change (Castells 1997; Touraine 1995), in some places institutionalized gangs and other groups of armed youth have moved into the vacuum created by the demise of the left. These groups are cynical about politics and are looking desperately for a better life today, not tomorrow. For them, the promises of modernity have proven to be illusory. Gangs are one price we pay for the failure of the modern project.

Institutionalized gangs are unlikely to either gradually die out or be elimi-nated by force. It might be profitable for social scientists to see them as partners at the table who need to be included in the polity, as Bursik and Grasmick (1993) controversially suggested a decade ago. In Touraine's sense, institutionalized gangs, too, are "subjects." Dealing with gangs as social actors requires a policy of both intolerance of violence and tolerance of informal, nonviolent economic activity. It requires more negotiation and less suppression. How we deal with the reality of gangs and others among the socially excluded is one of those markers that will shape the nature, and the future, of "civilization."

Notes

The author wishes to thank Mary Devitt, Paul Elitzik, David Perry, Jim Short, and the anonymous reviewers for their comments on earlier drafts of this paper.

An earlier version of this chapter was published in the *Journal of Contemporary Criminal Justice* (2005, vol. 21:153–69). Copyright © by Sage Publications, Inc. Reprinted by permission of Sage Publications.

1. While women play roles in these gangs, overwhelmingly they are groups of "armed young men," warriors fighting for masculinity, survival, and ethnic or religious identity.

13

Gang Membership and Community Corrections Populations: Characteristics and Recidivism Rates Relative to Other Offenders

David E. Olson and Brendan D. Dooley

D URING THE 1990S AND THROUGH 2003 correctional system populations in the United States—both institutional and community-based—experienced considerable growth. Between 1995 and 2003, for example, the number of adults in prison grew by 24 percent, to more than 1.2 million by 2003 (Harrison and Karberg 2004), adult parole populations climbed 14 percent to nearly 775,000, and adult probation populations grew to more than 4 million by 2003, 32 percent above 1995 figures (Glaze and Palla 2004). During this time awareness of gang membership increased, as did attempts to measure the prevalence and impact of gang membership in communities and correctional systems. The dramatic increase in the number and widespread dispersal of active gang members in the United States since the 1970s (Decker 2001b) has been attributed in part to the prolonged period gang members remain active (Hagedorn 1998b). The most recent annual National Youth Gang Center survey of law enforcement agencies reveals that there were nearly 800,000 gang members, affiliated with more than 24,500 gangs, nationwide in 2000 (Egley and Arjunan 2002).

Less is known of the prevalence of gang members within the U.S. correctional system. Based on self-reported information from surveyed inmates, the Bureau of Justice Statistics estimated that only about 6 percent of adult prison inmates were gang members (Bureau of Justice Statistics 1993). However, Lane (1989) estimated gang membership within prisons at 80 to 90 percent, and Knox's (2000) survey of prison staff produced a conservative estimate of roughly one-quarter of adult males and 8 percent of adult females in prison as gang-affiliated. Despite the fact that the majority of adults convicted of crimes are supervised in the community (e.g., on probation), little in the research literature has even attempted to examine the prevalence of gang membership among this population.

In the field of corrections, particularly community corrections such as parole and probation, attempts have been made to more effectively identify the risks of recidivating among offenders and the needs of these populations. However, the role of "gang membership" in these assessments is usually indirect. Reviewing best practices in community corrections classification and assessment, Latessa (2004) examines the evolution from "gut feelings" to actuarial risk and need assessment tools. While gang membership is not specifically addressed or examined in these assessments, some of the criminogenic characteristics and attitudes that gang members would be more likely to have, such as "procriminal associates," are taken into consideration (Kennedy 2004). The inclusion of gang membership as a specific variable in analyses of probationer or parolee recidivism is almost nonexistent and appears to be limited to juveniles released from correctional facilities in a few specific states: Arkansas (Benda, Corwyn, and Toombs 2001; Benda and Tollett 1999), California (Lattimore, Visher, and Linster 1995; Linster et al. 1996), and Arizona (Arizona Department of Juvenile Corrections Research and Development 2002). This limited body of research finds the independent role of gang involvement on recidivism to be fairly consistent, although varying somewhat when violent crimes are examined. For example, a study of roughly 250 juveniles (ten- to seventeen-year-olds) released from the Arkansas Division of Youth Services found gang members to be twice as likely as nongang members to be reincarcerated within a year (Benda, Corwyn, and Toombs; Benda and Tollett). Similarly, a study of nearly two thousand male nineteen-year-olds released from the California Youth Authority during the early 1980s found that institutional gang activity was associated with higher frequencies of postrelease rearrests (Linster et al.), but the same data found no relationship between gang activity and recidivism for violent crimes (Lattimore, Visher, and Linster). Results from Arizona, where more than 3,600 juveniles released from the Arizona Department of Juvenile Corrections were tracked, also found that juveniles involved in gangs were more likely to be returned to prison (Arizona Department of Juvenile Corrections Research and Development). Other research regarding the role of gang membership on involvement in crime is less consistent. Reexamination of an earlier study from the Seattle Youth Study data (Hindelang, Hirschi, and Weis 1981) found that, when the nature and level of self-reported delinquency was controlled, the gang/nongang rearrest odds were roughly similar (Brownfield, Sorenson, and Thompson 2001).

Limitations of these studies preclude firm conclusions regarding the role of gang membership on recidivism. First, only juvenile offenders have been studied, and juveniles account for a relatively small proportion of those arrested and are an incomplete representation of the gang population in the United States. Second, probation is the most frequently imposed sentence on convicted offenders in the United States, and this literature has not considered the role of gang membership in probationer recidivism. Finally, prior research inconsistently operationalizes recidivism, ranging from rearrest to reincarceration to self-reported involvement in delinquent behavior. This chapter examines and compares adult gang and nongang members among a sample of both prison releasees (parolees) and probationers.

Methodology

Data from two separate studies are combined in order to compare the characteristics and outcomes of gang and nongang members on community corrections in Illinois. Information collected as part of the 2000 Illinois Probation Outcome Study (see Olson and Adams 2002 for a more detailed description of the methodology) was examined together with data collected for a project specifically designed to study the influence of gang membership on adult parolee recidivism in Illinois (see Olson, Dooley, and Kane 2004, for a more detailed description of the methodology). Analyses confirmed no seasonality within either sample, and both samples were found to be representative of offender demographic characteristics, crime type, and jurisdiction type (e.g., urban versus rural).

The probation sample consisted of every adult (over age sixteen) probationer discharged from supervision in November 2000 (n = 3,364). Probation officers completed a data collection instrument containing a number of variables, including whether or not the probationer was considered to be "an active gang member." Probation officers made this judgment regarding gang membership based on a combination of presentence investigations, review of police reports, the probation intake interview/assessment, and their extensive interaction with the probationer during the course of supervision. Thus, some variation from one probation officer to another is likely. Answers to this question yielded an estimate of 6 percent of the adult probationers as gang members. Despite the limitations of relying on individual probation officers, across very different jurisdictions and information sources, we are fairly confident of the responses, particularly since probation officers were also allowed to select "unknown," an option used for 16 percent of the cases. Importantly, included among the probationer sample were adults convicted of both felonies and misdemeanors.

In the prison releasee/parolee sample, a similar sampling frame was used (all adults released from prison during November 2000) (n = 2,534), and a number of variables measuring socioeconomic, criminal, and substance abuse history and gang involvement were collected. From the data provided by the Illinois Department of Corrections (IDOC), 24 percent of the sample was identified as being gang members, based on an objective, multicriteria-based assessment completed by IDOC gang specialists specifically trained to make this determination. Given the point at which the gang membership determination was made for the parolees (during their period of incarceration), it is not known how many of these gang members would be considered "prison" gang members only, as opposed to "street" gang members.

Applying these sample estimates to the overall community corrections population in Illinois, it can be estimated that more than five thousand of the adults discharged from probation in Illinois during 2000 were gang involved, as were nearly eleven thousand of the adults released from prison onto parole in the state that year.

The analytic approach used for the analyses in this chapter involved a multistep model-building process. First, using chi-square analyses and analysis of variance (ANOVA), we compared gang and nongang members on probation and parole across a number of demographic, socioeconomic, and criminal and substance abuse history characteristics consistently found in the literature to be associated with recidivism. These variables include age, race, gender, marital status, educational achievement, whether or not the offender has children, jurisdiction type (e.g., rural versus urban), prior arrests, and whether or not the offender has a history of substance abuse. Next, recidivism among gang and nongang members was determined, measured here as rearrest for a new crime within two years following placement on either probation or parole. Finally, multivariate models, using both logistic and Cox regression, were developed to examine the independent effects on recidivism of various characteristics, including whether or not the probationer or parolee was a gang member.

Results

As can be seen in table 13.1, fairly consistent bivariate patterns are found between gang and nongang probationers and parolees across offender demographic, socioeconomic, criminal, and substance abuse histories. Among both probationers and parolees, gang members were more likely than nongang members to be younger, minority, and male, have educational deficits, be under supervision in an urban area, and have more extensive criminal and drug abuse histories. This pattern is consistent with the limited research that has been done comparing characteristics of gang versus nongang members under correctional custody. Analysis of a cohort of Nebraska prisoners found that gang members were younger, less likely to have a high school diploma, and less likely to be married or to have children, and they had more criminal life histories than their nongang counterparts (Krienert and Fleisher 2001). It is important to note that most of these characteristics have consistently been identified in the literature as factors that increase the likelihood of recidivism or failure under correctional supervision. Among probationers in the present study, gang members were, on average, just under twenty-three years of age, compared to an average age of almost thirty-two years among nongang members. While the age difference between gang and nongang parolees is less dramatic, the average age of gang members released to parole was just under thirty years of age, compared to the average age of almost thirty-three for nongang parolees. Other studies of offender recidivism consistently finds that the younger the offender, the higher the odds of rearrest after controlling for other factors (see Morgan 1994, 1995; Olson and Lurigio 2000; Petersilia 1997).

Although all individuals included in the sample were part of the "criminal population," since all had been convicted of a crime and sentenced to either prison or probation, it is clear that differences in prior criminal history influence the difference in the degree of involvement in crime (table 13.1). Sorted from lowest to highest are nongang members on probation (with an average of 3.3 prior arrests) to gang members on probation (with an average of 6.3 prior arrests) to nongang parolees (with 12.8 prior arrests) and gang member parolees (with an average of 14 prior arrests). Thus, in terms of prior involvement in crime (as indicated by prior arrests) nongang parolees could be considered "more serious" than the gang members on probation. Although the average of 14 versus 12.8 prior arrests among gang member parolees and nongang parolees is statistically different, the two populations are fairly similar on this measure of criminal history. On the other hand, the difference between the gang and nongang probationers is dramatic (6.3 versus 3.3).

For other characteristics examined, such as marital status, having children, and conviction offense type, differences between gang and nongang members were significant only among probationers. Gang member probationers were less likely to be married and to have children than were nongang probationers, but they were more likely to have been convicted for violation of drug laws. Substantive differences across these characteristics were not found among gang and nongang parolees.

Another consistent pattern appears across almost all the comparisons made in this study: Differences between the gang and nongang probationers were

TABLE 13.1

Comparison of Gang and Nongang Members across Illinois's Community Corrections Populations

	Probationers (n = 3,364)			Parolees (n = 2,534)		
	Nongang (94%)	Gang (6%)	Difference	Nongang (76%)	Gang (24%)	Difference
Average age (in years)	31.9	22.9	+++	32.9	29.5	+++
Percent nonwhite	40.9	89.0	***	69.5	87.9	***
Percent male	77.0	96.7	***	86.8	98.0	***
Percent without high school diploma/ GED	26.7	54.8	***	53.0	65.5	***
Percent married	24.8	5.7	***	18.1	15.3	n.s.
Percent with children	46.3	38.4	**	45.7	48.7	n.s.
Percent in urban area	77.1	92.8	***	89.2	94.4	***
Current conviction for a drug law violation	20.5	43.6	***	41.4	43.9	n.s.
Average prior arrests	3.3	6.3	+++	12.8	14	+
Illegal substance abuse history	52.6	81.9	***	48.5	57.8	***

*** = p < 0.001, ** = p < 0.01, * = p < 0.05, n.s. = not significant at p < 0.05 level based on chi-square test. +++ = p < 0.001, ++ = p < 0.01, and + = p < 0.05 based on ANOVA.

much larger than were those between gang and nongang parolees. The difference in educational deficit (percent without a high school diploma/GED) between the nongang and gang member probationers translates to roughly a 100 percent difference (27 percent versus 55 percent, respectively). By comparison, while there was a statistically significant difference in educational achievement between the nongang and gang parolees, the difference was not as dramatic (53 percent versus 66 percent). This pattern is evident also across age, race, gender, marital status, being supervised in an urban environment, prior arrests, and substance abuse history.

Thus, in most instances, gang members on probation and released to parole had more of the characteristics found in prior research to increase the odds of recidivism. It is not surprising, therefore, that clear and consistent differences in recidivism rates were found between gang and nongang members under community corrections supervision. Figure 13.1 presents these recidivism rates—defined as rearrest following either sentencing to probation or release from prison to parole—among gang members compared to nongang members *within* each of the two community corrections populations. Within two years of placement on probation, 64 percent of the gang members were rearrested for a new crime, compared to 30 percent of nongang probationers (p < 0.001). Similarly, 75 percent of the gang members released to parole were rearrested for

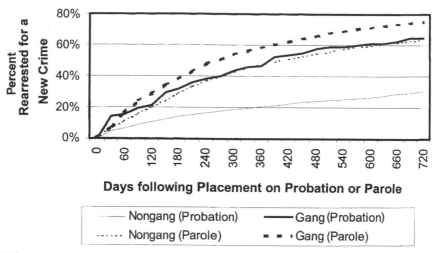

FIGURE 13.1
Cumulative Percent Rearrested following Placement on Community Corrections, by Gang Involvement and Supervision

a new crime within two years, compared to 63 percent of the nongang parolees ($p < 0.001$). Again, the magnitude of difference between the probationers and parolees is striking. The rearrest rate of gang member probationers within two years was more than double that of nongang probationers, whereas rearrest rate differences between the gang and nongang parolees was much smaller. It is also interesting to note, as is shown in figure 13.1, that the recidivism rate of the *gang members on probation* mirrors almost exactly the pattern of recidivism among the *nongang parolees*.

It is also interesting to note that, in general, there did not appear to be any statistically significant differences in terms of the nature of crimes for which gang and nongang members were rearrested in either the prison or probation samples. Among gang members and nongang members, and probationers and parolees, there was a fairly equal distribution of rearrests across drug law violations, property crimes, and violent offenses. Thus, while there were some differences in the overall rearrest rates, when only those who were rearrested were examined, it appears that the general types of crimes involved in these arrests did not differ substantially across the different populations examined.

These patterns remain in multivariate models measuring the independent effect of gang membership on recidivism, after statistically controlling for risk factors such as age, gender, race, education level, marital status, prior criminal and substance abuse history, jurisdiction type (e.g., rural versus urban), and time at risk (e.g., survival analyses). Specifically, in analyses of the probation population, Olson and Adams (2002) found, after statistically controlling for these other characteristics, that gang members were almost 3.5 times more likely than nongang members to get rearrested for a new crime. Similarly, in analyses of the parolee cohort, Olson, Dooley, and Kane (2004) found, after statistically controlling for these other characteristics and factors, that gang members were only about 20 percent more likely than nongang members to get rearrested for a new crime. Thus, not only did the gang members on probation and parole have more of the characteristics found in prior literature to increase recidivism (e.g., being young, male, less educated, etc.), but their gang membership in and of itself (i.e., after statistically controlling for these other factors) also increased their odds of rearrest. However, the magnitude of the gang effect on recidivism is quite different for probation and parolee populations. Although Olson, Dooley, and Kane found more substantive differences between gang and nongang member recidivism when specific age and offense types were examined and compared, overall the modest direct impact of gang membership on recidivism among parolees appears inconsistent with the results from the analyses of the probationers. The following section discusses some of the possible reasons for these differences and their implications for future research, practice, and policy.

Discussion

One of the most straightforward hypotheses as to why there is a much stronger "gang effect" on probationer than parolee recidivism has to do with the question, "Relative to what?" As can be seen in the comparisons presented in table 13.1, the adult probation population in Illinois, as in the rest of the country, is very diverse in terms of risks, needs, and criminality. Across age, race, gender, education levels, conviction offenses, and criminal histories, the adult probation population is more heterogeneous than the adult prison releasee population. Thus gang member probationers include a much broader array of offenders than do parolees, ranging from people convicted for the first time for driving under the influence of alcohol to serious repeat offenders. By comparison, less variation is evident among prison releasees, who comprise offenders with more extensive involvement in crime and who vary less across the other characteristics examined. Thus the gang member variable appears to be "capturing" some unique offender characteristics that distinguish gang members from nongang members, beyond what is being accounted for by the other variables examined (e.g., age, race, gender, education level, criminal history, etc.). On the other hand, given that the parolee population is much more homogenous, with less variation between gang and nongang members across the characteristics examined, gang member parolees are being compared to a relatively similar and more serious offender population. Thus among the parolees, gang membership does not dramatically differentiate the population beyond what is achieved by statistically controlling for other characteristics.

This research also has implications for community corrections policy and practice. Specifically, it appears that the inclusion of gang membership status within risk assessment instruments used by probation departments (or community corrections agencies supervising a diverse and heterogeneous group of offenders) is justified. Also, given the very large "base rates" of recidivism for gang members on probation (with almost two-thirds rearrested within two years and most probation revoked, resulting in prison sentences), the assignment of nearly all gang members on probation to some form of close supervision would also be warranted. It is also clear from the analyses and comparisons of the probation population that the identification of gang members can be used as a proxy for identifying a population with considerable needs, including educational services and substance abuse treatment. However, given the reality that many probation departments in the United States are organized and operate within specific geographic regions, such as county-level in Illinois, and the relatively low prevalence of gang membership among adult probation populations, it may be difficult in any one jurisdiction to focus exclusively on gang members through specialized caseloads.

On the other hand, the research presented here and elsewhere (Olson, Dooley, and Kane 2004) suggests that identification of gang members for purposes of parole supervision has less predictive benefit. Given that gang membership in and of itself "only" increased the odds of rearrest among the parolee population by 20 percent, and both the gang and nongang members released from prison onto parole had very high two-year rearrest rates, the challenge for parole agencies is to address high rates of risks and needs among all who are released from prison.

Thus the question "Are gang members more likely to recidivate than nongang members?" admits to a ready answer. When framed more narrowly, as "Are *offenders* identified as gang members more likely to continue their involvement in crime (i.e., recidivate) than *offenders* who are not gang members?" the answer is less clear. In the latter case, the answer appears to be mixed. Among probationers, which include a wide array of individuals who appear to be fairly heterogeneous, gang members in this study were much more likely to be rearrested, perhaps as a result of their gang involvement. On the other hand, after controlling for age, gender, education, substance abuse, and criminal history, rearreest differences between gang and nongang parolees are relatively small.

14

The Comprehensive, Community-wide Gang Program Model: Success and Failure

Irving A. Spergel, Kwai Ming Wa, and Rolando Villarreal Sosa

THE FOCUS OF THIS STUDY is a youth gang, social control program in Little Village that became a prototype for a comprehensive, community-wide approach to gang prevention, intervention, and suppression at five sites throughout the country. We indicate more briefly and schematically the process and impact of the model at the five other sites. Emphasis is on elements of interorganizational relationships, program structure, and worker contacts and services that produced lower levels of arrests (and self-reported offenses) for program youth, particularly for violence and to some extent for drug activities. Our research design was quasi-experimental. The Little Village program (A) in Chicago, the prototype site, was sponsored by the Illinois Criminal Justice Information Authority, with funding from the U.S. Department of Justice's Violence in Urban Areas Program, 1992–1997. Five of the programs—Mesa, Arizona (B); Riverside, California (C); Bloomington-Normal, Illinois (D); San Antonio, Texas (E); and Tucson, Arizona (F)—were sponsored and funded by the Office of Juvenile Justice and Delinquency Prevention (OJJDP), Office of Justice Programs, U.S. Department of Justice, between 1995 and 2000 (FY 1994).[1]

Earlier comprehensive youth gang programs generally adopted some form of traditional street work, social, and athletic activities, mediation between gangs, and occasionally youth counseling and job referral, to reduce intergang conflict. Collaboration among social agencies and community groups sometimes occurred, but with little or no collaboration with criminal justice agencies as well. In more recent decades, law enforcement agencies developed extensive suppression strategies and tactics aimed at street gang control and limited rehabilitation or prevention, sometimes in alliance with probation, parole, and district attorneys. However, there was no integration or systematic coordination of their efforts across various types of organizations (including social agencies) for purposes of interrelated community protection and social development of targeted gang members or youth at high risk of criminal gang involvement. For purpose of our discussion, we equate the terms *youth gang* and *street gang.*

Theory behind the Comprehensive Community-wide Gang Program Model

The comprehensive gang program model was informed primarily by concepts from community social disorganization and, to some extent, by differential association, opportunity, anomie, social control, and group process theories. Our community-based model was sensitized by the ideas and research findings of Battin-Pearson and colleagues (1998); Bursik and Grasmick (1993); Cloward and Ohlin (1960); Cohen (1980); Curry and Spergel (1988); Haynie (2001); Hirschi (1969); Klein (1971, 1995a); Kobrin (1951); Kornhauser (1978); Markowitz and colleagues (2001); Merton (1957); Morenoff, Sampson, and Raudenbush (2001); Sampson (1991); Sampson and Groves (1989); Sampson and Laub (1993); Shaw and McKay (1942); Short and Strodtbeck (1965/1974); Sullivan and Miller (1999); Sutherland and Cressey (1978); Suttles (1968); Thrasher (1927); Veysey and Messner (1999); and Zatz (1987).

Key assumptions of the model were that the youth gang problem, in its distinctive gang violence and drug-selling form, was increasingly present in marginal, low-income, minority, and socially isolated communities. It was not only represented by certain individual gang and gang member characteristics, but it was a response to the fragmentation of community and interorganizational efforts to adequately and interactively address the needs of youth for social development and social control and to protect the community through suppression of gang activity (Bursik and Grasmick 1993; Shaw and McKay 1942; Spergel 1995; Thrasher 1927). The model assumed that youth gangs were generally loosely structured, transitional organizations for the socialization of vulnerable youth between childhood and adulthood, particularly youth from disorganized or deviant families in socially and economically marginal neighborhoods (Klein 1971; J. Moore 1991; Vigil 1988). Local agencies and citizen organizations were often weak, with insufficient resources to address the gang problem in effective terms (Cloward and Ohlin 1960; Cohen 1955; Miller 1959; Sampson, Morenoff, and Earls 1999; Sampson, Raudenbush, and Earls 1997).

The comprehensive gang program model required criminal justice and social agencies to integrate and collaborate on key elements of control and social development, with participation from local neighborhood groups. Focus was not primarily directed to strategies of general community development, political or social reform, community policing, inclusive youth socialization, or even mediation of conflicts between gangs. These strategies were subsidiary to reducing the gang problem through an integrated social development, control, opportunities provision, and interorganizational mobilization approach. The model required the development of a lead agency and a street team of police, probation officers, and outreach youth workers (some former gang leaders)—interacting and working together—targeting delinquent/criminal gang youth and youth at high risk of gang membership who were also involved in delinquent activity (figure 14.1).

Earlier interdisciplinary or interagency community-wide, gang social control programs were not well developed. They lacked an appropriate range of strategies and collaboration with key agencies or community groups concentrated on or related to the gang problem. Evaluation research was deficient in describing the strategies, services, and activities of the different workers and the nature of their effects on program youth. Analyses of outcome also may not have used comparable nonserved youth and multivariate controls, including race/ethnicity, age, prior arrest history, duration in the program, gang membership, and risk period (Klein 1995a; Spergel 1995).

Our evaluation model (figure 14.2) for the six program sites was created as a guide to collecting and analyzing data and to explaining the interrelationship of program processes, structures, and results. Special interest was in (1) policy and organizational changes and worker efforts that contributed to program development and (2) the program's effects on youth behavior, especially factors that contributed to reduced levels of violence and drug crime arrests for program youth compared to similar nonserved youth in the same or comparable gang crime communities.

In order to explain changes in the targeted youth's behavior, data were collected at individual youth, program worker, and organizational levels (as well as, secondarily, at gang, family, and community levels). Key instruments used were individual youth interviews, individual youth police arrest histories, program worker records of service and contacts, organization administrator surveys, aggregate-level community crime statistics, U.S. census data, field observations, and program-related documents such as project applications for funding, progress reports, media reports, and local research studies. First we describe the program context in the prototype-A community, and then compare the nature of model implementation and results across all six communities.

Community Context
Social Disorganization Factors:

- **Demographic**
- **Socioeconomic**
- **Family Characteristics**
- **Ecological**
- **Cultural**

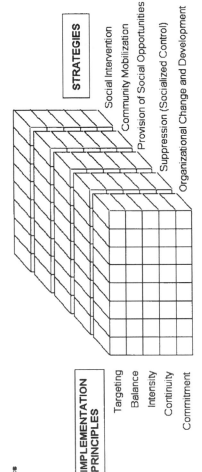

STRATEGIES

Social Intervention
Community Mobilization
Provision of Social Opportunities
Suppression (Socialized Control)
Organizational Change and Development

- Sustaining/diffusing model
- System change/legislative action
- Public/media relations
- Fund-raising
- Achieving program success
- Program analysis/evaluation
- Case management
- Staff selection/development
- Interagency coordination
- Organizing community interests/
- Sequencing strategies/tactics
- Planning
- Defining problems/issues
Lead Agency Management

Employment and Training
School Participation
Criminal Justice Participation
Social Services
Grassroots Involvement
Interagency Street Team
Steering Committee

PROGRAM ELEMENTS

**IMPLEMENTATION
PRINCIPLES**

Targeting
Balance
Intensity
Continuity
Commitment

FIGURE 14.1
Comprehensive Gang Program Model (Goal 1: Improve Community Interagency Capacity to Address Youth Gang Crime; Goal 2: Reduce Gang Crime)

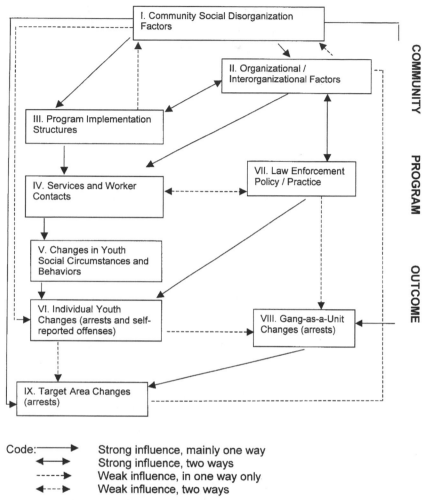

Code:⟶   Strong influence, mainly one way
    ⟷   Strong influence, two ways
   ----→   Weak influence, in one way only
   ◄---►   Weak influence, two ways

FIGURE 14.2
Evaluation Model: Program and Comparison Areas, Gangs, Youth (Comparison Area Components = I, II, V [partial], VI, VIII, IX)

Program Site A

The Little Village program (site A) took place in a very large metropolitan city, slightly earlier than the programs at sites B through F. The Little Village community (about four square miles), located eight miles from Chicago's business center, comprised an almost exclusively Mexican and Mexican American population of sixty thousand (U.S. Census Bureau 1992), plus an estimated thirty thousand undocumented residents. The city had one of the highest per capita gang homicide and gang violence rates of all very large cities. Both the city and the program area had long been known for a tradition of chronic, serious, gang violence problems.

The site A program community and its immediate surrounding area contained well-established institutions, including major medical, educational, and religious organizations, social agencies, a variety of city service facilities, light industry, and a thriving retail business sector. The community had been a place of first or second settlement for many successive and different immigrant populations. Its present occupants—lower-middle-class and marginal-income Latinos (mainly Mexican Americans)—began to establish residency about thirty years ago, replacing a Central European population. Three aldermanic districts cut through the area. Several major community organizations and service agency coalitions were present and operated across several areas. Local neighborhood-group and organizational concerns were with city services, overcrowded schools, high school dropouts, and high gang violence.

The idea of a comprehensive, community-wide, integrated suppression and social intervention gang program did not arise from the ideas or pressures of local neighborhood or city leaders. However, a new mayor had been elected and a new police superintendent appointed, and the mayor and other city and county leaders were concerned with the rise in both domestic and gang violence in the city. The associate director of the state criminal justice planning agency encouraged the director of the new research and development (R&D) unit of the Chicago Police Department (CPD) to apply for funding from the U.S. Justice Department's Urban Violence initiative. The senior author of this chapter, Irving Spergel, was asked to prepare a proposal for a demonstration community-based gang control project that focused on collaboration among agencies, including the police. The gang project was to be part of a set of violence control (including domestic violence) programs funded under the federal initiative. The gang project was initially required to target youth seventeen to twenty-four years of age.

The CPD agreed to be the lead agency of the project. The staff of the program was expected to comprise two full-time gang tactical officers and two part-time neighborhood relations officers, with three or four full-time adult probation officers and three youth workers who were part of the city's Department of Human Services gang outreach control program (located in the public schools). A local community advisory committee was also to be established. The project originally was to be administered by the commander of the Gang Crime Unit, with consultation from a liaison lieutenant from the police department's R&D unit. Spergel was expected to provide only initial technical assistance for developing the interagency collaboration but to have no program responsibility.

He was also to undertake an evaluation of the program. However, because the CPD was busy preparing for a community policing initiative, and other city departments were in the midst of a series of reorganizations, neither had much time for the project. When the Department of Human Services decided not to participate in the project, Spergel (who had already become involved in getting the program started) assumed the role of project coordinator, with responsibility for coordinating the efforts of the police and adult probation officers, as well as developing a unit of outreach youth workers. In the CPD reorganization, the centralized citywide Gang Crime Unit was dissolved and its gang officers replaced by tactical officers located at the local police districts.

The coordinator was under pressure to get the project running as soon as possible, particularly the direct-service-work component aimed at older adolescent and young adult gang members who were responsible for most of the serious violence. Former gang members who had worked with him in two previous projects in another area of the city were recruited as outreach youth workers. The workers, who were familiar with many gangs, quickly made contact with youth from the two targeted violent gangs in the area, both of which were related to or in coalition with other gangs in the city. The tactical police and adult probation officers assigned to the project were new to the area, with little knowledge of local neighborhood gangs.

The Little Village community was divided into two adjacent gang turfs. One of the gangs—the Latin Kings—had an estimated 1,200 members; the other—the Two Six—had 800 members. There were other, smaller gangs in the program area. Police incident data suggested that the two major gangs were responsible for 75 percent of the felony gang violence, including twelve homicides, on average, in the community in each of the two years prior to project operations. Each gang was organized into about fifteen subunits (or sections), operating on the streets of their respective territories. They engaged in a series of ongoing yet difficult-to-predict violent encounters with members of opposing gang sections. While most target gang youth used drugs, and about half sporadically sold drugs (particularly marijuana and powdered cocaine), they were not primarily or extensively involved in major drug-selling or drug transport operations. Other members of the same gangs were so involved, however.

The planned team approach was slow to get off the ground. Most of the outreach youth workers were from the two major gangs, had previously been arrested or served prison time, and were well known to members of each of the target gangs and to some of the veteran police in the district. Initially there was considerable suspicion and resistance among the project police, adult probation officers, and outreach youth workers to meeting with each other and sharing information about gang situations or gang youth. There was also no tradition of a close working relationship between county adult probation officers and city police. It took six months of weekly staff meetings, and many field contacts by project workers with each other, for them to feel comfortable and to gradually share information. Sharing names of targeted youth among the workers took three months and considerable prodding by the project coordinator.

Although coordination of information and collaboration of worker activity was essential, youth workers from the different gangs did not at first share information with other youth workers. Some were still somewhat identified with their respective gang groups, which may have been at war with each other in earlier years. Some, however, haltingly began to share a range of information about target youth gang violence. Probation and police officers more quickly exchanged information with each other about arrests and probation status of targeted youth. Such official information began gradually to be communicated to a few of the youth workers. In due course, youth workers, police, and probation officers were sharing information at biweekly staff meetings concerning violence occurring (or about to occur) in the community. After about a year, various project staff joined together to supervise graffiti paint-outs by target gang youth in their territories. Together they also supervised target youth in occasional basketball (and especially softball) games in neutral territory (usually on the University of Chicago's playing fields). Members of the gangs played against each other on opposing teams, with project staff participating.

Project workers were required to be on the street generally from 3:00 or 4:00 in the afternoon until midnight or later and engaged in crisis intervention, brief family and individual counseling and referrals, and surveillance and suppression activities. Workers did not necessarily perform their roles together, but they were in frequent communication by beeper and cell phone. At staff meetings, workers planned what to do with youth and how to handle crisis situations. Project efforts focused on individual gang youth who were active in carrying out or planning violent activities. The youth workers emphasized individual youth and family counseling, referrals for jobs, and social services. Little effort was directed to group services or conflict mediation between the gangs, that is, through peace and/or gang leadership meetings. Police and probation officers carried out their traditional law enforcement and supervision activities, targeting many of the same youth as the outreach youth workers and also referring target youth (and youth to be targeted) back to youth workers for services. Youth workers clarified information about serious gang assaults, aiding project police to determine who were, and were not, offenders. They also assisted probation officers in keeping abreast of information about youth and reminded youth to keep appointments with their probation officers.

A neighborhood advisory committee was formed, including representatives of several Catholic and Protestant churches, two Boys and Girls Clubs, a local community organization, a business group, other social agencies, the local alderman, and several local residents. Two large, local citizen meetings were held, but cohesion among the advisory committee members failed to develop. Local advisory committee leaders were unclear as to whether they wanted to develop individual service programs or an interagency coordinating group. Representatives of local community groups, social agencies, churches, and justice system agencies hardly communicated at all and were in varying degrees antagonistic to each other. Key established community agency and justice system leaders did not support the advisory committee. A major stumbling block was the inability of local youth agencies and the police to jointly sustain the program. Ultimately the neighborhood advisory group dissolved.

The project lasted five years, with the coordinator continuing on a year-to-year basis. The original plan was for him not to continue in this role after the first year of operations. Although supportive of the officers assigned to the project, the CPD chose not to integrate the project into its regular operations or its community policing program. Top-level police division officers insisted that the department's primary mission was suppression and not community organization or social work. The CPD was not interested in joint relationships and operations with other agencies and community groups in regard to the gang problem. Its stated interest in establishing a collaborative relationship with the Cook County Department of Adult Probation failed to develop. The R&D liaison police lieutenant to the project, who favored continuation of the project, maintained that the department had "deep pockets" and did not need the program. In frustration, he transferred back to work at a local police district during the course of the project. Three years of funding—$1.5 million—remained at the end of the project period.

Program Findings

The site A program sample (n = 195) consisted of all youth who were contacted and provided with a combination of services and controls for a period of more than one month, over a two-to-four-year period. All targeted youth were male, ranging in age from fourteen to twenty-four years (averaging eighteen years), almost all were of Mexican American or Mexican origin, and all identified themselves as gang members.

The research design for program evaluation called for two comparison samples in Little Village: a comparison group of youth (n = 208) who were from the same gangs as the program youth and who had been arrested with them, but who had not been provided with services; and a "quasi-program" comparison group of youth (n = 90), also coarrestees of program youth, who were provided with only limited (mostly recreational) services. Complete criminal histories were collected for all youth in each sample—program, comparison, and quasi program. Sixty-five percent of program youth were interviewed three times, at intervals ranging from a year to a year and a half. Youth in other samples were not interviewed (due to a lack of resources).

The chief accomplishments of the project occurred mainly through the work of the interdisciplinary street team. An array of integrated services was provided: crisis intervention, brief counseling, family contacts, educational/job referral and job placement, police surveillance, warnings, arrests, and probation intensive counseling. By the end of the project, a statistically significant reduction in gang crime, particularly violence and drug arrests, was found among program youth compared to youth in the comparison samples. Area-level gang violence arrest rates (but not drug arrest rates) were reduced in the Little Village area compared to six other high gang violence areas of the city.

Focus of the analysis was on differences in arrest patterns of program youth, quasi-program youth, and comparison samples, during the program and matched preprogram periods (based on the targeted program youth's length of time in the program). Mean total arrests for youth in their preprogram periods were high: program sample = 4.5; comparison sample = 4.0; quasi-program sample = 7.8. The difference was statistically significant between the quasi program and each of the other two samples ($p \leq 0.05$). However, there were no statistically significant differences between the samples with respect to preprogram serious violence arrests (homicide, aggravated assault, aggravated battery, and robbery). The patterns of total arrests for violence (including simple assault, simple battery, and illegal possession of a weapon, as well as serious violence) were similar. There were also no statistically significant differences across the three samples in preprogram arrests for property crime, drug or alcohol arrests, and a range of relatively minor offenses (e.g., disorderly conduct and mob action).

Multivariate analyses were conducted to determine whether there were differences in arrest changes for each of the different categories of offenses in the program sample and the two comparison samples. Various statistical models used controls for type of arrest, number of preprogram arrests, age category, and length of time in confinement during the program and preprogram periods. Interaction terms included age categories and preprogram arrest levels for each sample.

All the general linear models were significant ($p \leq 0.0001$), with preprogram arrests the strongest effect among all independent variables—that is, a regression effect: Youth in each sample who had high levels of preprogram arrests reduced their numbers of arrests in the program period, while youth with no or low levels of preprogram arrests increased their arrests in the program period. Age was another significant strong effect: There were differences in all the models across all subsamples. In general, arrests of youth nineteen and older declined, but arrests of the youngest age category—sixteen and under—increased. There was no significant difference in change in total yearly arrests, property arrests, or arrests for minor offenses among the samples.

There were major differences, however, in arrest levels for serious violence, total violence (felony and misdemeanor), and drugs between program youth and quasi-program youth, and especially between program youth and the non-served comparison youth. Reductions in serious violence arrests occurred for each of the samples, but were significantly different in the program sample compared to both the quasi-program and nonserved comparison samples: There was a 60 percent greater decrease (statistically significant) for the nineteen-and-older and seventeen-and-eighteen-year-old program youth subsamples than for the equivalent comparison and quasi-program subsamples. Reductions for program fourteen- to sixteen-year-olds were greater than those for the fourteen-to-sixteen-year-old quasi-program and comparison groups, but they were not statistically significant. The pattern of reduction was similar with respect to change in total violence arrests (see table 14.2).

Project workers made special efforts to increase school attendance and to aid youth in seeking and holding jobs (including getting them up in the morning). Although workers referred youth for drug treatment and made brief counseling contacts toward reducing drug use, they focused less on drug crime than on violent behavior of program youth. While drug use was pervasive, drug-selling behavior among program youth was limited. Most arrests for drugs among youth in the three samples were for possession of marijuana and powdered cocaine. Information on major drug operations (mainly involving the Mexican Mafia) was passed to police by a few of the youth workers in a controlled, indirect manner, resulting in important drug raids, arrests, and the closure of at least one bar and several drug houses. An adult criminal organization, the Mexican Mafia, was the primary agent for drug distribution and transport, and occasionally used program youth (and/or their parents) to sell and carry drugs from Mexico to Chicago.

We expected that, if program youth reduced their levels of violence arrests (or self-reported violence offenses), there would be an increase in drug offenses. All gang-problem communities in Chicago were undergoing increases in gang drug arrests in this period. This seemed to be part of a process of further natural development of established gangs, from primary interest in turf-based violence to primary but not exclusive or even organized interest in drug selling.

While community-area gang drug-related arrests increased by 1,000 percent (and area-level gang violence rates decreased) between the five-year preprogram period and five-year program period, they decreased for program youth over the same period (see table 14.2). In contrast, drug arrests increased for quasi-program and nonserved comparison youth. The decrease was significant for the program seventeen-to-eighteen and sixteen-and-under age subgroups, compared to the equivalent quasi-program and comparison age subgroups ($p = 0.02$).

We know of no other crime control programs—for example, the initiation of community policing in the area—that could have accounted for these program youth changes (Skogan and Hartnett 1997). A series of logistic regression equations statistically accounted for different types of project worker effects on program youths' attitudes and behaviors, which in turn contributed to lower levels of violence and drug arrests. Effective suppression contacts, as perceived by project police (and indicated in worker activity reports), were related to a reduction in a program youth's degree of affiliation with his gang. For example, compared to youth who did not change their affiliation, or changed to higher gang status, some youth changed from leaders to core members or regular members, peripherals, or nonmembers (odds ratio = 2.0; $p = 0.04$). Reduction in the youth's level of affiliation with the gang was significantly associated with lower violence and drug arrests. Suppression was also useful in persuading youth not to have unrealistically high income aspirations and to have more realistic ones (odds ratio = 2.71; $p = 0.006$).

Successful job referral and job placement of program youth (mainly by the outreach youth workers) simultaneously predicted the likelihood of youth spending less time with their gang friends (odds ratio 2.22; $p = 0.03$) and spending more time with wives or steady girlfriends (odds ratio = 2.48; $p \leq 0.01$). Worker success in getting youth back to school predicted a nonsignificant positive odds ratio of youth graduating or getting a GED (1.74; $p = 0.15$). The workers were more successful with older than younger youth in this regard (odds ratio 2.21; $p \leq 0.01$). Generally, holding a legitimate job was associated with significantly reduced levels of violence and drug arrests.

More program services and contacts—from all types of project personnel together, including youth workers, police, probation, and neighborhood organizers—predicted a reduced gap between the individual youth's income or job aspirations and expectations, that is, a more realistic appraisal of his chances for success in life. Similarly, the greater the dosage of worker contacts and services, the greater the reduction in the number of gang friends among these youth. Higher program dosage was also associated with reduced levels of violence arrests. Intensity and persistence in contacts and services clearly were required.

Collaborative project worker efforts—through interactive suppression, social support, and provision of social opportunities—effectively changed patterns of gang youth behavior, resulting in the pursuit of a more socially acceptable life course and the formation of relationships with more nongang peers.

Such changes in the youth's behavior were highly predictive of lower rates of gang violence.[2]

At the Little Village community level, the project was associated with lower levels of arrests for gang-motivated aggravated battery and assault over the preprogram and program periods, compared to six similar high gang violence Latino (Mexican American and Puerto Rican) community areas in the city during the first three years of project operations. The rate of decline in gang violence arrests at the program-area level dropped off slightly during the last two years of the project, when staff were increasingly discouraged and frustrated as it became clear that the city administration and the police department were not prepared to institutionalize the project approach.

Cross-Site Community and Program Characteristics and Changes in Arrest Patterns

In this section we summarize and compare the characteristics, importance, and success in implementation of the program code (figure 14.1) across the six sites (table 14.1). We use numbers of asterisks to indicate the degree of general importance of the eighteen basic program characteristics in implementing the model. We also indicate, through use of symbols, the extent to which each of the program characteristics was implemented at each site. The degree of importance of these program characteristics, but not the level of their implementation, was determined by the senior author. The level of implementation was determined by the findings of an evaluation survey completed by five to seven of the program leaders at each site, and by two or three national program evaluators familiar with the particular programs. The results of the survey were summed but not weighted for each site. Key factors accounting for successful or failed implementation were also identified for the sites.

We also identify selected gang effect factors at each of the six sites (table 14.2): level of the gang problem and its nature, gang structure, and race/ethnicity of gang members in the program and comparison youth samples, and in the program and comparison areas. Most attention is directed to a summary and comparison of key outcome factors from figure 14.2, especially changes in youth behaviors (V), individual youth outcome/arrests (VI), and target area outcome/arrests (IX). Arrows in the last three sections of table 14.2 indicate whether the individual youth in the program sample at each site significantly changed their arrest patterns, relative to youth in the comparison sample. A similar determination of whether program-area arrests were reduced relative to comparison-area arrests is also made between the preprogram and program periods. The area arrest assessments were based on gross police arrest statistics, without demographic controls at the six sites.[3]

TABLE 14.1
Program Implementation Characteristics: Degree of Importance and Levels of Implementation

	1.A. Program Implementation Characteristics (See also figure 14.1)	Degree of Importance to Program Success[†]	Levels of Implementation by Project Site[‡]					
			A	B	C	D	E	F
Program Elements (Structure)	[a]City/County Leadership	***	2	4	4	1	1	1
	[b]Steering Committee	**	1	4	3	1	1	0
	[c]Interagency Street Team/ Coordination	***	4	4	3	0	0	0
	[d]Grassroots Involvement	*	3	1	1	0	1	0
	Social Services: [e]Youth Work, [f]Individual Counseling, [g]Family Treatment, & [h]Recreation	**	3	3	3	2	3	3
	[i]Criminal Justice Participation	***	4	4	4	1	1	0
	[j]School Participation	**	1	3	3	3	2	0
	[k]Employment and Training	**	3	1	4	3	1	0
	[l]Lead Agency/Management/ Commitment	***	4	4	4	0	0	0
Strategies	Social Intervention: [m]Outreach & [n]Crisis Intervention	**	4	3	3	1	1	0
	Community Mobilization: [o]Interagency & [p]Grassroot	**	1	3	2	1	0	0
	Provision of Social Opportunities: [q]Education, [r]Job, & [s]Cultural	**	3	2	2	2	1	0
	[t]Suppression	***	4	4	3	0	0	0
	[u]Organizational Change & Development	***	2	4	4	0	0	0
Operating Principles	Targeting [v]Gang Members/[w]At-Risk Gang Youth	***	4	2	3	1	3	3
	[x]Balance of Service	***	4	3	3	0	0	0
	[y]Intensity of Service	*	4	3	3	1	0	0
	[z]Continuity of Service	**	2	1	2	2	0	2

TABLE 14.2
(Continued)

	1.B.	c, i, l,	a, c,	a, c,	–	–	–
Key Factors Δ Contributing to…	Success in Program Implementation	t, x	i, l, t, u	i, k, l, u			
	Failure in Program Implementation	–	–	–	c, l, t, u, x	c, l, t, u, x	c, i, l, t, u, x

---

† Importance of characteristics to success: *** = extremely, ** = moderately, and * = somewhat.

‡ Levels of Implementation: 4 = excellent, 3 = good, 2 = fair, 1 = poor, and 0 = none. A = Chicago, B = Mesa, C = Riverside, D = Bloomington-Normal, E = San Antonio, F = Tucson.
Δ refers to codes used in 1.A, Program Implementation Characteristics, and figure 14.1.

Factors Contributing to Program Implementation Success or Failure

A variety of interrelated program structures, strategies, and operating principles were assessed as necessary for the successful implementation of the comprehensive gang program model. At no site were all of the critical model factors fully implemented, although implementation appeared to have been more effective at site A, and to some extent at B and C, and less effective at sites D, E, and F. At sites A, B, and C, greater coordination of social intervention, services provision, and suppression contacts by workers predicted a reduction in violence and other types of arrests for individual youth. Certain program structure factors were correlated with declines in arrests for violence (and less often for drugs).

It was important to assign degrees of importance to model factors and determine the degree of their successful adaptation across the sites. The following seemed especially important: city and county governmental leadership committed to the model; development of an interagency street team and use of indigenous former gang influentials; coordination and interrelationship of strategies of social intervention, suppression, and provision of socioeconomic opportunities by police, probation, and outreach youth workers; and optimal lead agency management capacity, with a substantial effort directed to the development of a steering committee. The presence of these factors across sites A, B, and C was associated with a significant level of success in the reduction of the gang violence problem for program youth. The absence of these factors, or the lack of their substantial development, appeared to account for failure at the individual program youth level, and possibly at the program-area level. Other types of delinquency (arrest) patterns of gang youth (with the exception of drug arrests for program youth at site A, and to some extent at site B) were not generally affected at any of the six sites. The comprehensive gang program model approach appeared to be more effective in addressing distinctive gang-related violence than other delinquency or crime problems (table 14.2).

Gang Factors and Program Outcome

Gang-Problem Context Factors

The six project sites were located in a large metropolitan area, a medium-sized city, and smaller cities in the midwestern, southwestern, and far western parts of the country. The level of the gang problem, and especially the scope and severity of gang violence (but perhaps not drug-selling and drug-using activities of program youth), varied across the sites. Serious gang problems, particularly violence, were present in some cities but not in others. In none of the other five cities was the gang violence problem as severe and long-term as in the site A city. The gang drug problem existed with similar severity across all six cities, but without the presence of serious gang violence in the smaller cities. Youth gangs and/or delinquent groups were part of the history of each of the cities, but lethal gang violence was identified as a problem only recently in the cities of sites B through F.

The youth gang problem addressed by all the projects was defined mainly by government and public agency leaders, based on police arrest and probation data. The problem was concentrated among low-income minority groups, especially among Latino male youth in socially isolated and marginal sectors of each of the cities, particularly in areas undergoing significant population change. The gang problem, however, was not necessarily located in the lowest-income or the highest general-crime-rate areas of the six cities.

At some sites, youth identified by the project as gang members could have been classified by other agencies as members of "tagger" groups or ephemeral delinquent groups. Youth sometimes became members of different gangs in the same local areas over time. Gang youth engaged in a range of unlawful acts in the program and comparison areas. Property, drug, and minor crimes predominated at sites B through F, yet program youth generally were distinctively more violent and chronically delinquent than other delinquent youth at each of the sites (Klein 1971; Thornberry et al. 2003). It was difficult to classify the gang problem simply as emerging or chronic. Somewhat benign gang traditions existed in sites B through F, but in each city the gang problem became more salient with the arrival (or increase) of a low-income, isolated minority population, particularly the youth sector.

While OJJDP's (1994) comprehensive gang program initiative was concerned primarily with reducing gang violence, the drug problem was viewed by local program agency administrators at sites B through F as the most serious of gang

TABLE 14.2
Summary of Program Effect Factors

Program Youth/Project Area Characteristics		Project Site					
		A (Chicago)	B (Mesa)	C (Riverside)	D (Bloomington-Normal)	E (San Antonio)	F (Tucson)
Gang Factors	Level of site/problem	very high/chronic	low/emerging	moderate chronic/emerging	moderate/emerging	moderate chronic/emerging	high chronic/emerging
	Key problem(s)	violence & drugs	general delinquency	violence & drugs	drugs	property	violence & drugs
	Gang structure	large group, cohesive, decentralized	small group	large group, decentralized	large group, diffuse	small group, diffuse	small group, cohesive
	Race/ethnicity (gender)	Mex. Amer. (M)	Mex. Amer. (M & F)	Mex. & Afr. Amer. (M & F)	Afr. Amer. (M & F)	Mex. Amer. (M)	Mex. & Afr. Amer. (M & F)
Gang Membership Change	Program youth membership†	→	↑	×	↑	×	↑
	Project area membership	×	×	×	→	→	NA
Individual Youth Arrest Changes Program vs. Comparison Youth†	Total arrests	×	(↓)	×	×	×	×
	Violence arrests	→	(↓)	(↓)	×	×	×
	Drug arrests	→	(↓)	↑	↑	×	×
	Property arrests	×	↑	×	×	×	×
	Other arrests	×	→	×	×	×	×
Area Arrest Changes Program vs. Comparison Area‡	Total arrests	×	×	×	←	←	NA
	Violence arrests	→	→	→	←	←	NA
	Drug arrests	↑	→	→	×	←	NA
	Property arrests	×	→	×	×	←	NA
	Other arrests	×	×	×	×	←	NA

Levels of change: ↑ = increase, ↓ = decrease, × = no change, NA = data not available.

†Significant statistical changes were determined only at the individual youth levels: ↑ = increase, ≤ 0.001 to ≤ 0.05; ↓ = decrease, = ≤ 0.001 to ≤ 0.05; (↓) = marginal decrease, <0.06 to <0.015; × = no significant change; NA = data not available.

‡Relative difference between program and comparison areas: ↑ = more increase; ↓ = more decrease.

(and nongang) delinquency and crime problems (from surveys of eighty-six administrators at two program periods). The most frequent and serious gang-motivated and gang-related arrests for violence and drugs occurred only at site A. Large, cohesive, enduring gangs with many subunits were present only at site A. Gang members in four of the five other program sites were predominantly Mexican American; in one site they were predominantly African American. Across sites B through F, the minority youth—75 percent to 80 percent males—ranged in age from 12 to 20 years (median age about 16.5 years). The great majority of youth (85 percent) at these sites identified themselves as gang members, less often as associate or former gang members.

Arrest Changes

As in prototype site A, changes between the program and preprogram periods were the principal basis for determining program youth effects in sites B through F. Because of high interviewee dropout rates, self-report data were not as useful for program effect determinations as were police arrest data. Patterns of youth behavioral change (whether based on police arrest or self-report offense data) were similar over the same matched periods at each of the six sites.

The numbers of program and comparison youth at each site are shown in table 14.3. In order to compare changes in arrest patterns of individually matched program and comparison youth—over matched program and preprogram periods—multivariate analyses were also conducted at sites B through F, with statistical controls for age, race/ethnicity, gender, gang membership status, preprogram arrest history, confinement period, and length of time in the program. Program youth had statistically significant reductions in total arrests only at site B. Program youth did better than comparison youth in non-statistically-significant reductions in violence and drug arrests at sites A and B, but only in violence arrests at site C. Drug arrests increased for program youth compared to comparison youth at sites C and D. Also, property arrests went up, but other minor crime arrests went down at site B.

TABLE 14.3
Numbers of Youth at Each Site

Site	Program Youth	Comparision Youth	Total
A	195	298	493
B	109	258	367
C	234	135	369
D	101	134	235
E	110	120	230
F	126	101	227
Total	875	1046	1921

In general, the most positive effects for program youth were reductions in violence and drug arrests, particularly at sites A and B, with a mixed effect at site C. Program youth did not fare as well at sites D, E, and F, where differences in arrests of program youth and comparison youth for most types of offenses were not statistically significant. At the successful sites (A, B, C), youth in the program for two or more years rather than for shorter periods of time had statistically significant reductions in arrests. Surprisingly, whether the youth was presently a gang member, an associate gang member, or a nongang youth did not account for changes in arrest patterns of youth for the different types of offenses, although gang members typically were more chronically and seriously delinquent than were associate gang members, who were in turn more chronically and seriously delinquent than nongang youth. The most powerful predictor of change in arrest patterns at all the sites was *preprogram arrests*; that is, those who had more arrests in the preprogram period had fewer arrests in the program period, and those who had fewer arrests in the preprogram period had more arrests in the program period. This regression pattern, however, applied equally to program and comparison youth. The next most powerful and consistent predictors of reduced arrests of all types were *age* and *gender*. Across all sites, older adolescents and young adults, as well as females, generally did better than younger youth and males in reducing arrests.

Area-Level Arrest Changes

We could not convincingly determine whether changes in arrest patterns of program youth at the individual level were related to (or predicted) changes in arrest patterns at the community-area levels, except possibly for violence arrests at sites A, B, and C.

We attempted to measure changes in gang arrests for program and comparison youth at the program and comparison area levels, at each of the sites. Separate high-gang-crime comparison areas were carefully selected and matched to the program areas (the program and comparison youth samples were from the respective program and comparison areas, except in site A). The comparison areas were equivalent (if not almost identical) to the respective program areas in size, as well as in population, socioeconomic, and high-gang-crime characteristics. We measured changes in area gang arrests as defined by the local police departments, aggregating offenses consistent with the individual youth arrest-category measures: *total arrests*, *violence* (serious and less serious), *drug*, *property*, and *other arrests* (mainly mob action, disorderly conduct, resisting/obstructing a police officer, status offense).

Changes in gang arrests at the matched area level at each site were not necessarily expected to closely parallel those at the individual youth level. Arrests for sample youth included gang and nongang arrests; area-level arrests included only arrests defined by the local police as gang arrests. We could not control for age, race/ethnic, and gender factors but could for program and preprogram periods. The findings indicated that there were no changes in total gang arrests, gang property arrests, or gang "other" arrests that were different in the program areas than in the comparison areas. However, there was strong and consistent evidence that gang violence declined in the successful program sites (A, B, C), but did not in the unsuccessful sites (D, E, F). (We could not obtain local community-area gang arrest statistics at site F.) Gang drug arrests declined in the program areas relative to the comparison areas at sites B and C, but not at site A (where they rose in both the program and comparison areas—more in the program area than in four of the six comparison areas).

Implications for Policy and Theory

Evaluations of the demonstration programs and the utility of the comprehensive gang program model in the six different cities—large, medium, and small—during the middle and latter part of the 1990s clarified the nature of, and what to do about, the gang problem within a theoretical framework oriented primarily toward community social disorganization. The character and context of the youth gang problem was somewhat different across the sites. The evaluations indicated that reductions of gang violence, and to some extent drug-related crime, could be achieved through strong local government interest and support, appropriate public policy change or development, interorganizational collaboration, and interdisciplinary team worker efforts (especially involving former gang influentials as outreach youth workers), all founded on effective interactive community/agency leadership mobilization, social intervention, opportunities provision, suppression, and organizational change and development strategies.

Program youth and area levels of gang-related violence were reduced at three of the six sites. The findings of project success at these sites contrast to the findings of project failure in evaluations of classic community-based gang programs (Gold and Mattick 1974; Klein 1971, 1995a), and of a "total community" gang control project (Miller 1962). A more recent set of process evaluations of community-based but police-dominated gang suppression programs also indicate failure (Decker 2003). It is likely that all the failed projects lacked implementation of an adequate, combined, community-based, interorganizational, multistrategy, and interdisciplinary street-based intervention model to address the youth gang program.

The findings of the present evaluations also suggest that gang intervention theory may need to be modified. Gang and community theorists may have overemphasized the importance of single-dimensional individual, family, group, neighborhood, organizational, or larger societal factors relevant to the genesis and control of the delinquency gang problem (Bursik and Grasmick 1993; Hagedorn 1988; Klein 1971; Sampson, Morenoff, and Earls 1999; Skogan and Hartnett 1997). They may have insufficiently attended to government policies and especially to interorganizational relationships.

Gang program evaluations, when they exist, have been characterized by weak research designs; insufficient attention to use of comparison groups of individual, nonserved youth and comparable gang-problem areas; lack of use of individual- and area-level gang arrest histories (as well as individual youth self-reports of gang crime activities); inadequate definition of a "gang member," or level of gang involvement of youth; failure to specify services or controls provided to each program youth; and failure to use multivariate statistical models to assess individual youth outcome with attention to prior arrests (or self-reported offenses), age, and gender. Models to indicate causal routes between intervention, mediating, and outcome factors of program youth also need to be developed. A great deal more sophisticated, multidimensional research is required to understand the gang problem, and certainly to effectively evaluate gang program processes and outcomes (Decker 2003). We believe the evaluation research of the six sites we have described is a step in that direction.

Notes

Points of view in this chapter are those of the authors and do not necessarily represent the official positions or recommended policies of the U.S. Department of Justice or the Illinois Criminal Justice Information Authority, which were sponsors and funders of the particular program demonstrations and evaluations, or of the School of Social Service Administration of the University of Chicago, which provided supplementary support to complete the evaluations. For detailed case reports, including research methods, tables, and instruments, contact the Office of Juvenile Justice and Delinquency Prevention, Office of Justice Programs, U.S. Department of Justice, and the Illinois Criminal Justice Information Authority.

1. The lead agencies of the comprehensive community-wide interdisciplinary projects were (A) the Chicago Police Department; (B) the Mesa Police Department; (C) the Riverside Police Department (originally, the Office of Educational and Community Initiatives, University of California–Riverside); (D) Project Oz (youth-serving agency); (E) the San Antonio Police Department; and (F) Our Town Family Center (youth and family agency).

2. Gang violence was defined as any violence committed by youth in our samples (who were all gang youth)—whether the incident was of gang interest or not—based on arrest history and self-reports.

3. The site A area-level gang violence arrest reduction was also supported by additional measures and analyses, including a prevalence rate reduction of gang violence for seventeen- to twenty-five-year-old males (taken from U.S. census and CPD gang arrest data) and the perceptions of residents (n = 100) and organization representatives (n = 50) in Little Village compared to an adjoining, almost identical high gang-crime community, between the first and third years of the program.

15

Moving Gang Research Forward

James F. Short, Jr., and Lorine A. Hughes

S UBSTANTIVE CONCLUSIONS FROM the vast literature on youth gangs, reviewed in a variety of ways in the previous pages, are confusing, and often
contradictory; hence, our primary concerns are with methodological and theoretical issues. In this concluding chapter, we situate the study of gangs within
mainstream social and behavioral science and suggest in broad outline the sorts
of changes we feel might make these fields of greater usefulness to each other.
Some of these are under way, as is evident from the foregoing chapters, but the
agenda for gang research will require a great deal of change if this goal is to be
realized.

Much of this chapter is organized around themes that are developed in a
lengthy essay—"The Criminologists' Gang"—by Jack Katz and Curtis Jackson-
Jacobs (2004; hereafter Katz and JJ). Although the foregoing chapters are in
some measure responsive to this wide-ranging and scathing critique of gang
research and theory, issues are identified that require additional comment. We
begin with perhaps the most difficult issue of all: *causation.*

Taking Causation Seriously

Katz and JJ charge that gang studies lack "a good basis for thinking that gangs
cause crime" and that, as a result, "the field is structured on a quiet agreement
not to press the causal question" (93). Among many causal questions, we focus
on those that most concern Katz and JJ:

Do individuals become more criminal by virtue of joining or being in gangs?
Do gangs increase the level of criminal violence in society?

Taking gangs as collective phenomena, what accounts for their emergence, decline, spread, and evolution toward greater or lesser violence?

A good deal of research has addressed the first of these questions, albeit not entirely satisfactorily. Studies consistently find that, compared to their nongang counterparts, gang members are more likely to participate in criminal and violent activities. Moreover, analyses of longitudinal self-report data indicate that gang member involvement in crime and violence peaks during periods of active gang membership. Although such findings generally have been taken as powerful evidence of a gang "facilitative" effect (see Hall, Thornberry, and Lizotte, chapter 4 in this volume), this interpretation is open to question. Katz and JJ offer at least five "rival hypotheses," some of which are more plausible than others. As demonstrated in chapter 1, violence may indeed "cause youth to be seen as gang members" (Katz and JJ, 107) and sometimes "makes groups into gangs" (108; see also Thrasher 1927); but studies conducted over many years do not indicate that individuals typically join or remain in gangs because they want "to get involved in more violence" (107; see Coughlin and Venkatesh 2003; Short and Strodtbeck 1965/1974; Vigil 2002, 2003). The problem—in this Katz and JJ are certainly correct—is that we lack sufficient knowledge of the conditions and processes that result in the myriad observable forms of gang member behavior.

Katz and JJ also challenge empirically based affirmative answers to the second question. Because gangs are now quite widespread, they suggest that crime cannot be attributed to them but "must lie in the contingencies that turn gangs violent" (99). Although reports of gang prevalence in fact vary widely across the United States, the effects of such variations (and changes) have not been studied. However, we can reject on both theoretical and empirical grounds the further argument that because some communities and neighborhoods that do not have gangs "somehow produce crime rates from their youth population equivalent to those in 'gang-infested' areas . . . the relationship of gangs and violence, where it exists, is spurious" (99). Many studies demonstrate that membership in a gang exposes individuals to special circumstances that are conducive to violence: drive-bys, "wolf-packing" and other types of gangbangs (Sanders 1994; Short and Strodtbeck 1965/1974), as well as disputes related to status and impression management (Hughes 2004; see our further discussion of "the normative paradox," below). Unfortunately, however, empirical research and theory are insufficiently developed to specify the precise nature of the gang-crime relationship.

It is the third of Katz and JJ's questions that we believe is most important and that most intrigues us: how to account for gangs' "emergence, decline, spread, and evolution toward greater or lesser violence" (94). Because "social process moves on many levels at once" (Abbott 2001, 117), answers to this question require analysis at multiple levels.[1] For strategic research and analytic purposes, however, different levels of analysis typically are isolated from one another, as "fractals" of phenomena of interest (such as gangs or crime).[2] Indeed, *most gang studies regard gangs as a fractal of crime*. Methodological approaches to studies of gangs likewise become fractionated and isolated from one another—the ecology of gangs, for example, and survey versus ethnographic approaches to their study (Hughes 2005a; chapter 3 in this volume). Consequently, gang researchers bypass many types of inquiry that are important to understanding the causes and consequences of gang formation and change. We begin with issues at the macrolevel.

The Macrolevel of Explanation

Macrolevel studies seek answers to theoretical questions concerning how phenomena of interest relate to their community, organizational, social systemic, or structural contexts. Gang studies at this level have employed a variety of research methods to examine the relationship between neighborhood conditions and the behavior of gangs and their members, for example, a type of research well represented in these chapters. Because their impact on young people has drawn much less macrolevel research attention, we begin this section with a discussion of the large-scale social changes that are the focus of John Hagedorn's chapter 12.

Global changes and their significance for young people have been addressed by Hagedorn in a series of papers over nearly a decade (1998b, 2001, 2002a, 2002b, forthcoming-b; see also selections in Tonry 1997). Hagedorn argues that, as the industrial economy has been replaced by "network" and "information" societies (see Castells 1998/2000, 2000), forces with devastating effects have been unleashed, with the result that some traditional street gangs have been transformed and others have formed anew around powerful resistance identities based on fundamentalist religions, nationalism, hip-hop culture and "gangsta rap," and economic crime. Although his argument requires greater emphasis on *gangs as social actors* than most gang scholars recognize in their studies, examples of street gangs that have been transformed into entrepreneurial gangs with international ties to drug cartels and organized political activity (both in support of and in opposition to the status quo) have been well documented, from Thrasher to the present. Chicago's notorious El Rukns, for example, were transformed from a small south side street gang in the late 1950s, the Blackstone Rangers, to the Black P. Stone Nation, and later to a criminal organization willing to engage in terrorist activity against the United States (Papachristos 2005).[3]

Hagedorn's work and that of his contributors (Hagedorn forthcoming-b) constitute a large portion of the existing scholarly attention to the controversial nature of global changes and their effects on young people. Additional research is under way, however. With support from the Harry F. Guggenheim Foundation, the Social Science Research Council (SSRC) program on Global Security and Cooperation includes efforts to gather data on the "impact of armed conflict on children" in order to understand "youth in organized violence," "from participation in war and armed conflicts (including military and paramilitary groups) to organized forms of urban violence in gangs, protection rackets and street children organized around violent acts" (SSRC 2005, 25). A December 2004 workshop held in Pretoria, South Africa, brought together fieldworkers and scholars from Central and South America, Africa, Australia, and the United States (including John Hagedorn), to focus "on the development of better understandings of the contexts in which youth create, instigate, and are inducted into organized forms of violence, especially the situations that enable these organizations to flourish and evolve."[4]

> The workshop examined the role that organized forms of violence play in young people's lives; developed new theoretical and analytical insights on the issue of youth in organized violence; and encouraged a comparative analysis of the various forms of organized violence in which young people are engaged, providing perspectives that might not otherwise occur when viewing these in isolation. Drawing directly from their own field research, participants ... analyzed the complexity of the relationship between youth and organized violence and the various factors that contribute to their involvement ... for example, how issues such as poverty influence youth's involvement in violence in contexts as far-ranging as the Brazilian *favelas*, to youth gangs in the U.S. and Australia, and child soldiers in Sierra Leone, along with the prevalence of death squads and vigilantism in South Africa ... compared with situations such as the circumstances of child soldiers in Colombia and Sri Lanka, and protection rackets in Nigeria, as well as transnational issues such as the export of gang culture from Los Angeles to El Salvador. (SSRC 2005, 25)

The conditions giving rise to these concerns are real, albeit inadequately documented. Whether and how they relate to the traditional gangs on which the vast majority of youth gang research is focused has not been systematically studied; nor has the range of institutionalized gang adaptations.[5]

Are All Gangs, like Politics, Local?

Global developments notwithstanding, it remains the case that social life is fundamentally *local* in character[6] (Sampson 2002). Globalization affects commerce and communication, however, erecting barriers and creating both licit and illicit opportunities at the local level. As groups and individuals are bypassed by economies and are disenfranchised, some will form or affiliate with gangs; but treating "all gang members like mafia kingpins or terrorist masterminds is overestimating people who, more often than not, are petty delinquents" (Papachristos 2005, 55). The challenge is to document "the everyday realities of gang members on their own turf and in their own terms" (Katz and JJ 2004, 94)—the background conditions of most immediate concern to these young people (including how they are affected by global forces).

Katz and JJ note that no one except Mark Fleisher (1998) has "attempted to describe a 'day-in-the-life,' or what gang members do with others continuously and in detail, over any significant stretch of time" (101). More of this type of research is needed to counter the distortion that results from the widespread tendency to conflate gangs with crime. We need to know more about the reality of the daily lives of gang members, individually and collectively, not just on the streets, but also at work, in school, in family settings, and in relation to other social institutions. The advantages of this type of study extend beyond description, crosscutting multiple levels of explanation and forging linkages between them (Short 1998). Although better data on local conditions and group processes at the microlevel (interactional and situational) clearly are necessary, much can be learned from existing data sets, such as the brief and very different natural histories of the Nobles and the early Vice Lords, described in chapter 1. Field observations from Short and Strodtbeck's (1965/1974) Chicago study reveal a great deal about local street life and about gang members' relationships to each other, their families, and other community actors and institutions. Systematic analyses of these data are on our research agenda.[7]

The Normative Paradox

Studies strongly suggest that individual and group dynamics associated with crime and violence differ between gang and nongang members and situations and that being a gang member alters the character of interpersonal and intergroup interaction (e.g., Short and Strodtbeck 1965/1974). Yet there is much that we do not fully understand as to why this is so.

Among the most puzzling aspects of group dynamics in gang contexts is the role of group norms in both individual and collective behaviors. Early analyses of Short and Strodtbeck's data indicated that, even under provocative circumstances, participation in fights involving rival gangs varied greatly among gang members, suggesting that gang norms supporting fighting, toughness, and defense of the gang against rivals were insufficient to account for violent behavior (Short and Strodtbeck 1965/1974, 203–7; see also Hughes 2005b). Similarly, the strong and clear gang (and community) norm of active resistance by whites to black invasion of their communities was recognized and honored in quite different ways among white gang members, and was ignored by some (Short and Strodtbeck, 112–14). Yet Papachristos (2004c) finds that gang homicides differ from nongang homicides, and that gang homicides, in turn, differ in their normative referents. Intergang and intergang-nation homicides, for example, occur as a result of retaliation for external challenges to group solidarity, while intragang homicide and conflict result from internal challenges to norms related to group cohesion, and intranation homicide and conflict stem from status contests between groups among which gang norms prescribe group status equality.[8]

Retaliation and status concerns also figure prominently in other criminological research (e.g., Fagan and Wilkinson 1998; Kubrin and Weitzer 2003; Mullins, Wright, and Jacobs 2004; Wilkinson 2003). Donald Black (1993) and Mark Cooney (1998) note that the violence associated with such concerns appears to be overwhelmingly "moralistic" rather than "predatory." That is, it occurs in response to "a violation of standards of acceptable behavior" rather than as a means of achieving personal gratification (Cooney, 4). A pressing task for gang researchers is to determine the conditions under which violence in the gang context is (or is not) similarly motivated. Our recent analysis of Short and Strodtbeck's (1965/1974) Chicago gang data confirms the importance of status management and of retaliation as a pretext for disputes, especially those involving members of rival gangs (Hughes and Short 2005; see also Decker 1996), but other processes were also shown to influence the likelihood of violent/nonviolent dispute resolutions. Finer-grained comparative analyses will be necessary if processes related to specific behaviors are to be fully understood.

Gang and Youth Cultures

With few exceptions, gang researchers have neglected the relationships between gang and youth subcultures, variations of which have crossed virtually all international boundaries since James Coleman and his associates wrote so perceptively about the social forces that propelled youth culture following World War II (Coleman et al. 1974). Toward the end of their essay, Katz and JJ note that among the images of gang members portrayed in gang studies is that of "boys redefining their maintenance of childish ways with violent dispositions until they mature out of the extended youth that American affluence now makes possible for an 'underclass' that suits up for battle in designer-labeled clothes" (106). The irony of this image should not obscure the realities, however. Urban ethnographers such as Mercer Sullivan and Elijah Anderson have documented the attractions and distractions of symbolic elements of youth culture and the "code of the street."

> In each community the adolescent male peer group serves as a domain of interaction in limbo separated from household, school, and workplace. The cultural meaning of crime is constructed in this bounded milieu of interaction out of materials supplied from . . . the local area in which they spend their time almost totally unsupervised and undirected by adults, and the consumerist youth culture promoted in the mass media. Lacking the legitimate employment that would allow them to participate in this youth culture, they transform their local environment through criminal activities into sources of funds. (Sullivan 1989, 248–49)

> Youths typically place a high premium on eyewear, leather jackets, expensive sneakers, and other items that take on significance as status symbols. An impoverished inner-city youth who can acquire these material things is able to feel big and impress others, but these others may then attempt to relieve him of his property in order to feel big themselves and impress still others. (Anderson 1999, 78)

A further irony lies in the fact that many youth culture fads and fashions have their origins in the ghettos and barrios of cities. At least since the 1960s, Chicago gangs had subgroups of gospel and popular music singers who sang their "doo-wops" out on the street and practiced faithfully (Short 1998).[9] Upon rare occasions, they achieved a measure of success with recordings of their music. Dance styles such as the Watusi and the Horse were observed at an Egyptian Cobra–sponsored dance that was held in the Maxwell Street YMCA during the early 1960s, before they achieved recognition in youth culture (Short, 18). More recently, as Hagedorn notes, gang culture has become an important part of youth culture in many places, and the "trickle-up" of clothing fashions finds manufacturers seeking "a window on the world of the street" (Gladwell 1997, 78) to discern preferences among young people in U.S. cities.

We need to know a great deal more about youth and gang cultures and the role they play in gang formation and behavior. Too often, we fail to look beyond the gang context, to the relationship between gangs and the world around them. Indeed, most gang studies "refer primarily to other gang studies" (Katz and JJ, 97), ignoring research on young people in general and the broader social forces that influence them. Such exemplary works as Gary Schwartz's comparative examination of "youth and authority in America" have much to offer, however. In introducing his book, *Beyond Conformity or Rebellion: Youth and Authority in America*, Schwartz (1987, 3) writes:

> What is significant for the culture at large is going on within the youth culture. The ways in which young people define themselves in relation to their peers and adult authorities illuminates as much about the conflicts implicit in their parents' aspirations as it does about the meaning of youth culture identities and styles. Instead of thinking of youth as a force for conserving or changing societal institutions, we shall look at them as people who are working their way through tensions that exist in the environing culture.

If we are to understand the nature and behavioral consequences of gangs, closer attention must be paid to the interplay between youth and gang cultures. Here again, Thrasher's comparative perspective—the major theme of Klein's chapter 9—is badly needed.

Comparative Research

Katz and JJ argue that the field's neglect of "the causal question" has led to the virtual abandonment of "the healthy comparative perspective in which it was born" and the related inability to explain the allure of gangs over alternate forms of association:

> Thrasher's rich comparative description of forms of childhood social organization was ignored. Gang criminologists ridiculed the "play groups" that he abundantly described. Such innocent associations were absurdly innocuous in comparison with the seriously destructive gangs they studied. . . . Today, virtually no researcher documents gangs in comparison with the various other social forms in which adolescents associate (Katz and JJ 2004, 95).

Several of the foregoing chapters exemplify and/or urge comparative research. They note, for example, that differently structured youth groups (some of them street gangs) are associated with different behaviors (Klein; Sullivan) and that the role of street gangs in the lives of their members varies among young adult females (Fleisher), skinhead males (Simi), ethnic groups in Australia (White), and young people subject to powerful global forces (Hagedorn). Conflicting findings regarding the significance of neighborhoods for gang behavior (Hall, Thornberry, and Lizotte; Papachristos and Kirk) and of strategies for gang and violence control (Olson and Dooley; Spergel, Wa, and Sosa) add to the research agenda, as do relatively new research methodologies and theoretical perspectives (Fleisher; Papachristos; Sanders and Lankenau).

With its emphasis on cross-national comparisons, the Eurogang Research Program is the most ambitious street gang research effort ever undertaken. Although the number of chapters and contributors to the program's second volume is smaller than that of the first (see Klein et al. 2001), methodological and empirical advances are evident in the second such volume (Decker and Weerman 2005). The first volume represents an early summary of issues, methods, and preliminary findings from a broad spectrum of countries and contributors. The second, as the title indicates, is focused more on methods and findings regarding "European street gangs and troublesome youth groups."[10]

Despite its explicit focus on gangs *and* other problematic groupings, the Eurogang Program excludes from their concerns "crime cartels, terrorist groups, prison gangs, motorcycle gangs, and a whole host of youthful groups . . . which help one transition to adulthood without causing the authorities much trouble" (Klein 2005), thus effectively ruling out comparisons with these associations. Work toward a more inclusive typology clearly is needed.

The Role (and the Future) of Typologies

Both Sullivan's (2005; chapter 2 in this volume) and Maxson and Klein's (1995; see also Klein 2002) typologies are drawn from their own rich backgrounds of research. They approach the issue differently, however. Sullivan's typology is explicitly heuristic, while Maxson and Klein's (traditional, neotraditional, compressed, collective, and specialty) is meant to be operational in the service of comparative research and crime control. Sullivan distinguishes three "analytic categories of association," only one of which (named gangs) he considers a street gang. Klein and Maxson limit their typology to street gangs, as defined by the Eurogang research group on the basis of structural characteristics and crime patterns. Sullivan's typology (cliques, action-sets, and named gangs) includes groups that meet in the process of some coordinated activity (similar to Sarnecki 2001) and presumably could incorporate many groups specifically excluded by Maxson and Klein, such as skinheads and bikers.[11] However, with their "minimalist consensus" definition of street gangs and the coordinated research activity of the Eurogang program (a major feature of which is the use of standardized research instruments, including ethnographic guidelines), the Maxson and Klein typology lends itself to comparative research on an unprecedented scale (see Decker and Weerman 2005; Klein, chapter 9 in this volume; Klein et al. 2001). The comparative advantage of this program is evident in chapter 11, where Rob White uses the Eurogang definition in his survey of youth gang research in Australia.

The two typologies have elements in common. Both are street-oriented and, except for "action-sets," include durability as an indication of continuity of association. Both include involvement in illegal activity, Sullivan stressing the importance of public identity and Maxson and Klein stressing group identity with such activity. Neither satisfies the criticism that gang definitions that include illegal behavior are tautological, and both ignore issues related to gang emergence and development (Katz and JJ 2004; Short 1998). However, both are amenable to comparative study of conventional as well as illegal behavior, and both encourage contextual analysis and permit differentiation of cliques that may be part of some larger group.

Although the best typologies are useful for many purposes, different typologies may be necessary for different purposes. A typology of individuals may be useful for understanding and changing the behavior of individuals (see Moffitt 1993), for example, while a typology of groups may be necessary for understanding and changing the behavior of groups, as might be inferred from several chapters in this book. The ultimate goal, of course, is to integrate typologies in ways that would be most useful for both types of understanding and for developing practices and policies related to change and control.

Social Control and Social Policy

Scholars, citizens, politicians, and practitioners of many stripes quarrel over what to do with or to gangs. Attention to these and many other questions is important not only for causal understanding of gangs but also for public and policy reasons.

The importance of informal social control is a major theme throughout the history of social and behavioral science research and theory, clearly so in criminology and its parent disciplines (Sampson, Morenoff, and Earls 1999; Sampson, Raudenbush, and Earls 1997; Short forthcoming-a). It was uppermost in Shaw and McKay's work and in the Chicago Area Project that grew out of that work (Shaw and McKay 1942). Late in his book, Thrasher refers to Shaw's collaboration with W. I. Thomas on the idea "of solving the problems of difficult boys by formulating projects for them" (Thrasher 1927/1963, 511/353). Under two photographs, one of "a destructive gang" and below it the Boy Scout troop into which it was "transformed," he notes that the pictures illustrate

> how a project may be worked out for a whole group. The alternative method of
> handling a gang is to break it up and give the boys individual or group projects in
> a larger frame of reference, such as that provided by the Union League Boys' Club.
> The important point to be noted is that where the gang is broken up the social

world of the boy disintegrates and a new one must be substituted for it—not of the artificial type found in an institution, but one which will provide for a redirection of his energies in the habitat in which he must live.

Malcolm Klein and Cheryl Maxson's *Street Gang Patterns and Policies* (forthcoming) is a comprehensive review of what is known about gangs and crime control and the relationship between them. The Maxson-Klein typology figures less prominently in their "model for policy choices" than do other concerns, such as whether individuals or groups are to be the focus for change, program aims (prevention, intervention, or suppression), and the targeting of appropriate youths, group processes and structures, and community contexts. Informal control, in the form of work with families, schools, and job markets, is given less attention than are formally structured programs, in part because Klein and Maxson are interested above all in the planning that goes into structured programs and their careful evaluation.

Ironically, in view of the group nature of delinquent behavior (and certainly gangs), Klein and Maxson's review finds that fifty-five of the fifty-eight gang control efforts studied targeted individual gang members, while only nineteen were concerned with community contexts, five with group process, and none with gang structures. Gang suppression was the strategy employed by twenty-four of these efforts, prevention of nineteen, and only twelve used a gang intervention strategy. Klein and Maxson (forthcoming, chapter 8) offer some interesting comparative observations about gang control in different cultural contexts:

> In the far east, most notably China and Japan, accountability to one's group is paramount. Social change is oriented to the manipulation of the individual's accountability to his or her group affiliations. In Western Europe, individual responsibility tends to be located in community structures, with attendant greater use of social welfare approaches to problems of deviant behavior. Gangs in the far east are cast as group problems, and in Europe as social welfare and immigration problems. Yet in America, gangs are groups spawned in describable community contexts, but we respond to them much more as requiring individual change efforts.

The most comprehensive of the programs reviewed by Klein and Maxson is the "comprehensive, community-wide gang program model." The Little Village program, as it came to be known, utilized prevention, intervention, and suppression strategies aimed at changing both individuals and groups and working with community contexts. Although they are lavish in their praise of the comprehensiveness of the program and those that were patterned after it,

Klein and Maxson are critical of its implementation and dispute the modest success claimed by Spergel and colleagues in chapter 14.

Controversy of this sort is both healthy and necessary for the advance of knowledge and its application. It cautions us against the type of thinking that forms the basis of so much of the policy that has developed around gangs in the United States. Katz and JJ (2004, 106) speak eloquently—if somewhat exaggeratedly—to this issue:

> The deepest concern brought to the reading of gang criminology is that of defining the image of the low-income, minority male. Images matter. It is not an array of statistical correlations, but summarizing images, or, less politely, stereotypes, that go into the voting booth and that also haunt the shadows of policy making across all levels and branches of governmental power.

Given the current focus of gang control efforts, gang membership has become a huge and extremely difficult criminal justice problem that cries out for systematic study and policy attention. Although rigorous attempts to study the prevalence and experiences of gang members at all stages in the criminal justice system are rare, David Olson and Brendan Dooley find that recidivism rates among gang member probationers and parolees are higher than those among their nongang counterparts (chapter 13). The differences are especially great among probationers. Whether, or the extent to which, this may reflect police targeting of gang offenders who have been released on probation rather than incarcerated is unknown; however, gang membership appears to pose special problems for offenders and for agents of formal social control.

The formulation of sound policy clearly is needed now more than ever, as gangs continue to proliferate (see Egley, Howell, and Major 2004; Klein 1995a) and consume a greater share of criminal justice resources. Policy, however, depends on good research. It is our hope that this chapter will help push gang research in that direction. We turn now to some final observations.

Conclusion

A large number of problematic issues have been discussed in this brief chapter, and suggestions have been made as to how they might be addressed. Chapter 3's emphasis on contexts clearly applies to all these issues. Causation at all levels requires study of the "recurrent patterns of action" and the "recurrent structures" that constitute social life (Abbott 1999, 220), certainly including gang social life. As a way of identifying and bringing together such patterns and structures, contextualization requires attention to processes and mechanisms that are associated with gang formation and changes in form and behavior and study of gangs in different times and places. It also means placing gang behaviors in contexts of interaction in order to explain the mechanisms by which gangs "facilitate" behaviors. Contributing authors of previous chapters, by admonition or example, address contextualization in quite different ways, some more successfully than others. We suggest that greater effort to contextualize findings be made in studies of gangs at all levels of explanation. With Katz and JJ, we also urge that causation be elevated to a top priority in gang research, clearly including gang formation and change. Study of gang formation and change is especially important because it would obviate "the hoary issue of defining what a gang is" (Katz and JJ 2004, 116). The "meaning or meanings of gangs" would thereby be "empirically settled by finding the social processes that historically lead to different types." Only then will we be able "to set aside the dummy variable gang/non-gang youth that is employed by police" and many others (117). Finally, bringing the broader social and behavioral science literatures and the study of gangs together will ensure that they become mutually enriching.

Notes

1. Abbott is writing about the relationship between history and sociology and sociology's strategy of isolating historical epochs for causal analysis, but the point applies to all social life, certainly to youth gangs and gang members.

2. In general terms, *fractals* refer to different ways of looking at a given phenomenon, or a class of phenomena, for example, objectivist (or realist) versus constructionist, culture versus structure, or in level of explanation terms, macrolevel versus micro- or individual levels. Abbott (2001) refers to "fractal thinking" as a means of conceptualizing relational characteristics among fractals.

3. Reports from print and electronic media also contain much relevant information, for example, websites such as those referenced by Hagedorn in chapter 12 of this volume. *USA Today* of March 24, 2005, included articles titled "Ex-child soldier now Kenya's hottest rapper" and "Tragic challenge of child soldiers"; and the continuing role of gangs in Haiti's tragic history is often in the news.

4. Papachristos (2005) notes that the spread of gang culture, especially to Central and South America, almost certainly has occurred, in part, as a result of the U.S. policy of deporting thousands of immigrants with criminal records, as well as because of the Internet.

5. Katz and JJ also note that "historically critical events" may be "additional necessary conditions" for gang emergence and change over time. The events of September 11, 2001, and thereafter seem clearly to have influenced youth groups in many ways, but they have been little studied (see Calhoun, Price, and Timmer 2002; Hershberg and Moore 2002; Short forthcoming-b).

6. Longtime Speaker of the U.S. House of Representatives, Thomas P. "Tip" O'Neill, famously observed that "All politics is local." A recent RAND Corporation study avers

that "all *terrorism* is 'local,' or at least will start locally" (Wermuth 2004, 4, emphasis added).

7. We are grateful to Irving Spergel for making available to us data from this project for further study.

8. Papachristos (2004c) notes that these findings support Gould's (2003) theory that violence is most likely to occur among symmetric groups in contests of symbolic measures of social status.

9. Interference with practice occasionally led to threatened violence.

10. Two chapters present comparative data from the United States and the Netherlands and Scandinavian countries, respectively. Among advances in the second volume, greater attention is paid to the impact of family relationships and broader social and cultural forces on young people in the nations and communities being studied.

11. Interestingly, Pete Simi's chapter 10 finds that most skinhead gangs conform to the Eurogang definition of street gangs. Klein's earlier (1995a, 22) characterization of skinheads as "inside . . . working on their written materials; or if outside, they're looking for a target, not just lounging around" may have to be revised.

References

Abbott, Andrew. 1997. Of time and space: The contemporary relevance of the Chicago school. *Social Forces* 75:1149–82.

———. 1999. *Department and discipline: Sociology at one hundred.* Chicago: University of Chicago Press.

———. 2001. *Chaos of disciplines.* Chicago: University of Chicago Press.

Abbott, Andrew, and James Sparrow. Forthcoming. Structures of sociological action in World War II America. In *Sociology in America,* ed. Craig C. Calhoun. Chicago: University of Chicago Press.

Abdullah, Ibrahim. 2002. Youth, culture, and rebellion: Understanding Sierra Leone's wasted decade. *Critical Arts: A Journal of South-North Cultural and Media Studies* 16:19–37.

Aburish, Said K. 1998. *Arafat: From defender to dictator.* New York: Bloomsbury.

Adamson, Christopher. 2000. Defensive localism in white and black: A comparative history of Euro-American and African-American youth gangs. *Ethnic and Racial Studies* 23:272–98.

Addams, Jane. 1920/1960. *Twenty years at Hull-House.* New York: Signet.

Adimora, Adaora A., and Victor J. Schoenbach. 2005. Social context, sexual networks, and racial disparities in rates of sexually transmitted infections. *The Journal of Infectious Diseases* 191:S115–22.

Agar, Michael. 1996. Recasting the "ethno" in "epidemiology." *Medical Anthropology* 16:391–403.

Alter, M. J., E. E. Mast, L. A. More, and H. S. Margolis. 1998. Hepatitis C. *Infectious Disease Clinics of North America* 12:13–26.

Amnesty International. 2004. *2004 report.* www.amnestyusa.org/annualreport/index .html (accessed November 14, 2004).

Anderson, Carolyn J., Stanley Wasserman, and Bradley Crouch. 1999. A p* primer: Logit models for social networks. *Social Networks* 21:37–66.

Anderson, Elijah. 1992. Streetwise: Race, class, and change in an urban community. Chicago: University of Chicago Press.

———. 1999. *Code of the streets: Decency, violence, and the moral life of the inner city.* New York: W.W. Norton and Company.

Anderson, Erik. 1987. Skinheads: From Britain to San Francisco via punk rock. M.A. thesis, Washington State University.

Anderson, James F., Nancie J. Mangels, and Laronistine Dyson. 2001. A gang by any other name is just a gang: Towards an expanded definition of gangs. *Journal of Gang Research* 8:19–34.

Anti-Defamation League. 1989. Annual Report. New York: Anti-Defamation League.

———. 1995. Annual Report. New York: Anti-Defamation League.

———. 2004. Nazi Lowriders. www.adl.org/learn.ext_us/nlr (accessed March 12, 2004).

Arizona Department of Juvenile Corrections Research and Development, National Council on Crime and Delinquency. 2002. *Outcome evaluation fifth annual report.*

Asbury, Herbert. 1927. *The gangs of New York.* New York: Capricorn.

Aumair, Megan, and Ian Warren. 1994. Characteristics of juvenile gangs in Melbourne. *Youth Studies Australia* 13:40–44.

Ball, Richard A., and G. David Curry. 1995. The logic of definition in criminology: Purpose and methods for defining "gangs." *Criminology* 33:225–24.

Baron, Steven. 1997. Canadian male street skinheads: Street gang or street terrorist? *Canadian Review of Sociology and Anthropology* 34:125–54.

Batagelj, Vladimir, and Andrej Mrvar. 2004. *Pajek: Package for large networks.* Version 1.00. Ljubljana: University of Ljubljana.

Battin, Sara R., Karl G. Hill, Robert D. Abbott, Richard F. Catalano, and J. David Hawkins. 1998. The contribution of gang membership to delinquency beyond delinquent friends. *Criminology* 36:93–115.

Battin-Pearson, Sara R., Terrence P. Thornberry, J. David Hawkins, and Marvin D. Krohn. 1998. Gang membership, delinquent peers, and delinquent behavior. *OJJDP Juvenile Justice Bulletin.* Washington, DC: U.S. Department of Justice, Office of Justice Programs, Office of Juvenile Justice and Delinquency Prevention.

Bauman, Zygmunt. 1998. *Globalization: The human consequences.* New York: Columbia University Press.

Becker, Howard S. 1970. Practitioners of vice and crime. In *Pathways to Data,* ed. Robert W. Habenstein, 30–49. Chicago: Aldine.

———. 1999. The Chicago school, so-called. *Qualitative Sociology* 22:3–12.

Bell, Daniel. 1960. *The end of ideology: On the exhaustion of political ideas in the fifties.* New York: The Free Press.

Benda, Brent B., Robert F. Corwyn, and Nancy J. Toombs. 2001. From adolescent 'serious offender' to adult felon: A predictive study of offense progression. *Journal of Offender Rehabilitation* 32:79–108.

Benda, Brent B., and Connie L. Tollett. 1999. A study of recidivism of serious and persistent offenders among adolescents. *Journal of Criminal Justice* 27: 111–26.

Bennett, Andy, and Richard Peterson. 2004. *Music scenes: Local, translocal, and virtual.* Nashville, TN: Vanderbilt University Press.

Berbrier, Mitch. 2000. The victim ideology of white supremacists and white separatists in the United States. *Sociological Focus* 33:175–91.

Berkman, Lisa F., and Ichiro Kawachi, eds. 2000. *Social epidemiology.* Oxford: Oxford University Press.

Bessant, Judith, and Richard Hil, eds. 1997. *Youth, crime and the media.* Hobart, Australia: National Clearinghouse for Youth Studies.

Beyers, Jennifer M., Rolf Loeber, Per-Olof H. Wikström, and Magda Stouthamer-Loeber. 2001. What predicts adolescent violence in better-off neighborhoods? *Journal of Abnormal Child Psychology* 29:369–81.

Bhopal, Raj. 2002. *Concepts of epidemiology: An integrated introduction to the ideas, theories, principles and methods of epidemiology.* Oxford: Oxford University Press.

Bjorgo, Tore. 1998. Entry, bridge burning, and exit options: What happens to young people who join racist groups. In *Nation and race: The developing Euro-American racist subculture,* eds. Jeffrey Kaplan and Tore Bjorgo, 231–58. Boston: Northeastern University Press.

Black, Donald. 1993. *The social structure of right and wrong.* San Diego: Academic.

Blazak, Randy. 2001. White boys to terrorist men: Target recruitment of Nazi skinheads. *The American Behavioral Scientist* 44:982–1000.

Blee, Kathleen. 2002. *Inside organized racism: Women in the hate movement.* Berkeley: University of California Press.

Blumstein, Alfred, Jacqueline Cohen, Jeffrey A. Roth, and Christy A. Visher, eds. 1986. *Criminal careers and "career criminals."* Vol. 1. Washington, DC: National Academy.

Blumstein, Alfred, and Joel Wallman. 2000. *The crime drop in America.* New York: Cambridge University Press.

Blush, Steven. 2001. *American hardcore: A tribal history.* Los Angeles: Feral.

Boissevain, Jeremy. 1974. *Friends of friends: Networks, manipulators, and coalitions.* Oxford: Basil Blackwell.

Booth, Martin. 1999. *The Dragon Syndicates: The global phenomenon of the Triads.* New York: Carroll and Graf.

Borgatti, Steven, Martin G. Everett, and Linton C. Freeman. 1999. *UCINET: Software for social network analysis.* Boston: Analytic Technologies. www.analytictech.com (accessed November 21, 2004).

———. 2002. *UCINET 6 for Windows: Software for social network analysis.* Harvard: Analytic Technologies.

Bourdieu, Pierre. 1999. *Acts of resistance: Against the tyranny of the market.* Translated by Richard Nice. New York: The New Press.

Bowker, Lee H., and Malcolm W. Klein. 1983. The etiology of female juvenile delinquency and gang membership: A test of psychological and social structural explanations. *Adolescence* 18:739–51.

Brake, Michael. 1974. The skinheads: An English working class subculture. *Youth and Society* 6:179–99.

Bratton, William, and Peter Knobler. 1998. *Turnaround: How America's top cop reversed the crime epidemic.* New York: Random House.

Brotherton, David C., and Luis Barrios. 2003. *Between black and gold: The street politics of the Almighty Latin King and Queen Nation.* New York: Columbia University Press.

———. 2004. *The Almighty Latin King and Queen Nation: Street politics and the transformation of a New York gang city.* New York: Columbia University Press.

Brownfield, David, Ann Marie Sorenson, and Kevin M. Thompson. 2001. Gang membership, race, and social class: A test of the group hazard and master status hypotheses. *Deviant Behavior* 22:73–89.

Browning, Katharine, Terrence P. Thornberry, and Pamela K. Porter. 1999. *Highlights of findings from the Rochester Youth Development Study.* Bulletin. Washington, DC: U.S. Department of Justice, Office of Justice Programs, Office of Juvenile Justice and Delinquency Prevention.

Brymmer, Richard A. 1998. Hanging out with the good 'ole boys, gangsters, and other disreputable characters: Field research, quantitative research, and exceptional events. In *Fieldwork settings: Accomplishing ethnographic research,* ed. Scott Grills. Newbury Park, CA: Sage.

Bureau of Justice Statistics. 1993. *Survey of state prison inmates, 1991.* Washington, DC: U.S. Department of Justice, Office of Justice Programs.

Bursik, Robert J., Jr. 1988. Social disorganization and theories of crime and delinquency: Problems and prospects. *Criminology* 26:519–51.

———. 2002. The systemic model of gang behavior: A reconsideration. In *Gangs in America,* ed. C. Ronald Huff, 71-81. 3rd ed. Thousand Oaks, CA: Sage.

Bursik, Robert J., Jr., and Harold G. Grasmik. 1993. *Neighborhoods and crime: The dimensions of effective community control.* New York: Lexington.

Burt, Ronald S. 1991. *STRUCTURE.* Version 4.2. New York: Columbia University

———. 1992. *Structural holes.* Cambridge, MA: Harvard University Press.

———. 1997. The contingent value of social capital. *Administrative Science Quarterly* 42:339–65.

———. 2004. Structural holes and good ideas. *American Journal of Sociology* 110: 349–99.

Butts, Jeffrey A., and Jeremy Travis. 2002. *The rise and fall of American youth violence: 1980 to 2000.* Washington, DC: Urban Institute.

Caldiera, Teresa P. R. 2000. *City of walls: Crime, segregation, and citizenship in Sao Paulo.* Berkeley: University of California.

Calhoun, Craig, Paul Price, and Ashley Timmer, eds. 2002. *Understanding September 11.* New York: The New Press.

Campbell, Anne. 1991. *The girls in the gang.* 2d ed. Oxford: Blackwell.

Campbell, Bruce B., and Arthur D. Brenner. 2000. *Death squads in global perspective: Murder with deniability.* New York: St. Martin's.

Canetti, Elias. 1960/1984. *Crowds and power.* New York: Farrar, Straus, and Giroux.

Carney, Frank J., Hans W. Mattick, and John D. Calloway. 1969. *Action on the streets.* New York: Association.

Carrington, Peter J., John Scott, and Stanley Wasserman, eds. 2005. *Models and methods in social network analysis*. New York: Cambridge University Press.

Cartwright, Desmond S., and Kenneth I. Howard. 1966. Multivariate analysis of gang delinquency: Ecological influences. *Multivariate behavioral research* 1:321–71.

Cartwright, Desmond S., Barbara Tomson, and Hershey Schwartz, eds. 1975. *Gang delinquency*. Monterey, CA: Brooks/Cole.

Casey, Conerly. 2002. "States of emergency": Islam, youth gangs, and the politically unseeable. Unpublished manuscript, University of California, Los Angeles.

Castells, Manuel. 1997. *The power of identity*. Vol. 2, *The information age: Economy, society and culture*. Malden, MA: Blackwell.

———. 1998/2000. *End of millennium*. Vol. 3, *The information age: Economy, society and culture*. Malden, MA: Blackwell.

———. 2000. *The rise of the network society*. Vol. 1, *The information age: Economy, society and culture*. 2nd ed. Malden, MA: Blackwell.

Catalano, Shannan M. 2004. *Criminal victimization, 2003*. Washington, DC: Bureau of Justice Statistics.

Cates, Willard, Jr. 1999. Estimates of the incidence and prevalence of sexually transmitted diseases in the United States. *Sexually Transmitted Diseases* 26:S2–S7.

Cavan, Shari. 1972. *Hippies of the Haight*. St. Louis: New Critics.

Centers for Disease Control and Prevention. 2000. Gonorrhea-United States, 1998. *MMWR* 49:538–42.

———. 2001. Young people at risk: HIV/AIDS among America's youth. www.thebody.com/cdc/youth.html (accessed April 28, 2005).

———. 2003. HIV/AIDS Surveillance Report, 14. www.cdc.gov/hiv/stats/hasrlink.html (accessed April 28, 2005).

Cepeda, Alice, and Avelardo Valdez. 2003. Risk behaviors among young Mexican American gang-associated females: Sexual relations, partying, substance use, and crime. *Journal of Adolescent Research* 18:90–107.

Chesney-Lind, Meda, and John M. Hagedorn, eds. 1999. *Female gangs in America: Essays on girls, gangs and gender*. Chicago: Lake View Press.

Children in Organised Armed Violence. 2002. *From guerrillas to gangs*. www.paranaonline.org.br (accessed November 18, 2004).

———. 2003. Country reports, Rio de Janeiro, Viva Rio. www.coav.org.br (accessed November 14, 2004).

———. 2004. *Youth gangs using arsenal inherited from Haitian government*. www.coav.org.br (accessed November 14, 2004).

Chin, Ko-lin. 1996. *Chinatown gangs: Extortion, enterprise, and ethnicity*. New York: Oxford University Press.

Clarke, John. 1976. The skinheads and the magical recovery of community. In *Resistance through rituals*, eds. Stuart Hall and Tony Jefferson, 99–102. London: Hutchinson.

Clatts, Michael C., W. Rees Davis, Jo L. Sotheran, and Aylin Atillasoy. 1998. Correlates and distribution of HIV risk behaviors amongst homeless youth in New York City: Implications for prevention services and policies. *Child Welfare* 37: 195–207.

Clatts, Michael C., Robert Heimer, Nadia Abdala, Lloyd A. Goldsamt, Jo L. Sotheran, Kenneth T. Anderson, Toni M. Gallo, Lee D. Hoffer, Pellegrino A. Luciano, and Tassos Kyriakides. 1999. HIV-1 Transmission in injection paraphernalia: Heating drug solutions may inactivate HIV-1. *Journal of Acquired Immune Deficiency Syndrome and Retrovirology* 22:194–99.

Clatts, Michael C., Dorinda L. Welle, and Lloyd A. Goldsamt. 2001. Reconceptualizing the interaction of drug and sexual risk among MSM speed users: Notes toward an ethnoepidemiology. *AIDS and Behavior* 5:115–29.

Cloward, Richard A., and Lloyd E. Ohlin. 1960. *Delinquency and opportunity: A theory of delinquent gangs.* Glencoe, IL: The Free Press.

Coffin, Phillip O., Sandro Galea, Jennifer Ahern, Andrew C. Leon, David Vlahov, and Kenneth Tardiff. 2003. Opiates, cocaine and alcohol combinations in accidental drug overdose deaths in New York City, 1990–1998. *Addiction* 98:739–47.

Cohen, Albert K. 1955. *Delinquent boys: The culture of the gang.* Glencoe, IL: The Free Press.

Cohen Albert K., Alfred R. Lindesmith, and Karl Schuessler, eds. 1956. *The Sutherland papers.* Bloomington: University of Indiana Press.

Cohen, Albert K., and James F. Short, Jr. 1958. Research in delinquent subcultures. *Journal of Social Issues* 14:20–37.

Cohen, Bernard. 1969. The delinquency of gangs and spontaneous groups. In *Delinquency: Selected studies,* eds. Thorsten Sellin and Marvin E. Wolfgang, 61–111. New York: Wiley.

Cohen, Stanley. 1980. *Folk devils and moral panics: The creation of mods and rockers.* 2nd ed. New York: St. Martin's Press.

Coleman, James S. 1988. Social capital in the creation of human capital. *American Journal of Sociology* 94:95–120.

———. 1990. *Foundations of social theory.* Cambridge, MA: Harvard University Press.

———. 1994. A vision for sociology. *Society* 32:29–34.

Coleman, James S., Robert H. Bremner, Burton R. Clark, John B. Davis, Dorothy H. Eichorn, Zvi Griliches, Joseph F. Kett, Norman B. Ryder, Zahava·Blum Doering, and John M. Mays. 1974. *Youth: Transition to adulthood.* Report of the Panel on Youth of the President's Science Advisory Committee. Chicago: University of Chicago Press.

Coleman, James S., Elihu Katz, and Herbert Menzel. 1966. *Medical innovations: A diffusion study.* Indianapolis, IN: Bobbs-Merrill.

Collins, Jock, Greg Noble, Scott Poynting, and Paul Tabar. 2000. *Kebabs, kids, cops and crime: Youth, ethnicity and crime.* Sydney: Pluto.

Conrad, Peter, and Valerie Leiter, eds. 2003. *Health and health care as social problems.* Lanham, MD: Rowman and Littlefield.

Cook, Philip J., and John H. Laub. 1998. *The unprecedented epidemic in youth violence.* In *Youth violence,* eds. Michael Tonry and Mark H. Moore, 27–64. Vol. 24. Chicago: University of Chicago Press.

Cook, Thomas D., Shobha C. Shagle, and Serdar M. Degirmencioglu. 1997. Capturing social process for testing mediational models of neighborhood effects. In *Neighborhood poverty,* eds. Jeanne Brooks-Gunn, Greg J. Duncan, and J. Lawrence Aber, 94–119. Vol. 1. New York: Russell Sage Foundation.

Cooney, Mark. 1998. *Warriors and peacemakers: How third parties shape violence.* New York: New York University Press.

Coughlin, Brenda C., and Sudhir A. Venkatesh. 2003. The urban street gang after 1970. *Annual Review of Sociology* 29:41–64.

Covey, Herbert C. 2003. *Street gangs throughout the world.* Springfield, IL: Charles C. Thomas.

Covey, Herbert C., Scott W. Menard, and Robert J. Franzese. 1997. *Juvenile gangs.* 2nd ed. Springfield, IL; Charles C. Thomas.

Curry, G. David. 2000. Self-reported gang involvement and officially reported delinquency. *Criminology* 38:1253–74.

———. 2001. The proliferation of gangs in the United States. In *The Eurogang paradox: Street gangs and youth groups in the U.S. and Europe,* eds. Malcolm W. Klein, Hans J. Kerner, Cheryl L. Maxson, and Elmar G. M. Weitekamp, 79–92. Dordrecht, The Netherlands: Kluwer.

Curry, G. David, Richard A. Ball, and Scott H. Decker. 1996. Estimating the national scope of gang crime from law enforcement data. In *Gangs in America,* ed. C. Ronald Huff, 21–36. 2nd ed. Thousand Oaks, CA: Sage.

Curry, G. David, and Scott H. Decker. 1998. *Confronting gangs: Crime and community.* Los Angeles: Roxbury.

———. 2003. *Confronting gangs: Crime and community.* 2d ed. Los Angeles: Roxbury Publishing.

Curry, G. David, and Irving A. Spergel. 1988. Gang homicide, delinquency, and community. *Criminology* 26:381–407.

———. 1992. Gang involvement and delinquency among Hispanic and African-American adolescent males. *Journal of Research in Crime and Delinquency* 29: 273–91.

Davies, Andrew. 1998. Youth gangs, masculinity and violence in late Victorian Manchester and Salford. *Journal of Social History* 32:349–70.

Davis, Mike. 2004. Planet of slums. *New Left Review* 26 (March–April). www.newleftreview.net/NLR26001.shtml (accessed November 13, 2004).

de Certeau, Michel. 1984. *The practice of everyday life.* Translated by Steven Randall. Berkeley: University of California Press.

Decesare, Donna. 2003. From Civil War to gang war: The tragedy of Edgar Bolanos. In *Gangs and society: Alternative perspectives,* eds. Louis Kontos, David C. Brotherton, and Luis Barrios, 283–313. New York: Columbia University Press.

Decker, Scott H. 1996. Collective and normative features of gang violence. *Justice Quarterly* 13:243–64.

———2001a. The impact of organizational features on gang activities and relationships. In *The Eurogang paradox: Street gangs and youth groups in the U.S. and Europe,* eds. Malcolm W. Klein, Hans-Jurgen Kerner, Cheryl L. Maxson, and Elmar G. M. Weitekamp, 21–39. Dordrecht, The Netherlands: Kluwer.

———. 2001b. From the street to the prison: Understanding and responding to gangs. Paper prepared for the College of Justice and Safety Speaker's Series sponsored by the National Major Gang Task Force, February 9, in Richmond, Kentucky.

———. 2003. Policing gangs and youth violence: Where do we stand, where do we go from here? In *Policing gangs and youth violence*, ed. Scott H. Decker, 287–93. Belmont, CA: Wadsworth.

Decker, Scott H., and Kimberly Kempf-Leonard. 1991. Constructing gangs: The social definition of youth activities. *Criminal Justice Policy Review* 5:271–91.

Decker, Scott H., and Barrik Van Winkle. 1994. "Slinging dope": The role of gangs and gang members in drug sales. *Justice Quarterly* 11:583–604.

———. 1996. *Life in the gang: Family, friends, and violence.* Cambridge, UK: Cambridge University Press.

Decker, Scott H., and Frank M. Weerman. 2005. *European street gangs and troublesome youth groups: Findings from the Eurogang Research Program.* Lanham, MD: AltaMira.

Denzin, Norman. 1978. *The research act: A theoretical introduction to sociological methods.* New York: McGraw-Hill.

DeSena, Judith. 1990. *Protecting one's turf: Social strategies for maintaining urban neighborhoods.* Lanham, MD: University Press of America

Des Jarlais, Don C., Theresa Diaz, Theresa Perlis, David Vlahov, Carey Maslow, Mary Latka, Russel Rockwell, Vincent Edwards, Samuel R. Friedman, Edgar Monterroso, Ian Williams, and Richard S. Garfein. 2003. Variability in the incidence of human immunodeficiency virus, hepatitis B virus, and hepatitis C virus infection among young injection drug users in New York City. *American Journal of Epidemiology* 157:467–71.

De Soto, Hernando. 1990. *The other path: The invisible revolution in the Third World.* New York: Harper and Row.

Dillon, Paul, Jan Copeland, and Karl Jansen. 2003. Patterns of use and harms associated with non-medical ketamine use. *Drug and Alcohol Dependence* 69:23–28.

Douglas, Jack D. 1972. Observing deviance. In *Research on deviance*, ed. Jack D. Douglas, 3–34. New York: Random House.

Dowdney, Luke. 2003. *Children of the drug trade: A case study of children in organised armed violence in Rio de Janiero.* Rio de Janiero: 7Letras.

Eck, John, and Edward Maguire. 2000. Have changes in policing reduced violent crime? In *The crime drop in America*, eds. Alfred Blumstein and Joel Wallman, 207–65. New York: Cambridge University Press.

Egley, Arlen, Jr., and Mehela Arjunan. 2002. *Highlights of the 2000 National Youth Gang Survey.* Washington, DC: U.S. Department of Justice, Office of Justice Programs, Office of Juvenile Justice and Delinquency Prevention.

Egley, Arlen, Jr., James C. Howell, and Aline K. Major. 2004. Recent patterns of gang problems in the United States: Results from the 1996–2002 National Youth Gang Survey. In *American youth gangs at the millennium*, eds. Finn-Aage Esbensen, Stephen G. Tibbetts, and Larry Gaines, 90–108. Long Grove, IL: Waveland.

Egley, Arlen, Jr., and Aline K. Major. 2003. *Highlights of the 2001 National Youth Gang Survey.* Washington, DC: U.S. Department of Justice, Office of Justice Programs, Office of Juvenile Justice and Delinquency Prevention.

———. 2004. *Highlights of the 2002 National Youth Gang Survey.* Washington, DC: Office of Juvenile Justice and Delinquency Prevention.

Elias, Norbert. 1939/1994. *The civilizing process: The history of manners.* Oxford: Blackwell.

Elliott, Delbert S., David H. Huizinga, and Scott Menard. 1989. *Multiple problem youth: Delinquency, substance use, and mental health problems.* New York: Springer-Verlag.

Elliott, Delbert S., William J. Wilson, David H. Huizinga, Robert J. Sampson, Amanda Elliott, and Bruce Rankin. 1996. The effects of neighborhood disadvantage on adolescent development. *Journal of Research in Crime and Delinquency* 33:389–426.

Ennett, Susan T., Susan L. Bailey, and E. Belle Federman. 1999. Social network characteristics associated with risky behaviors among runaway and homeless youth. *Journal of Health and Social Behavior* 40:63–78.

Esbensen, Finn-Aage. 2000. *Preventing adolescent gang involvement.* Washington, DC: U.S. Department of Justice, Office of Justice Programs, Office of Juvenile Justice and Delinquency Prevention.

Esbensen, Finn-Aage, and David H. Huizinga. 1993. Gangs, drugs, and delinquency in a survey of urban youth. *Criminology* 31:565–89.

Esbensen, Finn-Aage, David Huizinga, and Anne W. Weiher. 1993. Gang and non-gang youth: Differences in explanatory factors. *Journal of Contemporary Criminal Justice* 9:94–116.

Esbensen, Finn-Aage, and Dana P. Lynskey. 2001. Youth gang members in a school survey. In *The Eurogang paradox: Street gangs and youth groups in the U.S. and Europe*, eds. Malcolm W. Klein, Hans J. Kerner, Cheryl L. Maxson, and Elmar G. M. Weitekamp. 93–114. Dordrecht, The Netherlands: Kluwer.

Esbensen, Finn-Aage, L. Thomas Winfree, Jr., Ni He, and Terrance J. Taylor. 2001. Youth gangs and definitional issues: When is a gang a gang, and why does it matter? *Crime and Delinquency* 47:105–30.

Etter, Greg. 1999. Skinheads: Manifestations of the warrior culture of the new urban tribes. *Journal of Gang Research* 6:9–21.

Everett, Martin G., and Stephen P. Borgatti. 1999. The centrality of groups and classes. *Journal of Mathematical Sociology* 23:181–201.

Fagan, Jeffrey. 1989. The social organization of drug use and drug dealing among urban gangs. *Criminology* 27:633–69.

———. 1990. Social processes of delinquency and drug use among urban gangs. In *Gangs in America*, ed. C. Ronald Huff, 183–219. Newbury Park, CA: Sage.

———. 1996. Gangs, drugs, and neighborhood change. In *Gangs in America*, ed. C. Ronald Huff, 39–74. 2nd ed. Thousand Oaks, CA: Sage.

Fagan, Jeffrey, Elizabeth Piper, and Melinda Moore. 1986. Violent delinquents and urban youths. *Criminology* 24:439–71.

Fagan, Jeffrey, and Deanna L. Wilkinson. 1998. Guns, youth violence, and social identity in inner cities. In *Crime and justice: A review of research*, eds. Michael Tonry and Mark H. Moore, 105–88. Vol. 24. Chicago: University of Chicago Press.

Fangen, Katrine. 1998. Living out ethnic instincts: Ideological beliefs among right-wing activists in Norway. In *Nation and race: The developing Euro-American racist subculture*, eds. Jeffrey Kaplan and Tore Bjorgo, 202–30. Boston: Northeastern University Press.

Farmer, Paul. 1994. *The uses of Haiti.* Monroe, ME: Common Courage Press.

Farrington, David P. 1987. Early precursors of frequent offending. In *From children to citizens,* eds. James Q. Wilson and Glenn C. Loury, 27–50. New York: Springer-Verlag.

———. 1988. Studying changes within individuals: The causes of offending. In *Studies of psychosocial risk: The power of longitudinal data,* ed. Michael Rutter, 158–83. Cambridge, UK: Cambridge University Press.

Farrington, David P., and Rolf Loeber. 2000. Epidemiology of juvenile violence. *Child and Adolescent Psychiatric Clinics of North America.* 9:733–48.

Ferber, Abby. 1998. *White man falling: Race, gender, and white supremacy.* Lanham, MD: Rowman and Littlefield.

Finckenauer, James O., and Elin J. Waring. 1998. *Russian mafia in America: Immigration, culture, and crime.* Boston: Northeastern University Press.

Finestone, Harold. 1957. Cats, kicks, and color. *Social Problems* 5:3–13.

———. 1967. Reformation and recidivism among Italian and Polish criminal offenders. *American Journal of Sociology* 72:575–88.

Finnegan, William. 1999. *Cold new world: Growing up in a harder country.* New York: Random House.

Fishman, Laura T. 1995. The Vice Queens: An ethnographic study of black female gang behavior. In *The modern gang reader,* eds. Malcolm W. Klein, Cheryl L. Maxson, and Jody Miller, 83–92. Los Angeles: Roxbury.

Fleisher, Mark S. 1995. *Beggars and thieves.* Madison: University of Wisconsin Press.

———. 1998. *Dead end kids: Gang girls and the boys they know.* Madison: University of Wisconsin Press.

———. 2001. *Adult male gang member residential mobility.* Washington, DC: U.S. Census Bureau.

———. 2002a. Doing field research on diverse gangs: Interpreting youth gangs as social networks. In *Gangs in America,* ed. C. Ronald Huff, 199–217. 3rd ed. Thousand Oaks, CA: Sage.

———. 2002b. *Women in gangs: A field research study.* Washington, DC: U.S. Department of Justice, Office of Juvenile Justice and Delinquency Prevention.

———. 2005. Fieldwork research and social network analysis: Different methods creating complementary perspectives. *Journal of Contemporary Criminal Justice* 21: 120–34.

Fleisher, Mark S., and Jessie L. Krienert. 2004. Life-course events, social networks, and the emergence of violence among female gang members. *Journal of Community Psychology* 2:607–22.

Fleisher, Mark S., and Christopher McCarty. 2004. Structural holes: Macher or nebesh. Paper presented at the 2004 International Network of Social Network Analysts, May 12–16, Portoroz, Slovenia.

Foote, Paula. 1993. Like, I'll tell you what happened from experience . . . Perspectives on Italo-Australian youth gangs in Adelaide. In *Youth subcultures: Theory, history and the Australian experience,* ed. Rob White, 122–28. Hobart, Australia: National Clearinghouse for Youth Studies.

Frank, Andre G. 1970. *Latin America: Underdevelopment or revolution.* New York: Monthly Review.

Freeman, Linton C. 1977. A set of measures of centrality based on betweenness. *Sociometry* 40:35–41.

French, Howard D. 2004. New boomtowns change path of China's growth. *New York Times,* July 28, 1.

Friedkin, Noah E. 1991. Theoretical foundations for centrality measures. *American Journal of Sociology* 96:1478–1504.

Friedman, Samuel R., and Sevgi Aral. 2001. Social networks, risk-potential networks, health, and disease. *Journal of Urban Health: Bulletin of the New York Academy of Medicine* 78:411–18.

Friedman, Samuel R., Benny J. Kottiri, Alan Neaigus, Richard Curtis, Sten H. Vermund, and Don. C. Des Jarlais. 2000. Network-related mechanisms may help explain long-term HIV 1 seroprevalence levels that remain high but do not approach population-group saturation. *American Journal of Epidemiology* 152:913–92.

Friedman, Samuel R., Alan Neaigus, Benny Jose, Richard Curtis, Marjorie Goldstein, Gilbert Ildefonso, Richard. B. Rothenberg, and Don. C. Des Jarlais. 1997. Sociometric risk networks and risk for HIV infection. *American Journal of Public Health* 87: 1289–96.

Gaines, Donna. 1994. The local economy of suburban scenes. In *Adolescents and their music: If it's too loud, you're too old,* ed. Jonathon Epstein, 47–65. New York: Garland.

Gatti, Uberto, Frank Vitaro, Richard E. Tremblay, and Pierre McDuff. 2002. *Youth gangs and violent behavior: Results from the Montreal Longitudinal Experimental Study.* Paper presented at the fifteenth World Meeting of the International Society for Research on Aggression, July, in Montreal, Canada.

Geis, Gilbert, and Mary Dodge. 2000. Frederic M. Thrasher (1882–1962) and The Gang. *Journal of Gang Research* 8:1–49.

Gladwell, Malcolm. 1997. Annals of style: The coolhunt. *The New Yorker,* March 17, 78–88.

Glaze, Lauren E., and Seri Palla. 2004. *Probation and parole in the United States.* Washington, DC: Bureau of Justice Statistics.

Goffman, Erving. 1963. *Stigma: Notes on the management of spoiled identity.* New Jersey: Prentice-Hall.

Gold, Martin, and Hans Mattick. 1974. *Experiment in the streets: The Chicago youth development project.* Ann Arbor: University of Michigan, Institute for Social Research.

Goldstone, Jack A. 2002. States, terrorists, and the clash of civilizations. In *Understanding September 11,* eds. Craig Calhoun, Paul Price, and Ashley Timmer, 139–58. New York: The New Press.

Gould, Roger V. 1996. Patron-client ties, state centralization, and the Whiskey Rebellion. *American Journal of Sociology* 102:400–29.

———. 2003. *The collision of wills: How ambiguity about social rank breeds conflict.* Chicago: University of Chicago Press.

Granovetter, Mark S. 1973. The strength of weak ties. *American Journal of Sociology* 78:1360–80.

Green, Donald P., Dara Z. Strolovitch, and Janelle S. Wong. 1998. Defended neighborhoods, integration, and racially motivated crime. *American Journal of Sociology* 104:372–403.

Greman, Sean, Marjie T. Britz, Jeffrey Rush, and Thomas Barker. 2000. *Gangs: An international approach.* Upper Saddle River, NJ: Prentice Hall.

Guerra, Carmel and Rob White, eds. 1995. *Ethnic minority youth in Australia: Challenges and myths.* Hobart, Australia: Australian Clearinghouse for Youth Studies.

Gunst, Laurie. 1995. *Born fi' dead: A journey through the Jamaican Posse underworld.* New York: Henry Holt.

Hagan, H., T. Reid, D. C. Des Jarlais, D. Purchase, S. R. Friedman, and T. A. Bell. 1991. The incidence of HBV infection and syringe exchange programs. *Journal of the American Medical Association* 266:1646–47.

Hage, Ghassan. 1998. *White nation: Fantasies of white supremacy in a multicultural society.* Sydney: Pluto Press.

Hagedorn, John M. 1988. *People and folks: Gangs, crime, and the underclass in a rustbelt city.* With Perry Macon. Chicago: Lake View.

———. 1990. Back in the field again: Gang research in the nineties. In *Gangs in America,* ed. C. Ronald Huff, 240–59. Newbury Park, CA: Sage.

———. 1998a. *People and folks: Gangs, crime and the underclass in a rustbelt city.* 2nd ed. Chicago: Lake View.

———. 1998b. Gang violence in the postindustrial era. In *Crime and justice: A review of research,* eds. Michael Tonry and Mark H. Moore, 365–419. Vol. 24. Chicago: University of Chicago Press.

———. 2001. Gangs and globalization. In *The Eurogang paradox: Street gangs and youth groups in the U.S. and Europe,* eds. Malcoln W. Klein, Hans-Jurgen Kerner, Cheryl L. Maxson, and Elmar G.M. Weitekamp, 41–58. Dordrecht, The Netherlands: Kluwer.

———. 2002a. Gangs and the informal economy. In *Gangs in America,* ed. C. Ronald Huff, 101–20. 3rd ed. Thousand Oaks, CA: Sage.

———. 2002b. Globalization, gangs, and collaborative research. In *The Eurogang paradox: Street gangs and youth groups in the U.S. and Europe,* eds. Malcolm W. Klein, Hans-Jurgen Kerner, Cheryl L. Maxson, and Elmar G.M. Weitekamp, 41–58. Dordrecht, The Netherlands: Kluwer.

———. Forthcoming-a. Gangs in late modernity. In *Gangs in the global city: Reconsidering criminology,* ed. John M. Hagedorn. Champaign: University of Illinois Press.

———, ed. Forthcoming-b. *Gangs in the global city: Reconsidering criminology.* Champaign: University of Illinois Press.

Hagedorn, John M., and David Perry. 2002. Contested cities. Paper presented at the American Society of Criminology Annual Meetings, November 13–16, in Chicago.

Hagedorn, John M., and Brigid Rauch. 2004. Variations in urban homicide. Paper presented at the City Futures Conference, July 8–10, in Chicago.

Hamm, Mark. 1993. *American skinheads.* Boston: Northeastern University Press.

Harris, Mary G. 1988. *Cholas: Latino girls and gangs.* New York: AMS.

Harrison, Paige M., and Jennifer C. Karberg. 2004. *Prison and jail inmates at midyear 2003*. Washington, DC: Bureau of Justice Statistics.

Hawkins, J. David, Todd Herrenkohl, David P. Farrington, Devon Brewer, Richard F. Catalano, and Tracy W. Harachi. 1998. A review of predictors of youth violence. In *Serious and violent juvenile offenders: Risk factors and successful interventions*, eds. Rolf Loeber and David P. Farrington, 106–46. Thousand Oaks, CA: Sage.

Hayden, Tom. 2004. *Street wars: Gangs and the future of violence*. New York: New Press.

Haynie, Dana L. 2001. Delinquent peers revisited: Does network structure matter? *American Journal of Sociology* 106:1013–57.

Hazlehurst, Cameron. Forthcoming. Observing New Zealand 'gangs', 1950–2000: Learning from a small country. In *Gangs in the global city: Criminology reconsidered*, ed. John M. Hagedorn. Champaign: University of Illinois Press.

Hazlehurst, Kayleen, and Cameron Hazlehurst, eds. 1998. *Gangs and youth subcultures: International explorations*. New Brunswick, NJ: Transaction.

Healey, Kathy, ed. 1996. *Youth gangs*. Sydney: Spinney.

Hebdige, Dick. 1979. *Subculture, the meaning of style*. London: Methuen.

Heckathorn, Douglas D. 1997. Respondent-driven sampling: A new approach to the study of hidden populations. *Social Problems* 44:174–99.

———. 2002. Respondent-driven sampling II: Deriving valid population estimates from chain referral samples of hidden populations. *Social Problems* 49:11–34.

Henry, Andrew, and James F. Short, Jr. 1954. *Suicide and homicide*. New York: McGraw-Hill.

Hershberg, Eric, and Kevin W. Moore, eds. 2002. *Critical views of September 11*. New York: Social Science Research Council and The New Press.

Hicks, Wendy. 2004. Skinheads: A three nation comparison. *Journal of Gang Research* 11:51–74.

Hill, Karl G., James C. Howell, J. David Hawkins, and Sara R. Battin-Pearson. 1999. Childhood risk factors for adolescent gang membership: Results from the Seattle Social Development Project. *Journal of research in crime and delinquency* 36: 300–22.

Hill, Karl G., Christina Lui, and J. David Hawkins. 2001. *Early precursors of gang membership: A study of Seattle youth*. Bulletin. Washington, DC: U.S. Department of Justice, Office of Justice Programs, Office of Juvenile Justice and Delinquency Prevention.

Hindelang, Michael J., Travis Hirschi, and Joseph G. Weis. 1981. *Measuring delinquency*. Beverly Hills, CA: Sage.

Hirschi, Travis. 1969. *Causes of delinquency*. Berkeley: University of California Press.

Hobsbawm, Eric. 1969. *Bandits*. New York: Pantheon.

Holmberg, Scott D. 1996. The estimated prevalence and incidence of HIV in 96 large U.S. metropolitan areas. *American Journal of Public Health* 86:642–54.

Holstein, James, and Gale Miller. 1990. Rethinking victimization: An interactional approach to victimology. *Symbolic Interaction* 13:103–22.

Homans, George C. 1950. *The human group*. New York: Harcourt, Brace.

hooks, bell. 1994. *Misogyny, gangsta rap, and the piano*. eserver.org/race/misogyny.html (accessed November 14, 2004).

Horowitz, Ruth. 1983. *Honor and the American dream: Culture and identity in a Chicano community.* New Brunswick, NJ: Rutgers University Press.

———. 1987. Community tolerance of gang violence. *Social Problems* 34:437–50.

———. 1990. Sociological perspectives on gangs: Conflicting definitions and concepts. In *Gangs in America*, ed. C. Ronald Huff, 37–54. Newbury Park, CA: Sage.

Howell, James C. 2003. *Preventing and reducing juvenile delinquency: A comprehensive framework.* Thousand Oaks, CA: Sage.

Howell, James C., and Scott H. Decker. 1999. *The youth gangs, drugs, and violence connection.* Bulletin. Washington, DC: U.S. Department of Justice, Office of Justice Programs, Office of Juvenile Justice and Delinquency Prevention.

Howell, James C., Arlen Egley, Jr., and Debra K. Gleason. 2002. *Modern-day youth gangs.* Bulletin. Washington, DC: U.S. Department of Justice, Office of Justice Programs, Office of Juvenile Justice and Delinquency Prevention.

Huff, C. Ronald. 1996. The criminal behavior of gang members and nongang at risk youth. In *Gangs in America*, ed. C. Ronald Huff, 75–102. 2nd ed. Thousand Oaks, CA: Sage.

Hughes, Lorine A. 2004. Impression management and the settlement of disputes involving youth street gang members. Paper presented at the annual meeting of the American Society of Criminology, November 16–20, in Nashville, TN.

———. 2005a. Studying youth gangs: Alternative methods and conclusions. *Journal of Contemporary Criminal Justice* 21:98–119.

———. 2005b. *Violent and non-violent disputes involving gang youth.* New York: LFB Scholarly.

Hughes, Lorine A., and James F. Short, Jr. 2005. Disputes involving youth street gang members: Micro-social contexts. *Criminology* 43:43–76.

Huisman, Mark, and Marijtje A. J. van Duijn. 2005. Software for social network analysis. In *Models and methods in social network analysis*, eds. Peter J. Carrington, John Scott, and Stanley Wasserman, 270–316. New York: Cambridge University Press.

Huizinga, David, Barbara J. Morse, and Delbert S. Elliott. 1992. *The National Youth Survey: An overview and description of recent findings.* Boulder: Institute of Behavioral Science, University of Colorado.

Human Rights and Equal Opportunity Commission. 2004. *Ismae—Listen: National consultations on eliminating prejudice against Arab and Muslim Australians.* Sydney: HREOC.

Human Rights Watch. 2002. *The Bakassi Boys: The legitimation of murder and torture.* www.hrw.org/reports/2002/nigeria2/index.htm#TopOfPage (accessed November 14, 2004).

———. 2004. *Stop the use of child soldiers.* hrw.org/campaigns/crp/index.htm (accessed November 14, 2004).

Hunt, Geoffrey P., and Karen Joe-Laidler. 2001. Alcohol and violence in the lives of gang members. *Alcohol Research and Health* 25:66–71.

Irwin, John. 1977. *Scenes.* Beverly Hills, CA: Sage.

Jamrozik, Adam, Cathy Boland, and Robert Urquhart. 1995. *Social change and cultural transformation in Australia.* Melbourne: Cambridge University Press.

Jankowski, Martin Sanchez. 1991. *Islands in the street: Gangs and American urban society.* Berkeley: University of California Press.

Jansyn, Leon R., Jr. 1966. Solidarity and delinquency in a street corner group. *American Sociological Review* 31:600–614.

Juarez, Paul D. 1992. The public health model and violence prevention. In *Substance abuse and gang violence,* ed. Richard C. Cervantes, 43–59. London: Sage.

Kaldor, Mary. 1999. *New and old wars: Organized violence in a global era.* Stanford, CA: Stanford University Press.

Kaplan, Jeffrey. 1995. Right-wing violence in North America. In *Terror from the extreme right,* ed. Tore Bjorgo, 44–95. London: Frank Cass.

Karmen, Andrew. 2000. *New York murder mystery: The true story behind the crime crash of the 1990's.* New York: New York University Press.

Kasarda, John D., and Morris Janowitz. 1974. Community attachment in mass society. *American Sociological Review* 39:328–39.

Katz, Jack. 1988. *Seductions of crime: Moral and sensual attractions in doing evil.* New York: Basic Books.

———. 2000. The gang myth. In *Social dynamics of crime and control: New theories for a world in transition,* eds. Susanne Karstedt and Kai D. Bussmann, 171–87. Portland, OR: Hart.

Katz, Jack, and Curtis Jackson-Jacobs. 2004. The criminologists' gang. In *The Blackwell companion to criminology,* ed. Colin Sumner, 91–124. Malden, MA: Blackwell.

Keiser, R. Lincoln. 1969. *The Vice Lords: Warriors of the streets.* New York: Holt, Rinehart and Winston.

Kelling, George L., and Catherine M. Coles. 1996. *Fixing broken windows: Restoring order and reducing crime in our communities.* New York: Simon and Schuster.

Kemerling, Garth. 2002. *Dictionary of philosophical names and terms.* www .philosophypages.com/dy/r.htm#reif (accessed September 21, 2004).

Kennedy, David M., Anthony A. Braga, and Anne M. Piehl. 1997. The (un)known universe: Mapping gangs and gang violence in Boston. In *Crime mapping and crime prevention,* eds. David Weisburd and Tom. McEwen. Monsey, NY: Criminal Justice Press.

Kennedy, S. M. 2004. A practitioners guide to responsivity: Maximizing treatment effectiveness. *Journal of Community Corrections* 13.

Kersten, Joachim. 2001. Groups of violent young males in Germany. In *The Eurogang paradox: Street gangs and youth groups in the U.S. and Europe,* eds. Malcolm W. Klein, Hans J. Kerner, Cheryl L. Maxson, and Elmar G. M. Weitekamp, 247–55. Dordrecht, The Netherlands: Kluwer.

Kipke, Michele D., Susan O'Connor, Ray Palmer, and Richard G. MacKenzie. 1995. Street youth in Los Angeles: Profile of a group at high risk for human immunodeficiency virus infection. *Archive of Pediatric and Adolescent Medicine* 149: 513–19.

Kirk, David S., and Andrew V. Papachristos. 2005. Exploring the neighborhood dynamics of black and Hispanic homicide: A spatial econometrics approach. Unpublished manuscript, Department of Sociology, University of Chicago.

Kitwana, Bakari. 1994. *Rap on gangsta rap: Who run it?* Chicago: Third World.

————. 2002. *Hip hop generation: Young blacks and the crisis of American culture.* New York: Basic Civitas.

Klein, Malcolm W. 1969. Gang cohesiveness, delinquency, and a street-work program. *Journal of Research in Crime and Delinquency* 6:135–66.

————. 1971. *Street gangs and street workers.* Englewood Cliffs, NJ: Prentice-Hall.

————. 1995a. *The American street gang: Its nature, prevalence, and control.* New York: Oxford University Press.

————. 1995b. Street gang cycles. In *Crime,* eds. James Q. Wilson and Joan Petersilia, 217–36. San Francisco: ICS.

————. 2002. Street gangs: A cross-national perspective. In *Gangs in America,* ed. C. Ronald Huff, 237–54. 3rd ed. Thousand Oaks, CA: Sage.

————. 2004. *Gang cop: The words and ways of Officer Paco Domingo.* Lanham, MD: AltaMira.

————. 2005. Introduction. In *European street gangs and troublesome youth groups: Findings from the Eurogang Research Program,* eds. Scott H. Decker and Frank M. Weerman. Lanham, MD: AltaMira.

Klein, Malcolm W., and Lois Y. Crawford. 1967. Groups, gangs, and cohesiveness. *Journal of Research in Crime and Delinquency* 4:63–75.

Klein, Malcolm W., Margaret A. Gordon, and Cheryl L. Maxson. 1986. The impact of police investigation on police-reported rates of gang and nongang homicides. *Criminology* 2:489–512.

Klein, Malcolm W., Hans-Juergen Kerner, Cheryl L. Maxson, and Elmar G. M. Weitekamp, eds. 2001. *The Eurogang paradox: Street gangs and youth groups in the U.S. and Europe.* Dordrecht, The Netherlands: Kluwer.

Klein, Malcolm W., and Cheryl L. Maxson. 2005. *Street gang patterns and policies.* Oxford: Oxford University Press.

————. Forthcoming. *Street gang patterns and policies.* New York: Oxford University Press.

Klein, Malcolm W., Cheryl L. Maxson, and Lea C. Cunningham. 1991. "Crack," street gangs, and violence. *Criminology* 29:623–50.

Knight, Nick. 1982. *Skinhead.* London: Omnibus.

Knox, George. 2000. *An introduction to gangs.* 5th ed. Peotone, IL: New Chicago School.

Kobrin, Solomon. 1951. The conflict of values in delinquency areas. *American Sociological Review* 16:653–61.

Kontos, Louis, David C. Brotherton, and Luis Barrios, eds. 2003. *Gangs and society: Alternative perspectives.* New York: Columbia University Press.

Kornhauser, Ruth R. 1978. Social sources of delinquency: An appraisal of analytic models. Chicago: University of Chicago Press.

Kovats-Bernat, J. C. 2000. Anti-gang, Arimaj, and the war on street children. *Peace Review* 12:415–21.

Krienert, Jessie L., and Mark S. Fleisher. 2001. Gang membership as a proxy for social deficiencies: A study of Nebraska inmates. *Corrections Management Quarterly* 5: 47–58.

Kubrin, Charis E., and Ronald Weitzer 2003. Retaliatory homicide: Concentrated disadvantage and neighborhood culture. *Social Problems* 50:157–80.

Lane, Jodi, and James W. Meeker. 2003. Fear of gang crime: A look at three theoretical models. *Law and Society Review* 37:425–56.

Lane, Michael P. 1989. Inmate gangs. *Corrections Today* 51:98–9, 126, 128.

Lankenau, Stephen E., and Michael C. Clatts. 2002. Ketamine injection among high risk youth: Preliminary findings from New York City. *The Journal of Drug Issues* 32:893–905.

———. 2004. Drug injection practices among high-risk youth: The first shot of ketamine. *Journal of Urban Health* 81:232–48.

Lankenau, Stephen E., Michael C. Clatts, Lloyd A. Goldsamt, and Dorinda Welle. 2004. Crack cocaine injection practices and HIV risk: Findings from New York and Bridgeport. *Journal of Drug Issues* 34:319–32.

Lankenau, Stephen E., Michael C. Clatts, Dorinda Welle, Lloyd A. Goldsamt, and Marya Viost Gwadz. 2005. Street careers: Homelessness, drug use, and hustling among young men who have sex with men (YMSM). *International Journal of Drug Policy* 16:10–18.

Latane, Bibb, James H. Liu, Andrzej Nowak, Michael Bonevento, and Long Zheng. 1995. Distance matters: Physical space and social impact. *Personality and Social Psychology Bulletin* 21:795–805.

Latessa, Edward J. 2004. Best practices of classification and assessment. *Journal of Community Corrections.* 12:4–7, 27–30.

Lattimore, Pamela K., Christy A. Visher, and Richard L. Linster. 1995. Predicting rearrest for violence among serious youthful offenders. *Journal of Research in Crime and Delinquency* 32:54–83.

Laumann, Edward O., and Franz Urban Pappi. 1973. New directions in the study of community elites. *American Sociological Review* 38:212–30.

Lee, Matthew T., Ramiro Martinez, Jr., and Richard Rosenfeld. 2001. Does immigration increase homicide: Negative evidence from three border cities. *The Sociological Quarterly* 42:559–80.

Leong, Laurence Wei-Teng. 1992. Cultural resistance: The cultural terrorism of British male working-class youth. *Current Perspectives in Social Theory* 12:29–58.

Leri, Francisco, Julie Bruneau, and Jane Stewart. 2003. Understanding polydrug use: Review of heroin and cocaine co-use. *Addiction* 98:7–22.

Leventhal, Tama, and Jeanne Brooks-Gunn. 2000. The neighborhoods they live in: The effects of neighborhood residence on child and adolescent outcomes. *Psychological Bulletin* 126:309–37.

Lien, Inger-Lise. 2002. The dynamics of honor in violence and cultural change. Unpublished manuscript, Norwegian Institute for Urban and Regional Research.

Linster, Richard L., Pamela K. Lattimore, John M. MacDonald, and Christy A. Visher. 1996. *Who gets arrested? Models of the frequency of arrest of the young, chronic, serious offender.* Sacramento: California Department of the Youth Authority.

Lizotte, Alan J., Terence P. Thornberry, Marvin D. Krohn, Deborah Chard-Wierschem, and David McDowall. 1994. Neighborhood context and delinquency: A longitudinal analysis. In *Cross-national longitudinal research on human development and criminal behavior*, eds. Elmar G. M. Weitekamp and Hans-Juergen Kerner, 217–27. Dordrecht, The Netherlands: Kluwer.

Long, Larry H. 1974. Poverty status and receipt of welfare among migrants and non-migrants in large cities. *American Sociological Review* 34:46–56.

Lorrain, Francois P., and Harrison C. White. 1971. Structural equivalence of individuals in social networks. *Journal of Mathematical Sociology* 1:49–80.

Lozusic, Roza. 2002. Gangs in NSW, *Briefing Paper 16*. Sydney: NSW Parliamentary Library.

Lyons, Elenor. 1995. New clients, old problems: Vietnamese young people's experiences with police. In *Ethnic minority youth in Australia*, eds. Carmel Guerra and Rob White, 163–78. Hobart, Australia: National Clearinghouse for Youth Studies.

MacLean, Nancy. 1994. *Behind the mask of chivalry: The making of the second Ku Klux Klan*. Oxford: Oxford University Press.

Maher, Lisa, David Dixon, Wendy Swift, and Tram Nguyen. 1997. *Anh Hai: Young Asian background people's perceptions and experiences of policing*. Sydney: UNSW Faculty of Law Research Monograph Series.

Marcuse, Peter. 1997. The enclave, the Citadel, and the ghetto: What has changed in the post-Fordist U.S. city. *Urban Affairs Review* 33:228–64.

Mares, Dennis. 2001. Gangstas or lager louts? Working class street gangs in Manchester. In *The Eurogang paradox: Street gangs and youth groups in the U.S. and Europe*, eds. Malcolm W. Klein, Hans-Jurgen Kerner, Cheryl L. Maxson, and Elmar G. M. Weitekamp, 153–64. Dordrecht, The Netherlands: Kluwer.

Mariner, Joanne. 2001. *No escape: Male rape in U.S. prisons*. New York: Human Rights Watch.

Markowitz, Fred E., Paul E. Bellair, Allen E. Liska, and Jianhong Liu. 2001. Extending social disorganization theory: Modeling the relationships between cohesion, disorder, and fear. *Criminology* 39:293–319.

Marsden, Peter V. 1990. Network data and measurement. *Annual Review of Sociology* 16:435–63.

———. 2002. Egocentric and sociocentric measures of network centrality. *Social networks* 24:407–22.

———. 2005. Recent developments in network measurements. In *Models and methods in social network analysis*, eds. Peter J. Carrington, John Scott, and Stanley Wasserman. New York: Cambridge University Press.

Martinez, Ramiro, Jr. 2002. *Latino homicide: Immigration, violence, and community*. New York: Routledge.

Massey, Douglas S. 1996. The age of extremes: Concentrated affluence and poverty in the twenty-first century. *Demography* 33:395–412.

Maxson, Cheryl L. 1999. Gang homicide: A review and extension of the literature. In *Homicide: A sourcebook of social research*, eds. M. D. Smith and Margaret A. Zahn, 239–54. Thousand Oaks, CA: Sage.

———. 2001. A proposal for multi-site study of European gangs and youth groups. In *The Eurogang paradox: Gangs and youth groups in the U.S. and Europe*, eds. Malcolm

W. Klein, Hans-Jurgen Kerner, Cheryl L. Maxson, and Elmar G. M. Weitekamp, 299–308. Dordrecht, The Netherlands: Kluwer.

Maxson, Cheryl L., and Malcolm W. Klein. 1990. Street gang violence: Twice as great, or half as great? In *Gangs in America*, ed. C. Ronald Huff, 71–100. Newbury Park, CA: Sage.

———. 1995. Investigating gang structures. *Journal of Gang Research* 3:33–40.

———. 1996. Defining gang homicide: An updated look at member and motive approaches. In *Gangs in America*, ed. C. Ronald Huff, 3–20. 2nd ed. Thousand Oaks, CA: Sage.

———. 2001. 'Play groups' no longer: Urban street gangs in the Los Angeles region. In *From Chicago to L.A.: Making sense of urban theory*, ed. Michael J. Dear. Thousand Oaks, CA: Sage.

Maxson, Cheryl L., and Monica L. Whitlock. 2002. Joining the gang: Gender differences in risk factors for gang membership. In *Gangs in America*, ed. C. Ronald. Huff, 19–35. 3rd ed. Thousand Oaks, CA: Sage.

Maxson, Cheryl L., Monica L. Whitlock, and Malcolm W. Klein. 1998. Vulnerability to street gang membership: Implications for practice. *Social Service Review* 72: 70–91.

Maxson, Cheryl L., Kristi J. Woods, and Malcolm W. Klein. 1996. Street gang migration: How big a threat? *National Institute of Justice Journal* 230:26–31.

McAdam, Douglas, and David A. Snow. 1997. *Social movements.* Los Angeles: Roxbury.

McCarty, Christopher. 2002. Measuring structure in personal networks. *Journal of Social Structure 3.* www.library.cmu.edu:7850/JoSS/McCarty/McCarty.htm (accessed November 5, 2004).

McCorkle, Richard C., and Terence D. Miethe. 2002. *Panic: The social construction of the street gang problem.* Upper Saddle River, NJ: Prentice-Hall.

McCurrie, Thomas. 1998. White racist extremist gang members: A behavioral profile. *Journal of Gang Research* 5:51–60.

McGloin, Jean Marie. 2005. Policy intervention considerations of a network analysis of street gangs. *Criminology and Public Policy* 4:607–35.

McKay, Henry D. 1969. Rates of delinquents and commitments: Discussion and conclusions. In *Juvenile delinquency and urban areas*, eds. Clifford R. Shaw and Henry D. McKay, 329–88. Chicago: University of Chicago Press.

McPherson, Miller, Lynn Smith-Lovin, and James M. Cook. 2001. Birds of a feather: Homophily in social networks. *Annual Review of Sociology* 27:415–44.

Merton, Robert K. 1957. *Social theory and social structure.* Glencoe, IL: The Free Press.

———. 1968. Self-fulfilling prophecy. In *Social theory and social structure*, ed. Robert Merton, 475–90. New York: The Free Press.

Messerschmidt, James W. 2000. *Nine lives: Adolescent masculinities, the body, and violence.* Oxford: Westview.

Meyer, Stephen. 2000. *As long as they don't move next door: Segregation and racial conflict in American neighborhoods.* Lanham, MD: Rowman and Littlefield.

Miller, B. A. 2000. *Anchoring whiteness: Race, class, community, and the politics of public schools.* Unpublished Ph.D. dissertation, New York University, New York.

Miller, Jody. 2001. *One of the guys: Girls, gangs, and gender.* New York: Oxford University Press.

Miller, Walter B. 1958. Lower class culture as a generating milieu of gang delinquency. *Journal of Social Issues* 14:5–19.

———. 1959. Implications of urban lower-class culture for social work. *Social Service Review* 33:219–44.

———. 1962. The impact of a "total community" delinquency control program. *Social Problems* 10:168–91.

———. 1966. Violent crimes by city gangs. *Annals of the American Academy of Political and Social Science* 364:96–112.

———. (1982 [Revised 1992]). *Crime by youth gangs and groups in the United States.* Washington, DC: U.S. Department of Justice, Office of Justice Programs, Office of Juvenile Justice and Delinquency Prevention.

———. 2001. *The growth of youth gang problems in the United States: 1970–98.* Report. Washington, DC: U.S. Department of Justice, Office of Justice Programs, Office of Juvenile Justice and Delinquency Prevention.

Moffit, Terrie E. 1993. Adolescence-limited and life-course-persistent antisocial behavior: A developmental taxonomy. *Psychological Review* 100:674–701.

Moore, David. 1994. *Lads in action: Social process in an urban youth subculture.* Brookfield, VT: Ashgate.

Moore, Jack. 1993. *Skinheads shaved for battle: A cultural history of American skinheads.* Bowling Green, OH: Bowling Green State University Popular Press.

Moore, Joan W. 1978. *Homeboys: Gangs, drugs, and prison in the barrios of Los Angeles.* Philadelphia: Temple University Press.

———. 1991. *Going down to the barrio: Homeboys and homegirls in change.* Philadelphia: Temple University Press.

———. Forthcoming. Female gangs: Gender and globalization. In *Gangs in the global city: Criminology reconsidered,* ed. John M. Hagedorn. Champaign: University of Illinois Press.

Moore, Joan W., and John M. Hagedorn. 2001. *Female gangs: A focus on research.* Bulletin. Washington, DC: U.S. Department of Justice, Office of Justice Programs, Office of Juvenile Justice and Delinquency Prevention.

Moore, Leonard J. 1991. *Citizen Klansmen: The Ku Klux Klan in Indiana, 1921–1928.* Chapel Hill: University of North Carolina Press.

Morenoff, Jeffrey D., Robert J. Sampson, and Stephen W. Raudenbush. 2001. Neighborhood inequality, collective efficacy, and the spatial dynamics of urban violence. *Criminology* 39:517–60.

Morgan, Kathryn D. 1994. Factors associated with probation outcome. *Journal of Criminal Justice* 22:341–53.

———. 1995. Variables Associated with Successful Probation Completion. *Journal of Offender Rehabilitation* 22:141–53.

Mullins, Christopher W., Richard Wright, and Bruce A. Jacobs. 2004. Gender, streetlife, and criminal retaliation. *Criminology* 42:911–40.

Murray, James. 1973. *Larrikins: 19th century outrage.* Melbourne, Australia: Lansdowne Press.

National Youth Gang Center. 1997. *The 1995 National Youth Gang Survey*. Washington, DC: U.S. Department of Justice, Office of Juvenile Justice and Delinquency Prevention.

———. 2000. *1998 National Young Gang Survey: Summary*. Washington, DC: U.S. Department of Justice, Office of Juvenile Justice and Delinquency Prevention.

———. Forthcoming. *National Youth Gang Survey: 1999–2001*. Washington, DC: U.S. Department of Justice, Office of Juvenile Justice and Delinquency Prevention.

Nelli, Humbert S. 1969. Italians and crime in Chicago: The formative years, 1890–1920. *American Journal of Sociology* 74:373–91.

New York City Police Department press release. May 13, 2004. www.ci.nyc.ny.us/ html/nypd/pdf/dcpi/2004-060.pdf

Nisbet, Robert A. 1980. *History of the idea of progress*. New York: Basic Books.

Nurco, David N., Timothy W. Kinlock., and Thomas E. Hanlon, 2004. The drugs-crime connection. In *The American drug scene: An anthology*, eds. James A. Inciardi and Karen McElrath, 346–60. Los Angeles: Roxbury.

Office of Juvenile Justice and Delinquency Prevention, U.S. Department of Justice. 1994. A comprehensive response to America's gang problem. *FY 1994 Discretionary Competitive Program Announcements*. Washington, DC.

Olson, David E., and Sharyn Adams. 2002. *An analysis of gang members and non-gang members discharged from probation*. Chicago: Illinois Criminal Justice Information Authority.

Olson, David E., Brendan Dooley, and Candice M. Kane. 2004. *The relationship between gang membership and inmate recidivism*. Chicago: Illinois Criminal Justice Information Authority.

Olson, David, and Arthur J. Lurigio. 2000. Predicting probation outcomes: Factors associated with probation rearrest, revocations, and technical violations during supervision. *Justice Research and Policy* 2:73–86.

Orcutt, James D., and David R. Rudy, eds. 2003. *Drugs, alcohol, and social problems*. Lanham, MD: Rowman and Littlefield.

Padilla, Felix M. 1992. *The gang as an American enterprise*. New Brunswick, NJ: Rutgers University Press.

Papachristos, Andrew V. 2001. *A.D., After the Disciples: The neighborhood impact of federal gang prosecution*. Peotone, IL: New Chicago School Press.

———. 2004a. Is murder transitive? Paper presented at the annual meeting of the American Society of Criminology, November 16–20, in Nashville, TN.

———. 2004b. Murder as interaction: The social structure of gang homicide in Chicago. Paper presented at the annual meeting of the American Sociological Association. August 14–17, in San Francisco.

———. 2004c. *Gang violence as social control*. Unpublished manuscript, Department of Sociology, University of Chicago.

———. 2005. Gang world. *Foreign Policy* 147: 48–55.

Park, Robert E. 1927. Editor's preface to *The gang: A study of 1,313 gangs in Chicago*, by Frederic M. Thrasher. Chicago: University of Chicago Press.

———. 1940. *Race and culture*. Chicago: University of Chicago Press.

Park, Robert E., and Ernest W. Burgess. 1924. *Introduction to the science of sociology.* Chicago: University of Chicago Press.

Parker, Howard, Lisa Williams, and Judith Aldridge. 2002. The normalization of 'sensible' recreational drug use: Further evidence from the North West England Longitudinal Study. *Sociology* 36:941–64.

Pattillo, Mary E. 1998. Sweet mothers and gangbangers: Managing crime in a black middle-class neighborhood. *Social Forces* 76:747–74.

Pearson, Geoffrey. 1983. *Hooligan: A history of respectable fears.* New York: Shocken.

Perkins, Douglas D., John W. Meeks, and Ralph B. Taylor. 1992. The physical environment of street blocks and resident perceptions of crime and disorder: implications for theory and measurement. *Journal of Environmental Psychology* 12:21–34.

Perrone, Santina, and Rob White. 2000. Young people and gangs. *Trends and issues in crime and criminal justice, No. 167.* Canberra: Australian Institute of Criminology.

Peters, Andy, Tony Davies, and Alison Richardson. 1998. Multi-site samples of injecting drug users in Edinburgh: Prevalence and correlates of risky injecting practices. *Addiction* 92:253–67.

Petersilia, Joan. 1997. Probation in the United States. In *Crime and justice: A review of research,* eds. Michael Tonry and Joan Petersilia, 149–200. Vol. 26. Chicago: University of Chicago Press.

Pinderhughes, Howard. 1997. *Race in the hood: Conflict and violence among urban youth.* Minneapolis: University of Minnesota Press.

Pinnock, Don. 1984. *The brotherhoods: Street gangs and state control in Cape Town.* Cape Town: David Philip.

Pitts, John. 2000. *The new politics of youth crime: Discipline or solidarity?* Basingstoke: Palgrave.

Polsky, Ned. 1967. *Hustlers, beats, and others.* Chicago: Aldine Publishing Company.

Portes, Alejandro, Manuel Castells, and Lauren A. Benton, eds. 1989. *The informal economy: Studies in advanced and less advanced countries.* Baltimore: The Johns Hopkins Press.

Poynting, Scott, Greg Noble, Paul Tabar, and Jock Collins. 2004. *Bin Laden in the suburbs: Criminalising the Arab other.* Sydney: Sydney Institute of Criminology.

Pudney, J., and B. Hooper. 1999. Police target gangs. *The Adelaide Advertiser,* March 8, 13.

Ragin, Charles C. 1987. *The comparative method: Moving beyond qualitative and quantitative strategies.* Berkeley: University of California Press.

Rich, Josiah D., Brian P. Dickinson, John M. Carney, Alvan Fisher, and Robert Heimer. 1998. Detection of HIV-1 nucleic acid and HIV-1 antibodies in needles and syringes used for non-intravenous injection. *AIDS* 12:2345–50.

Reuter, Peter. 1996. The mismeasurement of illegal drug markets. In *Exploring the underground economy,* ed. Susan Pozo, 63–80. Kalamazoo, MI: Upjohn Institute.

Rieder, Jonathan. 1985. *Canarsie: the Jews and Italians of Brooklyn against liberalism.* Cambridge, MA: Harvard University Press.

Rivera, Ramon J., and James F. Short, Jr. 1967. Significant adults, caretakers, and structures of opportunity: An exploratory study. *Journal of Research in Crime and Delinquency* 4:76–97.

Ro, Ronin. 1996. Gangsta: *Merchandizing the rhymes of violence*. New York: St. Martin's.

Robin, G. D. 1967. Gang member delinquency in Philadelphia. In *Juvenile gangs in context: Theory, research, and action*, ed. Malcolm W. Klein, 15–24. Englewood Cliffs, NJ: Prentice-Hall.

Rose, Tricia. 1994. *Black noise: Rap music and black culture in contemporary America*. Hanover, NH: Wesleyan University Press.

Rosenberg, P. S., R. J. Biggar, and J. J. Goedert. 1994. Declining age at HIV infection in the United States. *New England Journal of Medicine* 330:789–79.

Rosenfeld, Richard, Timothy M. Bray, and Arlen Egley. 1999. Facilitating violence: A comparison of gang-motivated, gang-affiliated, and nongang youth homicides. *Journal of Quantitative Criminology* 15:495–516.

Rotella, Sebastian. 1998. *Twilight on the line: Underworlds and politics at the U.S.-Mexico border*. New York: Norton.

Sampson, Robert J. 1991. Linking the micro-and macrolevel dimensions of community social organization. *Social Forces* 70:43–64.

———. 1997. Collective regulation of adolescent misbehavior: Validation results from eighty Chicago neighborhoods. *Journal of Adolescent Research* 12:227–44.

———. 2000. Whither the sociological study of crime? *Annual Review of Sociology* 26:711–14.

———. 2002. Transcending tradition: New directions in community research, Chicago style. *Criminology* 40:213–30.

———. 2003. Networks and neighborhoods: The implications for connectivity for thinking about crime in the modern city. In *Network logic: Who governs in an interconnected world*, eds. Helen McCarthy, Paul Miller, and Paul Skidmore, 157–166. London: Demos.

Sampson, Robert J., and W. Byron Groves. 1989. Community structure and crime: Testing social disorganization theory. *American Journal of Sociology* 94:774–802.

Sampson, Robert J., and John H. Laub. 1993. *Crime in the making: Pathways and turning points through life*. Cambridge, MA: Harvard University Press.

———. 1994. Urban poverty and the family context of delinquency: A new look at structure and process in a classic study. *Child Development* 65:523–40.

Sampson, Robert J., Jeffrey D. Morenoff, and Felton Earls. 1999. Beyond social capital: Spatial dynamics of collective efficacy for children. *American Sociological Review* 64:633–60.

Sampson, Robert J., Jeffrey D. Morenoff, and Thomas P. Gannon-Rowley. 2002. Assessing "neighborhood effects": Social processes and new directions in research. *Annual Review of Sociology* 28:443–78.

Sampson, Robert J., Stephen W. Raudenbush, and Felton Earls. 1997. Neighborhoods and violent crime: A multilevel study of collective efficacy. *Science* 277:918–24.

Sanders, Bill. 2005. *Youth crime and youth culture in the inner city*. London: Routledge.

Sanders, William B. 1994. *Gangbangs and drive-bys: Grounded culture and juvenile gang violence*. New York: Aldine de Gruyter.

Sarabia, Daniel, and Thomas E. Shriver. 2004. Maintaining collective identity in a hostile environment: Confronting negative public perception and factional divisions within the skinhead subculture. *Sociological Spectrum* 24:267–94.

Sarnecki, Jerzy. 2001. *Delinquent networks: Youth co-offending in Stockholm.* Cambridge, UK: Cambridge University Press.

Sassen, Saskia. 2002. Governance hotspots: Challenges we must confront in the post-September 11 world. In *Understanding September 11,* eds. Craig Calhoun, Paul Price, and Ashley Timmer, 106–20. New York: The New Press.

Savelsberg, Joachim J., Lara L. Cleveland, and Ryan D. King. 2004. Institutional environments and scholarly work: American criminology, 1951–1993. *Social Forces* 82:1275–1302.

Schneider, Eric. 1999. *Vampires, dragons, and Egyptian kings: Youth gangs in postwar New York.* Princeton, NJ: Princeton University Press.

Schwartz, Gary. 1987. *Beyond conformity or rebellion: Youth and authority in America.* Chicago: University of Chicago Press.

Sellin, Thorsten. 1938. *Culture conflict and crime.* New York: Social Science Research Council.

Shaw, Clifford R. 1927. Case study method. *Publications of the American Sociological Society* 21:149–57.

———. 1930. *The Jack-roller: A delinquent boy's own story.* Chicago: University of Chicago Press.

———. 1931. *The natural history of a delinquent career.* Chicago: University of Chicago Press.

———. 1938. *Brothers in crime.* Chicago: University of Chicago Press.

Shaw, Clifford R., and Henry D. McKay. 1931. *Social factors in juvenile delinquency: A study of the community, the family, and the gang in relation to delinquent behavior.* Vol. 2 of *Report of the National Commission on Law Observance and Law Enforcement.* Washington, DC: USGPO.

———. 1942. *Juvenile delinquency and urban areas.* Chicago: University of Chicago Press, 1969.

Shaw, Clifford R., and Maurice E. Moore. 1931. *The natural history of a delinquent career.* Chicago: University of Chicago Press.

Shaw, Clifford R., Frederick M. Zorbaugh, Henry D. McKay, and Leonard S. Cottrell. 1929. *Delinquency areas: A study of the geographic distribution of school truants, juvenile delinquents, and adult offenders in Chicago.* Chicago: University of Chicago Press

Shelden, Randall G., Sharon K. Tracy, and William B. Brown. 2001. *Youth gangs in American society.* 2nd ed. Belmont, CA: Wadsworth.

Short, James F., Jr. 1963. Introduction to *The gang: A study of 1,313 gangs in Chicago,* by Frederic M. Thrasher. Abridged ed. Chicago: University of Chicago Press.

———. 1990. New wine in old bottles? Change and continuity in American gangs. In *Gangs in America,* ed. C. Ronald Huff, 223–39. Newbury Park, CA: Sage.

———. 1996. Personal, gang, and community careers. In *Gangs in America,* ed. C. Ronald Huff, 221–40. 2nd ed. Thousand Oaks, CA: Sage.

———. 1997. *Poverty, ethnicity, and violent crime.* Boulder, CO: Westview.

————. 1998. The level of explanation problem revisited—the American Society of Criminology 1997 Presidential Address. *Criminology.* 36:3–36.

————. Forthcoming-a. Criminology, criminologists, and the sociological enterprise. In *Sociology in America*, ed. Craig C. Calhoun. Chicago: University of Chicago Press.

————. Forthcoming-b. The challenges of gangs in global contexts. In *Gangs in the global city*, ed. John M. Hagedorn. Champaign-Urbana: University of Illinois Press.

Short, James F., Jr., and John Moland, Jr. 1976. Politics and youth gangs. *Sociological Quarterly* 17:162–79.

Short, James F., Jr., Ramon J. Rivera, and Harvey Marshall. 1964. Adult-adolescent relations and gang delinquency. *Pacific Sociological Review* 7:59–65.

Short, James F., Jr., Ramon J. Rivera, and Raymond A. Tennyson. 1965. Perceived opportunities, gang membership, and delinquency. *American Sociological Review* 38:56–67.

Short, James. F., Jr., and Fred L. Strodtbeck. 1965/1974. *Group process and gang delinquency.* Chicago: University of Chicago Press.

Short, James F., Jr., Fred L. Strodtbeck, and Desmond S. Cartwright. 1962. A strategy for utilizing research dilemmas: A case from the study of parenthood in a street-corner gang. *Sociological Inquiry* 32:185–202.

Shurink, W. J. 1986. *Number gangs in South African prisons: An organizational perspective.* Paper presented at the Association for Sociology in Southern Africa, July, Durban, South Africa.

Silverman, David. 2001. *Interpreting qualitative data: Methods for analysing talk, text and interaction.* 2nd ed. London: Sage.

Silverman, Eli B. 1999. *NYPD battles crime: Innovative strategies in policing.* Boston: Northeastern University Press.

Simcha-Fagan, Ora, and Joseph E. Schwartz. 1986. Neighborhood and delinquency: An assessment of contextual effects. *Criminology* 24:667–703.

Simi, Pete, and Lowell Smith. 2004. Public enemy number one: A natural history. Paper presented at the Academy of Criminal Justice Sciences meetings, March 9–13, in Las Vegas, NV.

Simmel, Georg. 1908/1955. *Conflict and the web of group affiliations.* Translated by Kurt H. Wolf and Reinihard Bendix. New York: The Free Press.

Skogan, Wesley G. 1990. *Disorder and decline: Crime and the spiral of decay in American neighborhoods.* New York: The Free Press.

Skogan, Wesley G., and Susan M. Hartnett. 1997. *Community policing, Chicago style.* New York: Oxford University Press.

Skolnick, Jerome H., Theodore Correl, Elizabeth Navarro, and Roger Rabb. 1990. The social structure of street drug dealing. *American Journal of Police* 9:1–41.

Social Science Research Council. 2004. Meeting of the International Working Group. Pretoria, South Africa.

————. 2005. Children and armed conflict. *Items and Issues* 5:25.

Spergel, Irving A. 1984. Violent gangs in Chicago: In search of social policy. *Social Service Review* 58:199–226.

———. 1995. *The youth gang problem: A community approach.* New York: Oxford University Press.

Spergel, Irving A., and G. David Curry. 1988. *Survey of youth gang problems and program in 45 cities and 6 sites.* Chicago: University of Chicago, School of Social Service Administration.

Spitz, Marc, and Brendan Mullen. 2001. *We got the neutron bomb: The untold story of L.A. Punk.* New York: Three Rivers Press.

Spradley, James. 1970. *You owe yourself a drunk: An ethnography of urban nomads.* Boston: Little, Brown.

Standing Committee on Social Issues. 1995. A report into youth violence in New South Wales. Legislative Council, Parliament of New South Wales.

Stern, Susan B., and Carolyn A. Smith. 1995. Family processes and delinquency in an ecological context. *Social Service Review* 69:703–31.

Stratton, Jon. 1992. *The young ones: Working-class culture, consumption and the category of youth.* Perth: Black Swan.

Sullivan, Mercer L. 1989. *"Getting paid: Youth crime and work in the inner city.* Ithaca, NY: Cornell University Press.

———. 2005. Maybe we shouldn't study "gangs": Does reification obscure youth violence? *Journal of Contemporary Criminal Justice* 21:170–90.

Sullivan, Mercer L., Pedro Mateu-Gelabert, Barbara A. Miller, and Joseph Richardson. 1999. Gang emergence in New York City: Continuity and change in the social organization and symbolic representation of youth violence. *Report to the Office of Juvenile Justice and Delinquency Prevention.* New York: Vera Institute of Justice.

Sullivan, Mercer L., and Barbara Miller. 1999. Adolescent violence, state processes, and the local context of moral panic. In *States and illegal practices,* ed. Josiah McC. Heyman, 261–83. New York: Berg.

Sutherland, Edwin, and Donald R. Cressey. 1978. *Principles of criminology.* 10th ed. New York: J.B. Lippincott.

Suttles, Gerald D. 1968. *The social order of the slum: Ethnicity and territory in the inner city.* Chicago, IL: University of Chicago Press.

———. 1972. *The social construction of communities.* Chicago: University of Chicago Press.

Syme, S. Leonard. 2000. Forward to *Social epidemiology,* by Lisa F. Berkman and Ichiro Kawachi, eds. Oxford: Oxford University Press.

Tannenbaum, Frank. 1938. *Crime and the community.* Boston: Ginn and Company.

Taylor, Carl J. 1990a. *Dangerous society.* East Lansing: Michigan State University Press.

———. 1990b. Gang imperialism. In *Gangs in America,* ed. C. Ronald Huff, 103–15. Newbury Park, CA: Sage.

Thornberry, Terence P., Marvin D. Krohn, Alan J. Lizotte, and Deborah Chard-Wierschem. 1993. The role of juvenile gangs in facilitating delinquent behavior. *Journal of Research in Crime and Delinquency* 30:55–87.

Thornberry, Terence P., Marvin D. Krohn, Alan J. Lizotte, Carolyn A. Smith, and Kimberly Tobin. 2003. *Gangs and delinquency in developmental perspective.* Cambridge, UK: Cambridge University Press.

Thrasher, Frederic M. 1927 (abridged 1963). *The gang: A study of 1,313 gangs in Chicago.* Chicago: University of Chicago Press.

Tita, George E., K. Jack Riley, Greg Ridgeway, and Peter W. Greenwood. 2005. Reducing gun violence: Operation Ceasefire in Los Angeles. Research in Brief. Washington, DC: National Institute of Justice, U.S. Department of Justice. Office of Juvenile Justice and Delinquency Prevention.

Tonry, Michael, ed. 1997. *Ethnicity, crime and immigration: Comparative and cross-national perspectives.* Chicago: University of Chicago Press.

Touraine, Alain. 1995. *Critique of modernity.* Oxford: Blackwell.

———. 2000. *Can we live together? Equality and difference.* Stanford, CA: Stanford University Press.

———. 2001. *Beyond neoliberalism.* Cambridge, UK: Polity Press.

Tracy, Paul E. 1979. Subcultural delinquency: A comparison of the incidence and seriousness of gang and nongang member offensivity. Unpublished manuscript, University of Pennsylvania, Center for Studies in Criminology and Criminal Law.

UN-Habitat. 2003. *Slums of the world: The face of urban poverty in the new millennium.* Nairobi, Kenya: United Nations Human Settlements Programme.

United Nations Convention on Transnational Organized Crime. 2000. www.unodc .org/palermo.convmain.html (accessed November 14, 2004).

U.S. Census Bureau. 1992. *Census of population and housing, 1990.* www.census.gov (accessed February 10, 2005).

U.S. Department of Justice. 2001. *HIV in prisons and jails, 1999.* Bureau of Justice Statistics press release. www.ojp.usdoj.gov/bjs/pub/press/hiv99pr.htm (accessed November 29, 2004).

van Gemert, F. 2001. Crips in orange: Gangs and groups in the Netherlands. In *The Eurogang paradox: Street gangs and youth groups in the U.S. and Europe*, eds. Malcolm W. Klein, Hans-Jurgen Kerner, Cheryl L. Maxson, and Elmar G. M. Weitekamp, 145–52. Dordrecht, The Netherlands: Kluwer.

Venkatesh, Sudhir A. 1997. The social organization of street gang activity in an urban ghetto. *American Journal of Sociology* 103:82–111.

———. 1999. The financial activities of a modern American street gang. *NIJ Research Forum* 1:1–11.

———. 2000. *American project: The rise and fall of a modern ghetto.* Cambridge, MA: Harvard University Press.

Venkatesh, Sudhir A., and Steven D. Levitt. 2000. "Are we a family or a business?" History and disjuncture in the urban American street gang. *Theory and Society* 29:427–62.

Veysey, Bonita M., and Steven F. Messner. 1999. Further testing of social disorganization theory: An elaboration of Sampson's and Groves's "Community structure and crime." *Journal of Research in Crime and Delinquency* 36:156–74.

Vigil, James D. 1988. *Barrio gangs: Street life and identity in southern California.* Austin: University of Texas Press.

———. 2002. *A rainbow of gangs: Street cultures in the mega-city.* Austin: University of Texas Press.

————. 2003. Urban violence and street gangs. *Annual Review of Anthropology* 32: 225–42.

Voisin, D. R., L. F Salazar, R. Crosby, R. J. DiClemente, W. L. Yarber, and M. Staples-Horne, 2004. The association between gang involvement and sexual behaviours among detained adolescent males. *Sexually Transmitted Infections* 80:440–42.

Wacquant, Loic. 1999. Urban marginality in the coming millennium. *Urban Studies* 36:1639–47.

————. 2000. The new 'peculiar institution': On the prison as surrogate ghetto. *Theoretical Criminology* 4:377–89.

————. 2004. *Deadly symbiosis: Race and the rise of neoliberal penalty.* London: Polity.

Waldinger, Roger, and Mehdi Bozorgmehr, eds. 1996. *Ethnic Los Angeles.* New York: Russell Sage Foundation.

Wasserman, Stanley, and Katherine Faust. 1994. *Social network analysis.* New York: Cambridge University Press.

Weber, Max. 1921/1968. *Economy and society.* Vol. 1. Berkeley: University of California Press.

Weisel, Deborah L. 2002. The evolution of street gangs: An examination of form and variation. In *Responding to gangs: Evaluation and research,* eds. Winifred L. Reed and Scott H. Decker, 24–65. Washington, DC: National Institute of Justice.

Weitekamp, Elmar G. M. 2001. Gangs in Europe: Assessments at the millennium. In *The Eurogang paradox: Street gangs and youth groups in the U.S. and Europe,* eds. Malcolm W. Klein, Hans J. Kerner, Cheryl L. Maxson, and Elmar G. M. Weitekamp, 304–22. Dordrecht, The Netherlands: Kluwer.

Wellman, Barry. 1983. Network analysis: Some basic principles. *Sociological Theory* 1:155–200.

————. 1996. Are personal communities local? A Dumptarian reconsideration. *Social Networks* 18:347–54.

Wermuth, Michael A. 2004. *Empowering state and local emergency preparedness: Recommendations of the Advisory Panel to Assess Domestic Response Capabilities for Terrorism Involving Weapons of Mass Destruction.* Santa Monica, CA: RAND Corporation.

White, Rob. 1990. *No space of their own: Young people and social control in Australia.* Cambridge, UK: Cambridge University Press.

————. 1996. Racism, policing and ethnic youth gangs. *Current Issues in Criminal Justice* 7:302–13.

————. 2002. Understanding youth gangs. *Trends and issues in crime and criminal justice, No. 237.* Canberra: Australian Institute of Criminology.

————, ed. 1999. *Australian youth subcultures: On the margins and in the mainstream.* Hobart: Australian Clearinghouse for Youth Studies.

White, Rob, and Ron Mason. 2004. *Gangs in Perth: Student perspectives.* Report for the Office of Crime Prevention, Office of Premier and Cabinet, Western Australian Government.

White, Rob, Santina Perrone, Carmel Guerra, and Rosario Lampugnani. 1999. *Ethnic youth gangs in Australia: Do they exist?* [7 reports: Vietnamese, Turkish,

Pacific Islander, Somalian, Latin American, Anglo Australian, Summary Report].
Melbourne: Australian Multicultural Foundation.

Whyte, William F. 1943. *Street corner society: The social structure of an Italian slum.*
Chicago: University of Chicago Press.

Wikström, Per-Olof, and Rolf Loeber. 2000. Do disadvantaged neighborhoods cause
well-adjusted children to become adolescent delinquents? A study of male juvenile
serious offending, individual risk and protective factors, and neighborhood context.
Criminology 38:1109–42.

Wilkinson, Deanna L. 2003. *Guns, violence, and identity among African American and
Latino youth.* New York: LFB Scholarly Publishing.

Willis, Paul. 1981. *Learning to labor: How working class kids get working class jobs.* New
York: Columbia University Press.

Wilson, William J. 1987. *The truly disadvantaged: The inner city, the underclass, and
public policy.* Chicago: University of Chicago Press.

Wilson, William J., and Robert J. Sampson. 1995. Toward a theory of race, crime, and
urban inequality. In *Crime and inequality,* eds. John Hagan and Ruth D. Peterson,
37–54. Stanford, CA: Stanford University Press.

Winfree, L. Thomas, Jr., Kathy Fuller, Teresa V. Backstrom, and G. Larry Mays. 1992.
The definition and measurement of "gang status": Policy implications for juvenile
justice. *Juvenile and Family Court Journal* 43:20–37.

Wingood, Gina M., Ralph J. DiClemente, Rick Crosby, Kathy Harrington, Susan L.
Davies, and Edward W Hook III. 2002. Gang involvement and the health of African
American female adolescents. *Pediatrics* 110:57–61.

Wirth, Louis. 1928/1956. *The ghetto.* Chicago: University of Chicago Press.

Wolfgang, Marvin E., Terence P. Thornberry, and Robert M. Figlio. 1987. *From boy to
man, from delinquency to crime: Follow-up to the Philadelphia birth cohort of 1945.*
Chicago: University of Chicago Press.

Wood, Robert. 1999. The indigenous, nonracist origins of the American skinhead
subculture. *Youth and Society,* 31(2):131–51.

Wooden, Wayne, and Randy Blazak. 2001. *Renegade kids, suburban outlaws: From youth
culture to delinquency.* 2nd ed. Belmont, CA: Wadsworth.

World Bank Institute. 2000. *Street children: Latin America's wasted resource.* www1
.worldbank.org/deboutreach/summer00/ (accessed November 14, 2004).

Yablonsky, Lewis. 1962. *The violent gang.* New York: Penguin.

Yacoubian, George S., Jr. 2003. Tracking ecstasy trends in the United States with data
from three national drug surveillance systems. *Journal of Drug Education* 33:245–58.

Zatz, Marjorie S. 1987. Chicano youth gangs and crime: The creation of moral panic.
Contemporary Crisis 11:129–58.

Index

About the Contributors

Brendan D. Dooley, M.A., is currently pursuing a doctoral degree in the Department of Criminology and Criminal Justice at the University of Missouri at St. Louis. Mr. Dooley completed his M.A. in Criminal Justice at Loyola University Chicago; his thesis examined the relationship between gang membership status and probation "success." Mr. Dooley also previously served as a research analyst at the Illinois Criminal Justice Information Authority, where his research focused on prison gang status and recidivism.

Mark S. Fleisher, Ph.D., is Begun Professor and director of the Dr. Semi J. and Ruth W. Begun Center for Violence Research, Prevention and Education, Mandel School of Applied Social Sciences, Case Western Reserve University, Cleveland, Ohio. He has published numerous journal articles, book chapters, and books, including *Warehousing Violence* (Sage, 1988) and two award-winning books: *Beggars and Thieves: Lives of Urban Street Criminals* (University of Wisconsin Press, 1995) and *Dead End Kids: Gang Girls and the Boys They Know* (University of Wisconsin Press, 1998). He coedited *Crime and Employment: Issues in Crime Reduction for Corrections* (AltaMira, 2003). He has done gang research in Seattle, Kansas City (Missouri), Amsterdam, and Champaign, Illinois.

John M. Hagedorn has been studying gangs, drugs, and violence for more than twenty years. He has also participated in several international studies of gangs and is editor of the forthcoming *Gangs in the Global City: Exploring*

Alternatives to Traditional Criminology from the University of Illinois Press. He is currently at work writing a book, *Globalizing Gangs*, following the argument of his chapter in this volume.

Gina Penly Hall is a Ph.D. candidate in the School of Criminal Justice at the University at Albany. She is also a research assistant for the Rochester Youth Development Study. Her research interests include contextual and spatial influences on crime and delinquency, drug-related sentencing policy, and issues surrounding juvenile justice.

Lorine A. Hughes is an assistant professor in the Department of Criminal Justice at the University of Nebraska at Omaha. Her research interests include youth gangs, sex offenders, and computer crime.

David S. Kirk is a Ph.D. candidate in the Department of Sociology at the University of Chicago. His research interests include neighborhood and school effects on adolescent outcomes, criminology, urban sociology, the life course, and quantitative methods. His dissertation research explores the role of social context in explaining racial and ethnic differences in outcomes like school dropout, arrest, and imprisonment.

Malcolm W. Klein has been studying street gangs and responses to them for over forty years. His methods of study have included street observation; interviews with gang members, hundreds of police, and probation and social service workers; and archival analyses of police and court records. He has struggled with the often wide gap between academic knowledge about gangs and the beliefs and perceptions of practitioners such as police, prosecutors, and gang workers. He has also done extensive research studies on police handling of juveniles, community treatment of juvenile offenders, crime measurement, evaluation of criminal justice programs, and comparative juvenile justice systems. Recent publications include *The American Street Gang* (1995), *The Eurogang Paradox* (2001), and *Gang Cop* (2004). In 1997 he initiated the Eurogang Program, an ongoing consortium of over one hundred U.S. and European gang researchers and policymakers involved in understanding emerging street gang problems in Europe.

Stephen E. Lankenau, Ph.D., is an assistant professor at the University of Southern California, Keck School of Medicine, Department of Pediatrics. Trained as a sociologist, he has studied street-involved and other high-risk populations for the past ten years, including ethnographic projects researching homeless panhandlers, prisoners, sex workers, and injection drug users.

Currently he is principal investigator of a four-year NIDA study researching ketamine injection practices among young injection drug users in New York, New Orleans, and Los Angeles.

Alan J. Lizotte is professor of criminal justice and director of the Hindelang Criminal Justice Research Center at the University at Albany. He is also a co-principal investigator of the Rochester Youth Development Study. Among other things, his research interests include all aspects of firearms policy, ownership, and use, as well as using quantitative research methods to study the causes and consequences of various forms of antisocial behavior.

David E. Olson, Ph.D., is chairman and associate professor of criminal justice at Loyola University Chicago, a member of Loyola's graduate faculty, and a senior scientist at the Illinois Criminal Justice Information Authority. Prior to his appointment at Loyola, Dr. Olson was the director of the Illinois Statewide Drug and Violent Crime Control Strategy Impact Evaluation Program, where he oversaw the evaluation and monitoring of federally funded drug control efforts in the state. He has also served as staff to the Illinois Governor's Task Force on Crime and Corrections, the Illinois Legislative Committee on Juvenile Justice, and the Illinois Truth-in-Sentencing Commission, and has worked with a variety of local agencies during his eighteen years in the field of criminal justice. Dr. Olson received his B.S. in criminal justice from Loyola University in Chicago, his M.A. in criminal justice from the University of Illinois at Chicago, and his Ph.D. in political science/public policy analysis from the University of Illinois at Chicago, where he was the recipient of the Assistant United States Attorney General's Graduate Research Fellowship.

Andrew V. Papachristos is a Ph.D. candidate in the Department of Sociology at the University of Chicago. His dissertation research uses social network analysis to advance a structural theory of gang violence in Chicago. He is also currently involved in a four-neighborhood study of how the illegal and prosocial social networks of probationers influence offending patterns, gun markets, violence, and perceptions of neighborhood social order.

Bill Sanders, Ph.D., is a research associate within the Community, Health Outcomes, and Intervention Research (CHOIR) Program at the Saban Research Institute, Childrens Hospital Los Angeles. He has been researching young people in terms of "crime," drugs, violence, and gangs for fifteen years. His latest book, *Youth Crime and Youth Culture in the Inner City* (Routledge, 2005), offers interpretive accounts of young people's offending. Currently he is involved in a nationwide study of young injection drug users and is the principal investigator of a study exploring negative health outcomes among gang-identified youth in Los Angeles.

James F. Short, Jr., is professor emeritus of sociology at Washington State University. His research on youth gangs has moved from the street to the computer, the library, and correspondence with active field researchers.

Pete Simi is an assistant professor of criminal justice at the University of Nebraska at Omaha. He received his Ph.D. in sociology from the University of Nevada, Las Vegas, in 2003. His current research focuses on racist gangs and the politicization of youth and adult gangs.

Rolando Villarreal Sosa is a Ph.D. candidate in the Department of Sociology at the University of Wisconsin at Madison. He is responsible for much of the agency personnel survey and program youth services analyses of the Evaluation of the Comprehensive, Community-wide Approach to Gang Prevention, Intervention, and Suppression (five sites). His dissertation research explores the dynamics of familial and individual poverty among different Latino subgroups using data from the *Survey of Income and Program Participation* (SIPP). His research interests include poverty, immigration, social stratification, gangs and juvenile deviancy, and race and ethnicity.

Irving A. Spergel is the George Herbert Jones Professor Emeritus in the School of Social Service Administration at the University of Chicago. He has a master's degree in social work from the University of Illinois at Urbana and a Ph.D. in social work from Columbia University. He has been a street gang worker, supervisor, and gang program director in New York City and Chicago, and he has conducted street gang and community-based gang program evaluations in cities across the country. He was a UN Consultant on Youth Work in Hong Kong and a consultant on the development of social work training programs in Hong Kong and Russia. His major teaching experience at the University of Chicago has been in group work, community organization, and community development, as well as in youth gangs and gang work. His most recent research and development effort for a comprehensive gang program model and its testing in six cities has been sponsored by the Illinois Criminal Justice Information Authority and the Office of Juvenile Justice and Delinquency Prevention, U.S. Department of Justice (1997–2001). His most recent book is *The Youth Gang Problem: A Community Approach* (Oxford University Press, 1995). He is currently revising a book-length manuscript, *Reducing Youth Gang Crime: The Little Village Gang Violence Reduction Project.*

Mercer L. Sullivan received his Ph.D. in anthropology from Columbia University and his B.A. from Yale University. His studies have used comparative ethnographic data to explore the role of neighborhoods, schools, and other social contexts in adolescent development. He has also worked extensively with other social scientists in interdisciplinary projects integrating qualitative and quantitative approaches to the study of these problems. He is currently associate professor and director of the Graduate Program in the School of Criminal Justice at Rutgers University, on the Newark campus. His book *Getting Paid: Youth Crime and Work in the Inner City* was originally published by Cornell University Press in 1989 and has been reprinted several times. He has written extensively about delinquency and youth crime, the male role in teenage pregnancy and parenting, community development efforts in inner-city neighborhoods, and adolescent violence. He has worked with many public and private agencies, including the U.S. Bureau of the Census, Department of Health and Human Services, National Institute of Justice, Office of Juvenile Justice and Delinquency Prevention, and Department of Agriculture; the New York City Housing Authority; Manpower Demonstration Research Corporation; Mathematica; Public/Private Ventures; Social Science Research Council; National Research Council; and the Aspen Institute. He is a member of the National Consortium on Violence Research and the Selection Committee for the Scholars Program of the William T. Grant Foundation. He has served as editor of the *Journal of Research in Crime and Delinquency.*

Terence P. Thornberry is director of the Research Program on Problem Behavior at the Institute of Behavioral Science and professor of sociology at the University of Colorado at Boulder. He is also the principal investigator of the Rochester Youth Development Study, an ongoing panel study begun in 1986 to examine the causes and consequences of delinquency and other forms of antisocial behavior. His research interests focus on understanding the development of delinquency and crime over the life course and examining intergenerational continuity in antisocial behavior.

Kwai Ming Wa is a Ph.D. candidate in the Department of Education at the University of Chicago. His expertise focuses on modern psychometric methods, educational statistics, and research and evaluation methods. His special interests are conducting multivariate, multilevel data analyses and constructing educational and psychological growth and change models in the social sciences.

Rob White is professor and head of the School of Sociology and Social Work at the University of Tasmania, Australia. He has research and scholarly interests in areas such as juvenile justice, crime prevention, youth studies, corrections, and green or environmental criminology. Among his recent publications are *Controversies in Environmental Sociology* (editor), *Crime & Criminology* (with Fiona Haines), *Youth & Society* (with Johanna Wyn), *Juvenile Justice* (with Chris Cunneen), *Australian Youth Subcultures* (editor), *Crime & Society* (with Daphne Habibis), and *Crime & Social Control* (with Santina Perrone). He is in the final stages of completing a major national study of youth gangs in Australia.